500 THINGS EVERY TEEN SHOULD KNOW *Before* LEAVING HOME

Jack Greer
Heidi Tyline King
Laura Pearson
Pat Sherman

WEST
SIDE
PUBLISHING

Jack Greer is a writer living in Chicago.

Heidi Tyline King is a full-time writer who works from her home in Florida.

Laura Pearson is a freelance writer and editor who specializes in arts and culture reporting. She lives in Chicago and has written for numerous publications, both print and online. In many ways, writing helped her withstand the various trials of being a teenager (and she has *a lot* of impassioned poetry to show for it).

Pat Sherman is a freelance writer living in Cambridge, Massachusetts. She contributed to Publication International Ltd.'s *FYI Answers* series and has written for children, teens, and adults. Her most recent book is *Ben and the Emancipation Proclamation*.

Cover Photos: iStockphoto; Media Bakery; Shutterstock

West Side Publishing is a division of Publications International, Ltd.

Louis Weber, CEO
Publications International, Ltd.
7373 North Cicero Avenue
Lincolnwood, Illinois 60712

ISBN-13: 978-1-60553-644-6
ISBN-10: 1-60553-644-X

Manufactured in USA.

8 7 6 5 4 3 2 1

Contents

"I Didn't Know That!"

Well, here you are. After nearly two decades of life and a dozen years of schooling, you're ready to go off into the wide, wonderful world on your own. It's an exciting time, to be sure. But it can also be a little overwhelming. There's so much to figure out!

500 Things Every Teen Should Know Before Leaving Home was born of the reality that no matter how diligently your parents prepare you for life outside the nest, you will encounter situations, problems, and emotions that you won't know how to handle. How do we know? Because we've been there ourselves!

To create this book, we asked ourselves what we wished we'd known when we left home. As it turns out, the list is quite long—500 things long! It includes an abundance of practical issues, for which we give you straightforward advice. (See the Fast Fact at right for an example.) You'll find tips on everything from what to do if you drop your cell phone in water to how to give thoughtful gifts to what not to put in the microwave. Need help understanding your paycheck deductions? We've got you covered. Want to know how to write a sympathy note? No problem. We cover kitchen basics, survival skills, financial matters, cleaning, moving and leasing, etiquette, and so much more.

FAST FACT

When you wash and dry towels, it's best to skip the softener. The coating action of both liquid fabric softener and dryer sheets reduces towels' absorbency.

Of course, there's more to becoming an adult than simply learning practical skills. With this in mind, we've also included lots of advice about personal growth and development, as well as tips on how to navigate adult relationships, how to stay motivated when there's nobody around to prod you, and of course, how to adjust to the new dynamics with your siblings and parents now that you're an adult member of the family.

> ### Talk It Out
>
> The best way to be a good roommate is to communicate. You can have monthly "state of the union" talks or simply check in on a daily basis. Simple and direct communication is always best.

Leaving home for the first time is an exhilarating, nerve-racking, wonderful experience. With *500 Things Every Teen Should Know Before Leaving Home* as your guide, you can confidently venture into the great unknown—your future. We will be there to show you the way, with understanding and encouragement, and with very specific information and instructions, no matter what life throws your way.

So go forth, young person—the world is waiting for you!

1. How to Get Up in the Morning
(When You're Not a Morning Person)

For many teens, sunrise means one thing: Time for bed! But whether it's for an 8 A.M. class or that new 9-to-5 job, you'll have to start waking up early one of these days. Here are some tips that will help you get up, but we can't promise they'll turn you into a morning person.

1. **Put the alarm clock far away.** Getting up and walking to the alarm clock to turn it off will jump-start your body into "awake" mode.

2. **Drink a glass of water immediately.** The body dehydrates during the night. Drinking a glass of water right away tells your body it's time to get up. You can put the water right beside your alarm clock.

> ### You've Got Rhythm
> Your body's natural sleeping and waking cycle is called a "circadian rhythm." The circadian rhythms of many teens and young adults dictate that they rise later than children and older adults. This helps to explain why you're probably not a morning person.

3. **Hit the shower.** Taking a shower first thing in the morning— especially a cool one—helps to perk you up.

4. **Be productive.** It's a lot easier to wake up if you have something to do. Make a gym date with a friend, or schedule your computer to turn on and load up your projects at the same time each morning.

2. How to Stay Up Late
(When You're Not a Night Person)

If you get into your pajamas at 8 P.M. and are usually in bed by 9, then you probably don't consider yourself a "night person." Nevertheless, there may be situations—such as cramming for a test—for which you need to stay up late. Here are some suggestions:

1. **Prepare.** Figure out when you're going to have to stay up late and make sure you get plenty of rest in advance.

2. **Avoid caffeine and sugar.** They may provide a temporary burst of energy, but they will eventually cause you to crash. Avoid alcohol as well, as it will make you tired.

3. **Keep your environment on the cool side.** Turn down the heat so you don't get too cozy.

4. **Sit in a chair at a table.** If you sit on your bed or curl up on the couch, your body might go into R&R mode.

5. **Eat natural energy snacks.** Raw fruit and nuts are good choices.

6. **Stay engaged and in motion.** Even if you see the sun start to peek through the window!

3. The Truth About Energy Drinks

Study after study has shown that the "energy" from energy drinks comes primarily from two ingredients: caffeine and sugar. While caffeine does indeed have some health benefits when consumed in moderation—it has been shown to increase alertness, memory, and reaction time—too much of it can lead to all sorts of nasty side effects, including hypertension.

> ### Not Consequence-Free
> So what about the "sugar-free" formulations of these energy drinks? Well, avoiding the sugar is a definite plus. But according to a 2008 study by Australian scientists, drinking a single can of a popular sugar-free energy drink still significantly increases the chance of a heart attack or stroke.

Meanwhile, sugar has no nutritional value whatsoever. All it does is pad your waistline and increase your risk of diabetes. If you really need an energy boost, grab a cup of unsweetened black coffee, which has about the same amount of caffeine as some energy drinks.

4. Four Reasons Why Sleep Is Better Than Caffeine

No matter where we get it from, we love our caffeine. While caffeine has benefits when used in moderation—it's been shown to improve alertness and cognition in the short term and has some beneficial health effects in the long-term—too much of it can lead to nervousness, irritability, and a host of physical problems. So the next time you're tempted to reach for that coffee pot or soda can, remember that it might be better to catch a little shut-eye.

1. **Sleep helps cognition.** In study after study, participants who take puzzle-solving and other cognitive tests after sleep score considerably higher than those who didn't doze beforehand.

2. **Muscles need rest.** Your body can only go for so long before it starts to fail. Muscles need rest to repair and rebuild, and a jolt of caffeine isn't in the recipe for relaxation.

3. **Sleep improves motor skills.** Studies have shown that after a good night's sleep, people practicing a newly learned skill are almost twice as adept as those who didn't sleep well.

4. **Sleep might help weight control.** Researchers have discovered that lack of sleep triggers a drop in leptin, a hormone that tells the brain how many calories the body needs. Consequently, your body is tricked into feeling hungry.

5. What to Do When You Can't Go to Sleep

You need to develop good sleep habits if you want to get your shut-eye. Here are the basics.

✦ Don't drink coffee, tea, or other caffeinated beverages late in the afternoon or during the evening.

✦ Exercise at least an hour every day, but not right before bedtime.

✦ Eating a light snack before turning in is okay, but don't have a big meal close to bedtime.

✦ Gentle stretching can get your body ready to sleep.

- Open a window for a little fresh air, even in winter.
- Use earplugs to block out noise.
- Use a mask if you're sensitive to light.
- Make sure your blankets and sheets are appropriate for the weather.
- Don't use an overly soft pillow or mattress, either of which may leave you with an uncomfortable sinking feeling. Many people find that firmer is better.
- Try to go to sleep at around the same time on school and work nights.
- Try to avoid over-the-counter sleep aids. Ditto for "sleep-inducing" herbal supplements. If all else fails, get up and do something low-key for a while.

You Can't Live Without It

Teens need nine hours of sleep every night—one more than the eight hours recommended for adults. Sleep helps keep all your systems up and running; your body can't function without it.

Insomnia may also be a side effect of medication you are taking for another condition. Talk to your doctor to see if you can change this prescription or take your dose earlier in the day.

6. What Can You Afford?

Creating and following a budget will help you enjoy the things you want without plunging into debt. Although you may not want to do it, creating a budget is something you really *need* to do—and it's actually pretty easy. Before you start, gather all your financial records: bank statements, paycheck stubs, credit card bills, etc.

Calculate monthly income. Figure out how much money you bring in each month. If you have a regular salary, this is easy. If you have a variable hourly schedule or are a tipped employee, look at the last few months of income to get an average. This is how much money you have to spend each month.

Calculate monthly expenses. Monthly expenses are either fixed or variable. Fixed expenses—those that are the same each month, such as rent, cell phone bills, and car payments—are easy to track.

But the variable costs—groceries, eating out, gifts, and so on—are trickier. Again, you'll need to look at the last few months of bank, credit, and debit card statements to get a sense of how much you're spending each month. Even better, spend a few weeks keeping track of every penny before starting your budget.

Compare the two. If your income is less than your expenses, you've got to figure out how to cut down on the latter. You may need to cut back on fun stuff to make sure you're living within your means.

7. Learning the Difference Between Wants and Needs

1. *Food, water, shelter.*
2. *Vacations, designer jeans, video games.*

It's pretty obvious which of these are needs (#1) and which are wants (#2). But have you ever considered the difference between your own needs and wants? How many times have you said, "I need a latte"? In reality, you probably meant, "I really *want* a latte."

Taking inventory will make you aware of what you truly can't live without (there's not much) and what are merely exciting "extras." You may think you can't live without cable or the latest model of mobile phone, but try it. You may learn that there is some freedom in simplicity.

Needing Your Wants

Exciting news! Sometimes your wants can actually be things you need. Do you want a computer? Maybe you also need one for college. Similarly, you may want a cell phone but also need one for your job. Try to identify ways in which wants and needs intersect; they are worth investing in.

8. How Cooking at Home Saves Big Money

Going out to eat once in a while is a treat, but if you make it a habit you might find that you're blowing your monthly food budget in a week or two. Cooking at home has many advantages, not the least of which is that it's far cheaper than dining out every meal.

Here's a simple example of how cooking at home is cheaper. Olive Garden's "pasta with marinara" dish, which comes with breadsticks and salad, costs $10.50, not including tax and tip.

Now, let's figure out how much it would cost to make a similar dish at home.

✦ One-pound box of pasta: less than $2

✦ Jar of marinara sauce: less than $2

✦ Loaf of fresh bread: less than $2

✦ Pre-made bagged salad: less than $2

The total cost of these ingredients comes out to about $8, which is more than 25 percent cheaper than that restaurant meal. But it gets even better—the ingredients listed above make *three to four meals*, which means each meal is going to cost you as little as two bucks! You can save even more money by making your own salads and marinara sauce.

This is just one example. You'll find that cooking at home is a consistently cheaper option.

9. Take Control of Your Own Happiness

To take control of your own happiness, shift your focus to the things that make you happy! It can be easy to fixate on things that make you unhappy—a difficult exam, a tedious job, a speeding ticket, or a breakup, for example. But when was the last time you took inventory of all that's positive in your life? Make a list of who and what bring you joy. These could run the gamut from a great meal to a meaningful conversation, a sun-breaking-through-the-clouds moment to a college scholarship. Another way to take charge of your happiness is to allow yourself to be in the moment and feel what you feel. Denying or rejecting your emotions only leads to dissatisfaction and disappointment. If your schedule is too full, learn to say "no" to things. If your plans are too complicated, simplify. Take care of yourself—mentally, physically, and spiritually—and in so doing, you'll take care of your well-being.

10. Showing Up Is Half the Battle
(Small Things That Add Up When It Comes to Grades)

There's no trick to excelling at school, but there are plenty of ways to improve your academic performance—and maybe even earn that coveted "A." For starters, go to school! It may be obvious, but if you skip school, you'll never be able to make the grade. Next, come prepared. Preparedness doesn't just impress your teacher; it's also an instant confidence-builder. If you know you've done all you can do to complete an assignment or understand a concept, you will feel better equipped to participate in class and ask insightful questions. Introduce yourself to your teacher and approach him or her if you have a question or need to clarify what is expected of you. This way, you'll clear up any confusion and show your instructor that you are invested in the coursework. Lastly, take it one day at a time. If you get a syllabus at the start of the semester that is roughly the density of *War and Peace*, it can be a bit daunting. Just remember: This document outlines your work for the *entire* semester—you don't have to go home and do it all in one night!

11. Managing Stress

There are countless situations that bring about stress: spreading ourselves too thin, encountering conflict in a relationship, experiencing financial trouble, holding ourselves to impossible standards, missing the last episode of our favorite TV drama (*so* stressful!), etc. If you can identify the cause, you will be better equipped to deal with it. While a bit of stress can motivate us to finish projects or confront issues, prolonged stress takes a physical toll, contributing to depression and anxiety, an impaired immune system, and even cardiovascular disease. Here are some tips for managing stress:

1. Take time off—whether it's an entire day or simply 15 relaxing minutes.

2. Exercise or do a hobby that you enjoy to calm yourself down and feel rejuvenated.

3. Determine what's stressing you out and write it down. Expressing your frustrations and worries on paper can be very therapeutic and help provide perspective.

4. Talk to a friend or family member. He or she can provide perspective and encouragement. If necessary, seek advice from a health care professional.

12. What to Do if You Drop Your Cell Phone in Water

If you drop your mobile phone in water, all is not lost! The key to reviving a submerged cell phone is to act quickly. Rescue your phone from the water (swimming pool, bathtub, or—gulp!—toilet). Remove the battery (to reduce the risk of a short circuit), as well as the SIM card. Shake off as much water as possible, then dab the phone lightly with a paper towel, being careful to avoid pushing water back into any holes or grooves. Leave the phone out in a warm, dry place for a few hours, and don't turn it on until it has dried thoroughly. If the phone doesn't turn on or shows signs of water damage, you won't be able to replace it under warranty—a cell phone contains a moisture-sensitive sticker that indicates it was dropped into the drink. The good news is that some cell phones bounce back after taking a quick dip.

13. Five Things to Consider When Choosing an Apartment

Renting an apartment is a big deal. By signing a lease, you're agreeing to spend 12 months of your life in one place. But there is more to an apartment than the rent, the square footage, and whether utilities are included. Here are five things that are often overlooked in apartment searches.

1. **The floor it's on.** This is a matter of preference, but it is an important factor. First-floor units are more prone to break-ins, for example, but you won't have to deal with steps. Top-floor units can get hot in the summer, but you won't have anybody stomping around above you.

2. **The neighbors.** There's no getting around noise in apartment life, but having neighbors who crank Metallica until 3 A.M. every night is a bit much.

3. **The landlord.** Nothing can turn a dream apartment into a nightmare faster than a lousy landlord. Ask the previous tenants why they're moving out and what their opinions of the landlord are. You can also check online or with tenant unions to see if there have been any complaints lodged against the landlord.

4. **Windows.** Check out the windows before signing a lease, making sure they open and close smoothly, lock properly, and are fitted with unbroken screens.

5. **Electrical outlets.** It's frustrating to move into an apartment and find that there aren't enough outlets. The kitchen, bathrooms, bedrooms, and living rooms all should have outlets.

14. Why Choosing a Landlord Is as Important as Choosing an Apartment

So you've scoured Craigslist, walked around the neighborhood, and made a checklist of questions about laundry, utilities, and pets. You're all set, right? Almost. There's one more thing to consider before signing that lease: the landlord. Your landlord can be the difference between a great year of apartment life and a rotten one.

The landlord is going to be a major figure in your life. He or she has the keys to your apartment, fixes things that go wrong (or doesn't), and maintains the building. The landlord dictates the rules and deals with unruly tenants. Indeed, a reliable landlord is just as important as reliable heat or electricity.

Start your research by asking current tenants or the neighbors about the landlord. Ask the landlord to put you in touch with current residents; most good landlords will be happy to provide these "references." Call the Better Business Bureau or contact tenant unions, which maintain records of complaints about landlords, in the area. Finally, check out the U.S. Department of Housing and Urban Development (HUD) Web site, which has lots of information about tenant rights and tenant unions for each state. This may seem like a lot of trouble, but investigating a landlord before you sign that lease can save you a lot of grief later on.

> ## You've Got the Power
> Did you know that your lease is negotiable? If, when reading your lease before signing for an apartment (you *are* reading your lease, aren't you?), you notice an important clause is missing or disagreeable to you, ask the landlord if it can be amended. Just make sure to get it in writing before you sign on the dotted line.

15. Five Things to Do When You Move In

You've changed your address, returned the moving truck, and signed up for all your utilities. You're sitting on a pile of boxes in the middle of your new apartment. Now what?

Clean, clean, clean. If you couldn't do this before you moved in, definitely do it before you unpack! Someone else lived there before you, and it's unlikely they left the place in white-glove condition.

Put the "security" in security deposit. Take photos and note any damage or disrepair, and give this list to your landlord within the first couple of days after you move in. This will avoid any misunderstandings when it's time to move out.

Get to know your neighbors. This helps create a sense of community and safety, and you won't feel so awkward when you pass people in the hallway.

Consider the locks. Many landlords will change the locks between tenants, but some won't, which means everybody who's lived in your apartment—and their significant others—could potentially have a key to your place. Ask if the locks have been changed, and if the landlord says no, ask if it's okay to install a new deadbolt.

Check the smoke detectors. Even if the detectors are functioning, change the batteries, just to be safe.

16. Six Things to Do When You Move Out

For inexperienced apartment dwellers, the "moving-out" checklist often consists of one item: Pack. But when it's time to move out, packing your stuff into boxes is only half the battle. Here are six other tasks that you should have on your checklist.

1. **Clean.** Leaving the apartment clean for the next tenant is the courteous thing to do, and it's the best way to make sure you get your security deposit back. This means cleaning everything, from the fridge to the tub. Ask before you clean the carpets, though. Some apartment complexes will charge you a hefty fee for shampooing dirty ones.

2. **Cancel/change utilities.** If you move out and forget to tell the electric company, it'll just leave the lights on—in your name. Call the electric, gas, cable, and phone companies to cancel your service.

3. **Change your address at the post office.** The fastest way to change your address is through the U.S. Postal Service's online system. You can also fill out a change-of-address form and drop it off at the post office.

4. **Change your address everywhere else.** Contact your bank, telephone company, doctor's office, magazines' subscription services, and anybody else who needs your current address to inform them of the change.

> **Just the Essentials**
> Pack a box or duffel bag of "essentials." Because you'll need a few days to unpack after you move into your new place, it's helpful to have toiletries, a change of clothes, and a dish or two easily accessible right away.

5. **Get rid of junk.** Moving is a great time to get rid of stuff you never use. Have a yard sale, list a few things on eBay, or hit the recycling center—it'll make moving day a lot lighter.

6. **Label your boxes by room.** It makes unpacking a lot easier.

17. Five Ways to Be a Bad Tenant

The Internet is littered with stories about bad landlords. But for every bad landlord, there are probably three bad tenants. Here are five things that you as a tenant should not do.

1. **Begin improvement projects without consulting the landlord.** Even though you're living in the building, your landlord owns it. That means you need to ask him or her if it's okay before painting that sweet mural on the living room wall.

2. **Consistently be late with the rent.** Making a late rent payment once in a while happens. But if it happens too much, you begin to look irresponsible. If you must be late, notify your landlord and work out payment arrangements.

3. **Annoy your neighbors.** Playing music too loudly, leaving a barking dog on a patio all day, and leaving trash all over common areas are some of the ways you can get on your neighbors'—and your landlord's—bad sides.

4. **Don't clean your apartment.** An unclean apartment can attract cockroaches and other vermin, affects everybody in the building, and makes it harder for the landlord to rent out other apartments.

5. **Call the landlord at all hours for every little thing.** There are plenty of reasons to call the landlord—no heat in the dead of winter, for example. But don't call your landlord at 3 A.M. because the faucet is dripping.

FAST FACT

Having a good relationship with your landlord will not only make your day-to-day apartment life a lot more pleasant—it might save you money. Landlords may be less likely to raise the rent from lease to lease for tenants they want to stick around.

18. Understanding Security Deposits

For many first-time renters, the security deposit comes as a surprise. Why the heck do you need to pay an extra month's rent before you even move in?

The security deposit protects landlords from destructive or disappearing tenants. Most commonly, the security deposit is equal to a month's rent (though this can vary depending on the location and the particular landlord) and is due when you sign the lease.

If, after a tenant moves out, the landlord needs to repair, repaint, or clean the unit, that money comes from the security deposit. If the apartment is left in the same state it was when the tenant moved in, the security deposit is returned in full.

In some states, landlords are required to keep security deposits in a special interest-bearing account and give the tenant the interest each year, or at the end of his or her lease term. (Check out the Web site of the U.S. Department of Housing and Urban Development for state-by-state information.)

Clean, Then Clean Up

So how do you make sure you get your security deposit back? Simple: Leave the place as you found it (or even cleaner, if possible). But the process begins well before you move out. When you move into an apartment, take pictures and notes about its condition. Go over these with your landlord to prevent confusion about repairs when it comes time to move out.

As with any part of a rental agreement, it's important to clarify what will happen to your security deposit before signing a lease, and it's a good idea to ask your landlord what you can do to make sure you get your deposit back when the time comes.

19. Renter's Insurance

You've got your health insurance. You've got your auto insurance. But you probably don't think that you need insurance for your apartment. Your landlord has that, right?

Well, that's not exactly how it works. The landlord's insurance will cover damage to the building, but it won't cover damage to your possessions—or to people who might be visiting you.

Something else you don't want to learn the hard way: If your car is stolen and you've got personal items inside—say you're moving and you're storing some stuff in the car—your car insurance won't cover them. Only renter's insurance will.

Luckily, renter's insurance is widely available and very cheap, costing less per month than what some people spend at Starbucks in a week. Policies vary, but they usually cover loss or damage to possessions from theft, fire, water, and many other common problems. They also contain a liability component, which protects you in case, for example, somebody slips in your bathroom and then sues you for damages.

When shopping for renter's insurance, find out exactly what is covered before you buy. If you live in an area prone to tornadoes, for example, make sure tornado damage is covered. As with any insurance policy, lower coverage limits and higher deductibles will decrease your rates. Just be sure not to go too barebones—your coverage should match what your possessions are worth.

20. How to Follow a Recipe

For some people, cooking a meal can be like blundering through unknown territory without a map. A recipe is that map, guiding you through your meal preparation. The beauty of recipes is that anybody can follow one—if you know how. Check out the anatomy of a recipe.

Recipe information. The first part of the recipe will provide general information, such as the name of the dish, a short description, and the number of servings it prepares. (If you're planning to make more servings than the number indicated, you'll have to adjust your ingredients proportionally.) This section may also tell you how long the recipe will take to prepare.

Recipe ingredients. The ingredients, and how much you need of each one, are usually listed in the order in which they are used. Make sure you have all the ingredients before you start.

Recipe instructions. Follow the recipe's instructions in order. If you come across unfamiliar terms, look them up. If you're using a cookbook, it may have a glossary of cooking terms to consult. If not, or if you're still unsure about a technique, there are many Web sites and online videos with step-by-step instructions.

FAST FACT

A word about servings: This is not the same as the number of people the recipe serves. A recipe that makes four servings doesn't serve four people—unless they only take one helping.

21. How to Stock Your Pantry

If you've ever planned on making a meal, then opened the cupboard to discover all you had on hand was a bag of rice, a half-empty box of cereal, and all-purpose flour, then you know the importance of keeping a well-stocked pantry. No one likes to spend a lot on groceries, but here's a little food for thought: By springing for some nonperishable essentials and supplementing them with perishables (milk, fruits and vegetables, bread, and meat), you'll be all set to cook whatever, whenever! Some essentials to add to your shopping list include: applesauce (for a quick side dish) · baking soda (for baking and cleaning) · balsamic vinegar (for marinades and salad dressing) · a few cans of beans (for soups, casseroles, tacos, etc.) · butter or margarine · cereal (for breakfast—or any time!) · cinnamon (for sprinkling on toast or in applesauce) · crackers · flour · garlic salt · granulated sugar · honey · Italian seasonings (basil, oregano, rosemary, etc.) · jam · ketchup · maple syrup · mayonnaise · mustard · assorted nuts (for snacks, salads, or baking) · oatmeal · olive oil · pancake mix · parmesan cheese · pasta · pasta sauce · peanut butter · pepper · pizza sauce · salsa · a few cans of soup (for a quick meal) · soy sauce (for stir-fry and sauces) · vegetable oil (for cooking and frying) · white wine vinegar (for flavoring and salad dressing).

22. How to Plan a Menu

Planning meals in advance will save you money and time, and it can help you eat healthier, too. You'll cut down on trips to the grocery store and take advantage of sales, both of which will be a boon to your food budget. You'll also eat out less frequently, since you'll know that you've got lasagna or a stew waiting for you at home.

Here are some tips to help you get started.

1. Consider what dishes you like to eat, then consult cookbooks or Web sites to find recipes for them.

2. Figure out how many meals you can get out of each recipe and when you'll want to eat the dishes you'll cook. Make a chart for the week and fill it in.

3. Consult grocery store flyers for sales and adjust your plans accordingly. Make a grocery list.

4. Think in terms of food groups: breads/grains, fruit, vegetables, dairy, and meat/protein. This makes meal planning much easier, and your meals will be better balanced.

5. Use a Web site to help plan your menu. Sign up for e-mail reminders, so your daily menu will come right to your inbox.

23. Cooking Ahead Saves Time and Money

Many people love to cook but feel that they don't have the time. That's why preparing more than one meal at a time is such a good idea—it saves time, and it also saves money. Buying ingredients in bulk for larger cooking projects is cheaper in the long run than buying smaller sizes. And since your meals are already prepared, you won't be tempted to eat out on the nights when you just don't feel like cooking.

✦ **Pick a day on which you have enough time to cook the meals you want.** You'll probably need an entire afternoon or evening.

✦ **Plan your meals.** Decide if you want to make main dishes that contain some of the same ingredients so you can buy in larger quantities and save some cash. Another option is to make large quantities of whatever you're cooking, then freeze some for a different week. Savvy shoppers plan their meals around what's on sale at the grocery store that week.

Cold Comfort

For real convenience, divide entrees into meal-sized containers that you can refrigerate or freeze. When you get home at night, all you'll need to do is pop one of the containers in the microwave, and a few minutes later, dinner will be served!

✦ **Multitask.** For example, if you're planning to make a meatloaf and a stir-fry, first get all the ingredients ready. Then, you can stir-fry on the stovetop while baking the meatloaf in the oven. You can also look for recipes that call for baking in the oven at the same temperature. If both fit into the oven, you'll save on gas and/or electricity if you bake them at the same time.

✦ **Store your food properly.** Most leftovers can be stored in the fridge for three to four days. If you plan to eat the meals over a longer period of time, freeze them in freezer bags or freezer-safe plastic or glass containers.

24. What You Should Keep in Your Car's Glove Compartment

If you own a car, you need to keep some essential items in your glove compartment. By essential, we don't mean brochures, napkins, receipts, or gum wrappers. If your glove box is jam-packed with this stuff, it might be time to clean it out and fill it with the real essentials: your vehicle registration form (only the most up-to-date version), a current insurance card (any expired cards can be thrown away, as they are no good to you), the owner's manual to your vehicle, an emissions form (if your state requires emissions testing), and a pad of paper and a pencil (to write down any important information you might need after an accident). You might also include a list with contact information for a mechanic, your insurance agent, and a tow company. The glove compartment is also a good place to keep a list of oil changes and tire rotations, as well as repair work, so you can make sure that you're up-to-date on vehicle maintenance.

25. Ten Things to Have in Your Car at All Times

For most of us, the car is a sort of traveling junk drawer. But if you have a breakdown in the middle of nowhere, is a frisbee going to do you any good? Here are ten items you should always have in your car.

1. **Flashlight.** Ever tried to change a tire in the dark? It's not easy.

2. **Map.** Even if you have a GPS unit, a good road map is essential.

3. **Insurance card and registration.** These are the things police officers ask for during traffic stops.

4. **Blanket/warm clothes.** It gets cold waiting for a tow truck in the middle of winter.

5. **Cell phone charger.** At the bare minimum, you should have a cell phone charger that plugs into a cigarette lighter. Even better, stash a prepaid phone in the glove compartment for emergencies.

6. **First-aid kit.** Keep this beneath one of the front seats for easy access.

> ### Enroll the Patrol
> While 911 is usually the best number to call for emergencies, many states have cell phone codes that you can call to report emergencies to the highway patrol. These vary from state to state, so it's important to learn which numbers work in your area.

7. **Jumper cables.** Everybody leaves the headlights on all day at least once.

8. **Road flares.** Placed beside your car, these will alert other drivers that you are stranded and prevent them from hitting you.

9. **Ice/snow scraper.** It's hard to see out the windshield when it's completely covered in ice.

10. **Nonperishable food and water.** Even if you never get stranded for days, there will be plenty of times you'll be glad that you have water and snacks in the car.

26. Car Insurance: What You Need to Know

If you own a car, you don't have a choice about carrying auto insurance; every state requires it. The question is, what kind of coverage do you need and how much is it going to set you back every month? You'll want to consider the risks and the costs to determine the right insurance package for you.

The Basics. There are four kinds of coverage you need to know.

✦ *Liability.* Pays for accidental bodily injury and property damages to others, including any court costs incurred.

✦ *Collision.* Covers damages to your vehicle.

✦ *Comprehensive.* Pays for loss or damage to the car that does not result from auto accidents. (Theft and flooding are good examples.)

✦ *Personal Injury Protection (PIP).* Pays for the insured driver's medical expenses, regardless of fault.

Learn the Laws. Each state has its own car insurance laws. Forty-seven states require liability insurance, although the sufficient coverage amount varies. Fifteen states require PIP coverage.

Avoid double coverage. Compare your auto insurance policy to your health insurance to make sure you aren't being charged twice for the same coverage.

Find your comfort level. After basic coverage, decide what other protections are necessary. For example, rental reimbursement keeps out-of-pocket expenses to a minimum if you need to rent a car while yours is being repaired.

Don't overinsure. If auto insurance costs you more than 10 percent of your car's value, drop everything but the coverage that the law requires. It doesn't pay to have your car insured for more than it's worth.

Save money. Increasing your deductibles, improving your credit, and paying an annual premium are some ways to save money on insurance.

27. Where to Find a Job

When you're looking for a job, you likely will spend hours upon hours perusing job-search Web sites, and you may send dozens of résumés electronically into the ether. But there's more to job-hunting than surfing the Web. Here are some suggestions for other ways to find work.

1. **Use your contacts.** If you're looking for a job, let people know about it. Discreetly e-mail well-connected acquaintances and ask if they'd be willing to alert you to any job openings.

2. **Carry an up-to-date copy of your résumé with you.** You never know when you may meet a potential employer or job-related contact.

3. **Join a professional organization in your field.** This will give you access to information about job openings, as well as net-working opportunities.

4. **Research companies for which you'd like to work.** Find one or more employees who hold positions in the area that most interests you. Send an introductory e-mail or letter and/or make an introductory phone call. Ask to set up an informational meeting.

5. **Consider freelancing.** This will keep your skills sharp and may even lead to a part-time or full-time position.

28. How to Write a Standout Résumé

Writing a résumé can seem intimidating, but don't let that blank sheet of paper get you down. Start with the basics, such as contact information, education, and experience (making sure that you have the dates correct). Then concentrate on making your résumé stand out. Incorporate some keywords that are relevant to the job for which you're applying—perhaps even words or phrases lifted directly from the job description. Employers look for these buzzwords as they sift through résumé piles. Remember, they'll only give your résumé about 30 seconds, so you need to grab their attention. If you're just entering the workforce, don't worry about your lack of professional experience. Instead, punch up your résumé with other types of relevant experience—volunteer work, community projects, leadership roles, research, etc. Be sure to check for typos, grammatical errors, and formatting inconsistencies. Use a readable font, and let a friend or family member read it for content as well as for any mistakes you missed. Make sure it says exactly what you want, without any errors, before hitting "Send" or dropping it in the mail.

29. Five Things Not to Put on Your Résumé

Your résumé is your introduction to a prospective employer, but unfortunately, even excellent résumés are easy to overlook. Chances are, your résumé is going to be thrown into a pile with 100 others that look very similar. While you want your résumé to stand out, you don't want it to be for the wrong reasons. Avoid the following when writing your résumé.

1. **Irrelevant job experience.** When you're just starting out in the workforce, you won't have much experience, but you still don't need to put that junior-high babysitting job on a résumé that you're submitting for a bank position.

2. **Personal information.** Your prospective employer doesn't need to know your physical characteristics, religious preference, political affiliation, or sexual orientation.

3. **Cute fonts.** A résumé submitted in Comic Sans script is going straight into the garbage.

4. **References/references upon request.** References are a given; you don't need to waste résumé space on them. Have references available on a separate sheet of paper in case a prospective employer asks about them.

5. **A photograph.** Attaching a photograph to a résumé is a huge no-no. Employers do not care what you look like, and it's against the law to use personal appearance to judge a candidate.

30. How to Ask for a Reference

Whether you're seeking higher education or trying to get your foot in the corporate door, a good reference can make the all the difference between "Not quite" and "Yes!"

Who should you ask to provide references? Teachers, academic advisors, and work supervisors are natural choices. If you're looking for your first job, organizations for which you have provided volunteer service can be excellent sources of references.

Here's how to make the request.

✦ Put it in writing. Send an e-mail or write a letter.

> **What If the Answer Is No?**
>
> Ouch! Rejection hurts, but don't argue. Send a short e-mail saying, "Thank you for letting me know that you feel that way." Then turn your attention to finding a reference who really *is* on your side.

✦ If you have been out of contact with your prospective reference for a while, be sure to reintroduce yourself: "I took American History with you last year." Or, "I was the marketing assistant the summer of 2009."

✦ Get to the point. "I'd like to use you as a reference."

✦ Remind the prospective reference of a specific accomplishment, such as a paper you wrote, a project you worked on, or an idea that you offered.

✦ Add something about your prospective reference, too. "You made history come alive for me." Or, "Your management style inspired me." Don't lay it on too thick—just let your reader know you think highly of him or her.

✦ Be clear about how the reference will be used. "I'm applying for a job at the Widget Co." Or, "I'm applying to Gigantic University."

✦ Thank your potential reference.

✦ Follow up with a phone call a week or two later to make sure your request was received.

31. How to Dress for an Interview

Interview attire depends largely on the kind of job for which you're applying: A bank has a different dress code than a restaurant, for example. But if you're not sure, it's always better to be overdressed than underdressed. In many cases, the interview is the first personal interaction you'll have with your potential employers, and you want to make a good impression. If you're a guy, a tie is usually appropriate, and you should choose slacks instead of jeans. A sport coat is often a good intermediate look.

While many companies look for unique individuals, be careful about displaying tattoos and unusual piercings. Employment experts recommend always covering up tattoos and removing piercings for an interview. Don't dress in a revealing or flamboyant manner, and avoid powerful colognes and perfumes.

FAST FACT

Looks may not be everything, but they account for about 55 percent of another person's perception of you, according to image consultants.

Though you might feel constricted and awkward in your interview attire, remember that it's just for a couple of hours, and it might make all the difference.

32. Five Questions to Ask at a Job Interview

During a job interview, you'll be answering a lot of questions from your potential employer, but you should come prepared with a few questions of your own as well. Asking questions shows that you're genuinely interested in the company as well as the interviewer. Why is this important? Because you want to work there too!

Here are some potential queries to help you get started.

✦ What's the single most important thing that the person hired for this position can do for the company?

✦ How will my work be evaluated and by whom?

✦ If employees have suggestions about improving products, services, or work procedures, is there a system in place for presenting them to management?

Remember, people like to talk about themselves, so it's good to ask your interviewer things like:

✦ How did you start out with this company?

✦ What do you enjoy most about working here?

Don't ask about salary, vacation time, sick leave, or holidays. There will be plenty of time for that later—after they've offered you the job, of course.

33. Which Fork Do I Use?

If you've ever dined in a fancy restaurant and been puzzled by the abundance of flatware, you're not alone. Here are some guidelines for multifork establishments.

1. In general, you want to work from the outside in. The salad fork is farthest to the left. Place it on the salad plate when you are finished.

2. The next fork is for your entrée, and the small, inner fork is for dessert.

> ## What to Wear
>
> Although restaurant dress codes are more relaxed than they used to be, some fine dining establishments require men to wear jackets or shirts with collars. To be safe, call ahead and ask for the dress code and what it specifically means. If you are given loose parameters (such as "Jeans discouraged" or "Jackets preferred"), press for a little more information.

3. Spoons and knives are on the right. The outermost spoon is for soup, and there may also be a teaspoon (for coffee or tea).

4. Place your napkin in your lap, try to keep your elbows off the table, and don't reach across other people's plates. Instead, ask politely if another diner can pass you what you want.

34. Restaurant Etiquette

For many young adults, dining out in a "real" restaurant is something of a new experience—at least it is if they're paying. If you haven't been in charge before, here are some things you need to know to make the experience pleasant for all involved.

Reservations. Be on time. When you're late, you inconvenience the restaurant and the dozens of other diners who are waiting for tables or have reservations after you. Call if you'll be more than a few minutes late. If you must cancel, do so as soon as you know you won't make it.

Dress code. Most restaurants won't refuse you service if you're dressed inappropriately, but that doesn't mean wearing a Speedo and t-shirt to dinner is okay. If you're unsure about the dress code, simply call and ask what is appropriate.

Cell phones. Your dining neighbors don't need to hear about your previous night's exploits. Similarly, put the phone away when the waiter is interacting with your table.

A Matter of Respect

Always remember that restaurant employees are human beings and deserve to be treated with respect. There's an old adage in the industry: "Somebody who is nice to you but not nice to the waiter is not a nice person."

Sending food back. It's okay to send food back if it's been cooked incorrectly or you're allergic to it; it's not okay if you don't like it or you're no longer hungry.

Tipping. Because servers make little to no hourly wages, tipping is standard practice in American restaurants. As of 2010, the standard tip is 18 percent of the total bill before tax is applied. You can always give more if the service was good or less if you felt service was bad.

Never reduce the tip because the food was bad. Servers bring the food to the table—they don't cook it.

35. When to Send Your Food Back at a Restaurant

You're at a fancy steakhouse for a special occasion, but when the medium-rare steak that you ordered arrives, it's so overcooked that you can barely cut into it. What should you do? Despite popular myths to the contrary, the majority of restaurants are very understanding—and apologetic—when a guest sends a dish back. Here are four situations when it's always okay to send back your meal.

1. **The food is dangerous or offensive to you.** If you have a food allergy or a religious objection to certain kinds of food, it's okay to ask the waiter to take it away, particularly if the menu doesn't make it clear that certain ingredients are in the dish.

> ### How Rare?
> When ordering meat, don't assume that the restaurant's idea of "medium-rare" is the same as yours. When in doubt, ask the waiter to clarify how the food is cooked. Nothing incurs the wrath of a chef faster than having perfectly prepared food sent back to the kitchen. And nobody wants to eat food cooked by a wrathful chef.

2. **The food is prepared incorrectly.** If you ordered a steak done rare and it comes out looking like a hockey puck, you're perfectly within your rights to send the food back. The same goes for chicken, which should be cooked all the way through; undercooked chicken can lead to salmonella infection.

3. **It's not what you ordered.** Mistakes happen, even in the best of restaurants. Sometimes the server will bring the wrong dish, or perhaps he or she misunderstood what you were saying when you ordered. But there's no reason to force yourself to eat something you don't want if you didn't order it.

4. **There's literally a fly in your soup.** Or a bug in your salad. Or a hair in your taco. Or any other foreign object in your food.

36. How to Split a Check

Who ordered the taco special? Vegetarian chili? Extra guacamole? Stop the madness before it begins by telling your waiter that you want separate checks before you place your order. If the group is too large or the waiter too busy, do the following.

1. Choose one person to act as accountant.

2. Decide if everybody will put in cash or if one person will pay with a credit card and be reimbursed.

3. Decide on a percentage for a tip. In most cities, it should be around 18 percent.

4. When the check comes, get a pad of paper. (You might have to ask the waiter for one.) The accountant should write down everyone's name on a slip.

5. Go through the bill. Under each name, the accountant should write what that person ordered and how much it cost.

6. Have the accountant add up the total and add in the tip. (Most cell phones have a calculator that can be used for this.)

7. Pass each person his or her slip.

8. Everyone should double-check their items and total.

9. If everyone's paying cash, write on the slip how much cash you put in. For example, if you owe $13.50 and you only have a $20 bill, write $20.00 so the accountant can figure your change. Pass cash and slip to the accountant.

10. If one person is paying by credit card, he or she should receive the slips along with either cash or an "IOU" for a later date.

37. When to Tip

Tipping is customary in America. In fact, many servers earn their livings solely from tips. A rule of thumb is to leave 18 percent of the total bill, excluding tax. Some people leave less if they feel their service was poor, but it is up to the patron's discretion to decide this. If you feel your service was extremely poor, ask to speak with a manager quietly. Make your complaints brief and specific; don't just walk out without saying anything or without leaving a tip. If you're paying with a credit card, you can either add the tip to the charge slip or leave it in cash on the table.

And don't forget to tip others in the service industry. Tip hair-stylists 10 to 20 percent of the bill, products and tax excluded. Tip skycaps at airports $1 per bag. And tip doormen $1 to $5, depending on how much help they provide.

38. What to Do When You Can't Stand Your Best Friend's Significant Other

You love your friends; you may not always love their lovers.

Sometimes it's a habit that rubs you the wrong way. Other times, you may have a serious conflict of personal, social, or ethical values. How can you keep the peace?

First, give it time. Some people feel shy, nervous, or defensive when faced with a lot of introductions. The bad habits and prickly attitude may fade after a while.

Recognize that there may be a bit of jealousy on your part, too. It's easy to feel put out when a good friend is suddenly wrapped up in someone else.

Try to schedule a little time alone with your friend. Don't criticize the new significant other. Just listen—there may be something you don't know that paints him or her in a much better light.

What if there really are irreconcilable differences? It's okay to let the significant other know you don't agree with his or her views—just don't turn every encounter into a fight.

Don't give your friend the ultimatum, "It's me or him/her!" When you're alone together, explain that you care about your friend, but you can't befriend the significant other. You may have to maintain your distance for a while.

Keep the door open, however. You'd want your friend to do the same for you!

39. How to Spot a Lie

Most people tell lies every once in a while. In fact, 98 percent of teenage respondents in one study admitted to lying at least once. If it's a "white lie"—a lie designed to spare someone's feelings—it might not be a big deal. But big lies not only hurt feelings, they can ruin relationships—especially if lying becomes a habit. Psychologists suggest that you look for these clues.

1. **Body language.** Sometimes our bodies tell a different story than our words do. Liars will often cover their mouths, rub their noses, or otherwise fidget in inadvertent "avoidance" poses when they are lying.

2. **Changing stories.** Liars often get small details incorrect when repeating lies.

3. **Eye contact.** Psychologists say that most people make eye contact at least half the time. If a person avoids your eyes, he or she may be lying.

> ### Lyin' Eyes
>
> Blinking might be the most universal sign of lying, according to a study at Portsmouth University in England. Researchers found that liars blink less frequently than normal while telling a lie. Their blinking rate goes way up immediately afterwards.

4. **Cadence and tone.** Is the person talking faster or slower than normal, or in a higher or lower pitch? This may be a sign that he or she is telling a falsehood.

40. How to Maintain Old Friendships

When you leave home and/or your childhood friends move away, you may wonder how best to preserve old friendships. Even though cities, states, or even countries separate you and your buddies, you can still keep in touch. Be proactive about keeping up with these friends, making a point to e-mail, call, text, or write letters whenever possible. Communicate regularly so you can stay up-to-date on each other's lives (and so that each time you talk, it doesn't necessarily have to be a three-hour-long game of conversational catch-up). It's likely that you and your friends will undergo changes while you are apart; try to be as open and accepting of these changes as possible, both in them and in you. Practice mutual respect, forgiveness, and acceptance, and be sure to express gratitude for their friendships. As the children's song goes: "Make new friends, but keep the old. One is silver and the other gold."

41. Preventing the "Freshman 15"

Changes in routine, activity level, emotional outlook, and diet—not to mention the loss of the structure and stability you experienced while living at home—all contribute to a phenomenon called "the freshman 15." This is the popular term for the extra pounds that many first-year college students tend to gain between high school graduation and the end of freshman year. Here are some tips that will help keep your weight steady.

✦ **Limit alcohol consumption.** Alcohol has a lot of calories, plus you tend to eat more when you drink.

✦ **Exercise regularly.** Many students are physically active in high school but slow down in college. Walk to class, take the stairs, and join an intramural team to maintain your metabolism level.

✦ **Eat breakfast.** Even if it's just a granola bar or bowl of cereal.

✦ **Drink lots of water and stay away from carbonated beverages.** Sugar-laden sodas can pack on the pounds.

✦ **Grab a piece of fruit every time you leave the dining hall and tuck it into your backpack.** That way, you'll have a healthy snack on hand when you get hungry.

✦ **Think about your day and determine when you will have time to eat before you get hungry.** Eating on the fly is a big factor in weight gain. Planning ahead can curb impulse eating.

✦ **College dining hall buffets make it very easy to overeat— especially high-calorie foods.** Even the salad bar can be a trap if you load up on cheese and high-fat dressings.

42. Five Unhealthy Foods That Masquerade as Nutritious

Maintaining a healthy diet isn't easy, but marketing gurus make it even tougher by disguising their sugary, fatty products as "health foods." Here are five foods whose nutrition labels don't match their reputations.

1. **Protein bars.** Most protein bars are loaded with sugar and saturated fats.

2. **Sports drinks.** Most of these drinks are packed with more sugar than electrolytes. Stick with water.

> ### Fat-free Doesn't Mean Calorie-free
> Food marketing departments often stick "fat-free" labels on their products in the hope that you overlook the enormous amounts of sugar they contain.

3. **Store-bought smoothies.** Smoothie chains often load their concoctions with high-calorie and high-fat ingredients such as ice cream, sugar, and chocolate.

4. **Restaurant salads.** Many restaurants load salads with toppings that turn them into 1,300-calorie gut bombs. Dressing on the side, please.

5. **Dried fruit.** Fresh fruit is healthy, but be wary of dried fruit, which is often loaded with sulfur and crystallized sugar. Health experts say that eating "candied" dried fruit isn't much different from eating candy itself.

43. Three Reasons to Avoid Fast-food Restaurants

Fast-food restaurants are convenient, quick, and relatively affordable. Unfortunately, fast food also is often fat food. When hunger strikes, consider the following before dining at a fast-food joint.

1. **Cost.** The average fast-food meal costs between $5 and $10. For that same amount of money, you could buy five to ten pounds

of whole grains and eat for days—and be a lot healthier.

2. **Sanitation.** According to an undercover report by the television program *Dateline,* the average fast-food restaurant isn't particularly clean. Reporters found cockroaches in soda cups, worms in salads, and dead rats in the kitchens of fast-food restaurants around the country. Still hungry?

3. **Nutrition.** Or lack thereof. The average McDonald's chicken sandwich gives you more than two-thirds of your recommended daily intake of sodium, while the massive quantities of fat in most fast food can cause endothelial dysfunction, a disorder of the blood vessels, among other health problems.

44. How to Eat Healthy at a Fast-food Restaurant (*If You Must Eat at a Fast-food Restaurant*)

Fast food is unhealthy. It's loaded with fat, sugar, and salt, and it lacks nutrients. But sometimes you can't resist hitting a fast-food restaurant on your way to school or work. Make the healthiest possible choices by following these guidelines.

Get a salad; don't use the dressing. When is a salad unhealthy? When it's loaded with fatty dressings. Get the dressing on the side or skip it altogether.

Skip the soda. That soda could cost you more than 400 calories. Self-serve soda machines are even more potentially disastrous. Drink water instead.

Keep it small. Bigger isn't necessarily better, especially when it comes to 1,000-calorie "super-size" gut bombs from fast-food chains.

Avoid the fryer. Don't order anything that's been fried—the oil adds enormous amounts of calories and fat. Yes, this includes french fries.

45. Basic First Aid

Knowing basic first aid keeps minor accidents from becoming full-blown emergencies. For more serious injuries, the professionals are just a phone call away: Just dial 911.

Pulled muscles and sprains. Try the RICE treatment. *Rest* the injured body part. *Ice* the area to reduce swelling. *Compress* the area, which also reduces swelling. *Elevate* the injured part by propping it higher than the heart to decrease swelling and pain.

Puncture wounds. Apply gentle pressure to stop the bleeding. If bleeding continues or blood spurts out after several minutes of pressure, call 911 and continue to apply pressure. If the bleeding stops, gently clean the wound and use sterilized tweezers to remove any debris. Apply a thin coat of an antibiotic ointment over the wound, then cover it with a bandage.

Burns. Soothe minor burns that affect the outer layer of skin with cold water, *not* ice. After 15 minutes, dry and cover with gauze. Do not apply ointment, and do not break blisters. For serious burns that char the skin and burn into deeper layers of skin, call 911, then only remove clothing that comes off easily; do not pull fabric from the burned area. Cover the burns with a clean cloth and apply pressure only if they are bleeding.

Insect stings. Scrape out the stinger and clean the area with soapy water. Apply ice for ten minutes or more to control swelling, and hold the area lower than the level of the heart. Take acetaminophen or ibuprofen for pain, if necessary.

46. First-Aid Kit Essentials

With a well-stocked first-aid kit, you can treat everyday mishaps like cuts, bruises, and insect stings in a snap, and you'll also be prepared for more severe injuries. Although you may have many of these items on hand, assembling a kit is a good way to double-check, and it will save valuable time if an accident occurs. Any shoebox-size container or even an extra-large reclosable plastic bag will work to store your kit.

+ Phone numbers for poison control, local emergency services, a personal physician, and an emergency contact
+ First-aid manual
+ Flashlight
+ Disposable gloves
+ Matches (to use as a light source or to sterilize a needle)
+ Hand sanitizer with alcohol (to disinfect hands if soap and water aren't available)
+ Cotton balls
+ Adhesive bandages in various sizes
+ One-inch-wide adhesive tape
+ Elastic bandage or wrap (for sprains or pulled muscles)
+ Cotton swabs
+ Four-inch square gauze pads
+ Instant cold pack
+ Medicine dispenser (for taking liquid medicine)
+ Sewing needle (for removing splinters)
+ Thermometer
+ Tweezers
+ Scissors
+ Saline solution (for flushing eyes)
+ Antihistamine (for allergic reactions)
+ Nonaspirin pain reliever
+ Aspirin (for heart attack)
+ Ipecac syrup (to induce vomiting)
+ Antibiotic ointment

Check Kit Out

Every six months or so, check the supplies in your kit. Check expiration dates and replace any items you have used or that have expired. Check the batteries in the flashlight and the thermometer.

- Hydrocortisone cream (for itching and swelling)
- Antidiarrhea medication
- Bottled water

47. What to Do if You Make a Mistake

We all make mistakes, but handling them gracefully is a sign of mature adulthood. Here are four steps to follow the next time you blunder.

1. **Admit your mistake.** A mistake is compounded by a refusal to "own" it.

2. **Apologize—and mean it.** There's nothing worse than somebody who says "I'm sorry" when they obviously aren't.

3. **Fix your mistake.** Do this quickly. Correcting your flub will help you learn—and will help ensure that you don't make the same mistake again.

4. **Learn from your mistake.** Identify what went wrong. Even better, identify the underlying cause. Was it a lack of concentration? A lack of know-how? A lack of confidence? Isolating and fixing the root of the problem will keep you from repeating it. Remember these famous words: "The only real mistake is the mistake from which we learn nothing."

48. How to Deal with Embarrassment

There are myriad ways to mortify yourself. Remember that everyone is embarrassed at some point! So *when* you next embarrass yourself (it's not a question of *if*), here's how to deal with it. First, don't obsess over the incident or devote a ton of energy to replaying it in your head. People will eventually forget what happened and time will minimize the incident's impact. Apologize to the appropriate people, if necessary, but again, don't dwell on it. The adage, "This too shall pass," is true. If possible, make light of your embarrassing occurrence: If you laugh, others will likely feel more at ease. Laughing will also keep you from taking things too seriously and help you get on with your life.

49. How to Apologize

We toss around the words "I'm sorry" very casually in conversation ("I'm sorry to bother you"; "I'm sorry I missed your call"), but when you've really messed up, how do you convey that you're truly sorry? Apologizing meaningfully can be difficult, but it's also incredibly important. First of all, you need to know for what you're apologizing. Then, you must be sincere and take full responsibility for your actions or words. Try to apologize at a time and in a place that is best for the recipient. (Muttering "I'm sorry" after an argument then scurrying out the door is not the most thoughtful course of action.) Avoid placing blame or making excuses. After you've apologized, be patient; don't expect the recipient's mood to change immediately. Ask to be allowed to rectify the situation, if that's possible. Then be sure you follow through and mean it.

50. Repairing a Hole in Your Pocket

If you're singing, "There's a hole in my pocket!" because there is one and, "With what shall I fix it?" because you don't know, then you need some practical answers. Here they are.

1. Thread a needle with thread that matches the color of the pocket. Double the thread for a stronger fix. Make a knot.

2. Turn the pocket inside out and check whether the hole is in the seam or in the fabric.

3. If the hole is in the seam, line up the two pieces of material and the seam. You can pin the pieces together or just hold them in place. Begin stitching at a spot about a half-inch away from the hole, working from right to left using small backstitches. Continue until you stitch about a half-inch beyond the formerly open seam. Make a knot, and cut the thread.

4. To repair a hole in the pocket's fabric, cut a patch that is a bit larger than the hole (approximately three-quarters of an inch larger on all sides) out of some other sturdy fabric, pin it in place, and sew around the patch using an angled stitch. Remove the pins, then revel in your new hole-free pocket!

51. How to Replace a Button

Threading a needle is the hardest part of sewing on a button. You can master this simple skill in ten minutes or less. All you need is a sharp needle that's small enough to fit through the buttonhole, thread that matches the thread color on the garment's other buttons, and scissors.

Knot a Problem

To make a knot, bring the two ends of the thread together and wrap them loosely two or three times around your index finger near the first joint. Push the thread to the end of your finger with your thumb so that the thread twists together and rolls over itself. Holding the loop with one hand, pull the ends of the thread through the center of the loop with your other hand until a knot forms. Pull taut.

1. Cut a 20-inch piece of thread, then thread the needle. Align the two ends and make a knot.

2. Place the button where it belongs and hold it there. Take the needle, and from underneath the garment, push it up through the fabric and one of the holes in the button. Pull the thread all the way through tightly, but not *too* tightly or the fabric will pucker. Push the needle down through the adjacent buttonhole, pulling the thread taut.

3. Continue working up and down through all buttonholes, making several passes through each one and keeping the thread taut. The button should lie flat and close to the top of the fabric but be loose enough to move with your fingers.

4. On the last stitch, bring the needle up through the fabric but stop before going through the buttonhole; instead, bring the needle out underneath the button. Wrap the thread tightly around the stitches that hold the button in place, then push the needle through the fabric to the underside of the garment. Make a loop with the thread and pass the needle through it three times, then pull tight to form a knot. Cut the thread close to the knot.

52. How to Fix a Hem

The most effective way to repair a hem is to slip off the garment, iron the hem to its original position, and whipstitch it into place.

If you don't know how to sew, try using fusible hem tape—a no-sew product that resembles double-sided tape. It's available in the notions or craft sections of variety, drug, and fabric stores. Iron the tape between the hem and pant leg to hold the hem in place. Fabric-glue products also work, but they might require a curing time before you can wear the garment. Low-temperature glue applied with a glue gun works wonders on jeans and other thick fabrics, but it will bleed through thinner materials.

53. How to Unstick a Zipper

A stuck zipper can really get you down. Here's how to solve the problem.

✦ Don't yank. Gently try to tug the zipper up and down to loosen it.

✦ Check for bits of thread or cloth that may be caught inside the teeth. Tease them out with tweezers, a needle, or even your fingers. If you remove the obstruction, the zipper should move freely again.

✦ For more stubborn problems, you'll need a lubricant. Use liquid hand or dish soap because they will wash out of clothing. Rub the soap around the zipper pull, working it into the stuck area and the zipper teeth below it. A sliver of hard soap will do if you don't have liquid, but it might not work as well.

> **What's with the YKK?**
>
> Your zipper pull is likely marked with the letters YKK. The initials stand for Yoshida Kogyo Kabushikigaisha, a Japanese firm that is the largest zipper-manufacturing company in the world.

✦ After the zipper is dislodged, pull it all the way down and then all the way up.

✦ You can add extra lubrication to a metal zipper by rubbing the point of an ordinary lead pencil against the teeth.

If you can't fix the zipper or it breaks, it can be replaced. Take the garment to a dry-cleaning establishment; these businesses often employ seamstresses and tailors who do repairs and tailoring.

54. How to Cram for a Test

It's the night before a big test and you haven't started studying. Whoops—time to cram! Here are some tips.

Know what you need to study. If you weren't paying attention when the instructor said what was going to be on the test, contact a classmate to get the scoop. Review your notes. See what you underlined or starred and what points the professor emphasized: These are good indicators of the topics on which you might be tested.

Write it down. Rewrite your notes to solidify the knowledge in your brain. Write key points down on index cards that you can use to quiz yourself halfway through your study session. Go back through your textbook to look for key words and highlighted passages.

Read materials provided by the instructor. Take any practice tests or quizzes in your textbook, as instructors may pull questions directly from them.

Use memorization tricks. Utilize the three "R's": Repetition, rhyming, and rewriting.

55. Staying Alert While Studying

That economics chapter about soy farming isn't fascinating material, but you've got a test on it in about twelve hours. How are you going to stay alert while cramming? Here are a few pointers.

1. **Get uncomfortable.** Sitting in a comfy couch or chair (or worse, sitting or lying in a bed) while studying is a good way to fall asleep. Study at the dining table or in a hard-back chair.

2. **Use proper lighting.** Turn on some bright lights and wake up.

3. **Drink water.** Drinking coffee keeps you awake, but water perks you up too—a full glass of cool water every couple of hours is invigorating.

4. **Move around.** Do something to stretch your muscles and get your blood flowing. Aerobic exercise is good for getting the blood pumping and stimulating your brain.

> ## Sugar, Nay!
>
> Don't load up on sugary drinks and junk food when you're pulling an all-nighter. The initial sugar high will lead to a major crash sooner than you think.

5. **Snack.** Avoid eating big meals, as they make you feel sluggish and dull afterwards. Small, light meals every few hours will give you the energy you need to stay alert.

56. Memory Tricks

If you have trouble remembering passwords, addresses, PIN numbers and more, try some of the following memory tricks.

Use your senses. You'll remember something much better if you connect it with multiple senses. Try to incorporate smell, touch, taste, sound, and sight—or as many of them as possible—to aid your recall.

Use humor. If you can attach a funny word, name, or mental cue to something you want to remember, you're more likely to recall it.

Repeat. If you want to memorize a password or phone number, repeat it (or write it) over and over…and over…

57. Sharpen Your Memory

Even if you weren't born with boffo recall, you can improve it. Build your brainpower with these memory-making tips.

Eat memory-enhancing foods. Green tea and chocolate boost memory, while omega-3 fatty acids in fish and nuts maintain brain function. Vitamins A, C, and E promote and preserve memory, and the mineral magnesium is critical for brain function and performance.

Get enough sleep. Sleep is the brain's equivalent of hard-drive defragmentation. A tired brain has trouble processing information, let alone filing it away for later use.

Exercise. Exercising relieves stress, enhances sleep, and increases blood flow to the brain.

Stimulate your brain. Try new hobbies and sports. Work crossword puzzles and read. Challenging your brain strengthens neural connections.

58. How to Remember Names

These memory tricks will help you confidently greet acquaintances—even those you've met only once—by name.

Use the person's name several times in conversation. Repeating the name will help you remember it.

Read the name out loud. If you are handed a business card, read the name and make an association that will help you remember it.

Write it down. Write down the name or names of people with whom you've spoken right after a job interview or important meeting, along with a description or something the person said.

Fudge a bit. Ask for a last name—people often will repeat their first names when they tell you their surnames. Or ask for a business card. Or introduce the person to someone else by saying, for example, "Do you know Pat?" The mystery person may then complete the introduction, revealing his or her name.

59. What to Do When the Power Goes Out

When the refrigerator stops humming or you're plunged into darkness, what should you do?

First, check to see if the outage is only in your building or if it covers a larger area. If power is on in part of your home but not in others, check your circuit breakers or fuse box for an overloaded circuit. These can be reset or replaced to restore power. If your entire building has lost power, check with your neighbors—often you can just look out the window to see the extent of an outage. If the cause is external, call the power company.

While you wait, be safe. Don't walk around outside if there might be damaged or downed power lines. These are often live and dangerous. Unplug your electrical equipment and appliances except for the refrigerator and/or freezer. Leave one light switch on so you know when the power comes back on. Sometimes electricity will surge when it is restored, so wait 15 minutes before you plug items back in. This allows the electrical current to level out.

60. What to Do When the Basement Floods

Water in the basement is every homeowner's nightmare. If your basement is flooded, follow these guidelines.

✦ Beware electrical hazards. Water and electrical appliances don't mix. Turn off all electrical appliances, or even the entire electrical system—but *only* if it's safe. (Avoid electrical devices and outlets submerged in water, as well as the water itself, which could be carrying an electrical current.) Don't turn appliances back on until everything is dry.

✦ If your basement doesn't have a sump pump, use a "wet-vac"—a special vacuum cleaner designed to suck up water. If you don't own a wet-vac, you can rent one. Or you can hire a professional.

✦ After you've removed the water, use a bleach-and-water solution to clean the floors and walls (make sure to ventilate the area while you're working) to kill bacteria and prevent the growth of mold and mildew. Rent a steam cleaner from your local hardware store to clean the carpets. If the water was tainted with sewage, toss the carpets and use a stronger bleach-water solution. Run a dehumidifier and fans to help dry out the room.

61. What to Do if the Smoke Alarm Goes Off

A blaring smoke alarm makes a terrifying noise for a reason: You need to get up and get out! Do not stop to look for valuables or try to identify what caused it to sound. Once outside, call the fire department. Even if you don't smell smoke or see flames, stay outside until the fire department arrives and gives the all-clear.

Sometimes smoke that is created while cooking causes the alarm to go off. Even if this happens repeatedly, do not, under any circumstances, disconnect the alarm. (If you are forced to take out the battery during a meal preparation, make sure you replace it when you're finished cooking.)

Develop a plan of action for a fire emergency. For example, devise an escape route with your roommates, and identify a meeting place outside of the house. A little time spent planning now can prevent tragedy down the road.

62. What to Do When the Tornado Siren Sounds

If you're inside a building when the tornado siren goes off, immediately head for the basement. If there is no basement, put as many walls as possible between you and the outside. Seek shelter in an interior room on the lowest level of the building, away from windows. Once there, get underneath a sturdy table if possible. Sit hunched over with your arms protecting your head and neck.

If you're driving, don't be tempted to try to outrace the tornado. Even SUVs are easily whipped away by tornado-force winds. Instead, get out of your car immediately and find shelter in a nearby building (not a mobile home). If there are no buildings, look for a depression or ditch in

Watch or Warning— What's the Dif?

A tornado watch means only that the conditions are right for a tornado. A tornado warning, on the other hand, means that twisters have been spotted in the area.

which you can lie down flat. Make sure it's away from trees, bridges, and underpasses, which can collapse during tornadoes. Cover your head with your hands.

63. Staying Connected with Your Family After You Leave Home

Getting established outside of the family home shouldn't mean cutting yourself off from the family. It's important for you—and for them—to stay in touch. Find a balance between enjoying your new freedom and maintaining contact with your family. Being "friends" with your parents and siblings on social networks such as Facebook is a great way to stay in touch. They can keep up with your life without constantly calling you. Of course, you'll need to be careful about what gets posted on your wall. Make time to call—even a 15-minute phone call will let family members know that you care about them. Asking your parents for advice—whether it's about how to make spaghetti sauce or a major life decision—is another great way to stay connected. You're still free to take it or leave it.

What Happened to My Room?

Moving out can be hard for you, too—especially if you come home to find that your old bedroom is now Mom's office. Staying in touch will keep these "surprises" to a minimum.

64. Home for the Holidays

The first few holidays you spend at home after moving out can be stressful—especially if your parents still treat you like a kid. And let's be honest—everyone reverts to childlike behavior when they go home. Here are some strategies for handling the holidays.

✦ **Make time to do family things.** Your parents want to see you. It's fine to spend time with old friends, but remember that your family misses you too.

✦ **Respect your family.** When you're on your own, you stay out until all hours every night. But when you're at home, you have other people's schedules to consider.

- **Discuss ground rules.** Explain that you want to abide by the house rules but that you also want to be treated as the adult you have become.
- **Keep your parents posted.** It's only fair to tell your parents your plans. After all, they have lives too, so they need to know if you'll be home for dinner or staying out late. And they worry!

65. How to Be Away from Home for the Holidays

What if you can't get home for the holidays? You can still make the holiday season a special time. Here are some holly-jolly ideas.

1. Get together with other "orphaned" friends and throw a holiday bash. Divide the cooking and decorating responsibilities and perhaps include an inexpensive or gag gift exchange.

2. Get temporarily "adopted" by a local family—maybe from your school or church—and participate in their holiday traditions.

3. Call or use a webcam with voice chat to stay connected with your family during the holiday season.

4. Have a holiday-theme film fest/slumber party with friends.

66. How to Survive Homesickness

Even if you are glad that you moved away from home, you still can feel homesick. Longing for the familiar is part of the adjustment process. It's normal to be happy one day and sad the next. Feeling uncomfortable or out of place, lonely, and nervous are common signs of homesickness. Here are some ways to ease the transition.

Call home. Hearing Mom or a friend say that everything will be okay sometimes makes it so.

Another Shade of Blue

If you can't shake feelings of sadness, cry without a reason, feel overly tired, or lose your interest in work, school, and activities you normally enjoy, you could be depressed. Talk to a professional counselor on campus or get a referral from a physician.

Go out. Go someplace with an energetic vibe, such as a local park or coffee shop. Make an effort to meet people by starting a conversation or a pickup game of Frisbee, for example.

Get involved. Join a sports team, club, gym, or community service program.

Try something new. If there's something you always wanted to do or learn, now is a good time to start. It's also a great way to meet like-minded people.

67. Laundry Basics

Now that you're responsible for the laundry, it seems more complicated than biochemistry. Here's how to get from a pile of dirty laundry to stacks of clean clothes.

Sort. For the best results, sort your laundry into whites (these can take bleach, hot water if you want to use it, and a hot dryer setting), darks, lights (in-between colors), and delicates (fabrics that require special handling).

Check pockets. Remove everything from all pockets before your clothes go into the washing machine or you will regret it.

Read labels. The labels will tell you if the garment is dry-clean only (which usually means that it shouldn't be machine-washed); which cycle to use for the washing machine; whether the garment can be dried and, if so, on what setting; whether it's safe to use chlorine or nonchlorine bleach; and more. Don't ignore the manufacturer's instructions unless you are ready to part with that piece of clothing.

Re-sort. Make more piles based on the label instructions. Also re-sort based on fabric weight. Dress shirts, for example, shouldn't be washed with heavy cotton clothes, even if they all can be washed in the permanent press cycle.

Pretreat. Look for stains and use a spray or solid stain remover on them before you put them in the washing machine. Once washed and dried, the stain will be hard—if not impossible—to remove.

68. When to Use the Cold and Hot Water Cycles

Laundry newbies are often paralyzed when it comes to choosing which water temperature to use. Don't worry—it's really not that complicated.

You will rarely need to use the hot water cycle. In fact, more and more laundry experts recommend washing *everything* in cold water, and many detergent manufacturers have come out with cold-water products. For most items the difference in cleanliness between hot and cold water is negligible, and because 90 percent of washing-machine energy usage comes from heating water, you can seriously cut down on your energy bill—and support the environment—by using cold water exclusively.

> ### *Adeiu*, Allergens
> If you've got allergies, consider using hot water for your sheets and towels. A recent study showed that washing fabric in hot water (above 140 degrees) eliminates 100 percent of dust mites, while washing the same items in cold or warm water eliminates only about 6 percent of the pests.

Heavily soiled and some stained items often require hot water to get clean, however, and many experts suggest using hot water for underclothes because it can kill bacteria lurking there. Some fabrics shrink and fade in hot water, however, so check the tags on the items you're washing. If a stained or filthy item should only be washed in cold water, pretreat it with a stain remover.

69. Don't Put These in the Dryer

If you're not careful about what you toss in the dryer, you might be in for an unpleasant surprise. Here are a few items that shouldn't go into the dryer.

Shoes. Although some of them *might* survive the dryer, it's generally a bad idea to dry shoes. The rubber and plastic on the soles could easily melt, and the leather will crack and shrink. If your shoes get wet, try stuffing them with newspaper to absorb moisture.

Leather. Leather will shrink and crack when dried in a dryer.

Silk. The hot air of a dryer will dull and shrink silk, so you should air-dry silk clothing (and sheets) on a clothesline or rack.

Wool. Most types of wool will shrink when exposed to heat. Air-dry your wool sweaters (lay them on a rack or on a thick towel on the floor, reshaping them while wet).

70. When to Use the Permanent Press Setting on the Dryer

Take Action

The permanent press setting doesn't guarantee that your clothes will be wrinkle-free. Remove your clothes from the dryer immediately after the cycle ends. Clothing and linens that sit in a machine or laundry basket will wrinkle, regardless of the cycle on which they were dried.

The permanent press setting dries clothes by using a special cool-down feature that runs near the end of the cycle to help minimize wrinkling so that they look like they've been pressed. The permanent press cycle will also tumble the clothes periodically after the cycle is done, until the items are removed; this also helps prevent wrinkles from setting in.

Clothes marked as "permanent press" aren't the only ones that can go into a permanent press dryer cycle. In fact, according to manufacturer Maytag, it's a good idea to *always* use the dryer's permanent press setting, regardless of the type of fabric being dried.

Because it uses cool air during the permanent press cycle, the dryer uses less electricity or gas. That means you're helping to save the environment—and your pocketbook too.

71. Deconstructing the Fabric Care Label

Following the fabric-care instructions on clothing labels will help your clothing last longer and stay cleaner. Here are some common terms that are used on labels and what they mean.

Machine wash. It's safe to launder these clothes in the washing machine. This instruction is often followed by a recommended water temperature. If no setting is indicated, stick with cold.

Wash separately. This means the colors may run, so wash the item on its own first and later perhaps with like colors.

Hand wash only. Wash and rinse in a basin. The label will tell you whether you can wring it out.

Dry clean only. In general, don't put these garments in the washing machine.

Tumble dry. Safe for the dryer; there should be a temperature or cycle setting—such as "Tumble Dry Low"—indicated as well.

Dry flat. Don't put the garment in the dryer, and don't hang it—lay it flat to dry.

Non-chlorine bleach only. Non-chlorine bleach is also known as "color-safe" bleach. Regular chorine bleach will fade or remove the color from fabrics that are marked this way.

72. What Is Fabric Softener?

Fabric is often soft, but it doesn't always come out of the washer or dryer that way. Fabric softener helps fabric *remain* soft after laundering. It's also useful for reducing static cling.

Fabric softener comes in two forms: liquid and dryer sheets. Dryer sheets are much easier to use—just throw one into the dryer with the wet clothes. The liquid variety requires a little more effort—it needs to go into the washer during the start of the rinse cycle. Putting it in at the wrong time could stain the clothes.

So which is better? It's not clear. Many people swear by dryer sheets, but some studies have shown that liquid softener may work better with some synthetic materials. Decide for yourself.

> **FAST FACT**
>
> When you wash and dry towels, it's best to skip the softener. The coating action of both liquid fabric softener and dryer sheets reduces towels' absorbency.

73. How to Make a Bed

A neatly made bed will help you sleep comfortably, and it will make your room look more attractive.

1. Starting with clean sheets, place the fitted sheet (the one with the elastic at the corners) on the mattress pad and secure each corner. Smooth it out.

2. Lay the flat sheet on top of the fitted sheet with the right or decorated side facing down. Align the top edge of the sheet with the top of the mattress. Make sure the sides of the sheet that are hanging down are even, then tuck the bottom edge of the sheet under the mattress. Make hospital/military corners at the bottom corners; if you don't know how, look online for instructions. Hospital corners keep the sheets tucked in more securely and will make your bed look like a well-wrapped present. You can leave the sides hanging down or tuck them in as far up the bed as you like.

3. Add a blanket or comforter on top of the sheet for warmth. You can enclose a comforter in a duvet cover—which is like a pillowcase for it—to help keep it clean. Duvet covers are also decorative.

4. Fold the top of the flat sheet over the top of the blanket so that the decoration or hem of the sheet is revealed.

5. If you don't use a duvet cover, you can add a bedspread for decoration and to keep the blanket clean.

> ### Go Euro
> Some people like sleeping the European way: They use a bottom sheet but no top sheet. On top, they use a duvet-covered comforter.

6. Put pillowcases on the pillows and fluff them. Place them at the head of the bed.

74. How Often to Change the Sheets

Generally speaking, you should change linens once a week. That's because we all shed skin cells (bedbugs' and dust mites' favorite meal), bodily fluids, and hair that collect on sheets and pillowcases. How grungy your linens get, however, depends on your own personal habits. If you don't bathe every day or wear clean pajamas, or if you use the bed for more than sleeping (i.e., to eat, study, watch movies, or have sex), then your sheets will get dirty faster and you'll need to change them more frequently. If you are sick, consider changing the pillowcase every night. And be sure to change the sheets after you've recovered.

75. How to Fold a Fitted Sheet

The secret to folding a fitted sheet is to take your time and work in a large open space where you can lay the sheet flat. There is more than one way to get the job done, and they all are easier to show than to tell (a premise supported by the number of online videos available on the subject). Here are the basics; if you need visual aids, surf the Web.

✦ Lay the sheet flat on a bed or a table so that the elasticized edges are curved over the top surface of the sheet. The sheet will look like a square with rounded corners.

✦ Smooth wrinkles from the center of the sheet to the edges. Fold each long side to the center of the sheet so that the edges meet in the middle. Picture a window with two shutters that open to either side; when the edges of the sheet are folded to the center, they resemble the window with the shutters closed.

✦ Fold the left side over the right side so that the edges of the sheet are hidden inside.

✦ Fold the sheet longways so that the ends meet; fold over two more times to finish.

76. Don't Let the Bedbugs Bite

A bedbug infestation isn't dangerous, but it can deprive you of sleep and drive you crazy. Signs of a bedbug infestation include small, itchy welts on the body (from bites), small dots of blood on the sheets (from smashed bedbugs), and empty brown husks around the bed (from molting bedbugs). Once you have bedbugs, there's very little you can do about it. They're nocturnal, elusive creatures that hide everywhere—under floorboards, behind electrical switches, and in the seams of mattresses. Not only that, but they are are able to survive more than a year without eating and in a wide range of temperatures.

Experts resoundingly agree that the only real way to eradicate bedbugs is to call a pest control service. While this can be costly, it may be a small price to pay for a good night's sleep.

77. How and Why to Use a Debit Card

There are many advantages to using a debit card when you're first starting out. Since most retailers accept them, it will free you from carrying around lots of cash, and you can always withdraw money from an ATM if need be. A debit card gives you that flexibility without exposure to the financial risk inherent in using a credit card. This is because debit cards deduct money directly from your bank account—usually your checking account, but some debit cards also deduct from your savings. You can only spend money that you actually have, so you'll avoid racking up debt.

How to Debit Safely

"Skimming" is an increasingly popular way of committing debit card fraud. Thieves install fake card readers on ATMs and gas pumps to steal your information—and your funds. The best way to stay safe is to only use ATMs at banks or other places you trust—and to check your bank balance frequently.

To use a debit card, simply present it to the cashier. who will swipe it and ask you if you wish to use debit or credit. After choosing debit, you'll be asked to type a personal identification number, or PIN, into a keypad. The store's computer connects with your bank, and the bank will send back an approval code. You may or may not have to sign anything—when a tip is part of the bill, for example, you'll need to sign a receipt. Some establishments have self-swipe machines. The process is the same, but you'll do the swiping.

Be sure to record all your transactions as soon as you're able so you can keep track of how much money you have available. Since a debit card is tied to your actual bank balance, you'll be charged overdraft fees if you spend more than what's in your account.

78. How to Avoid and Handle Credit Card Balances

Credit cards eliminate the need to carry much cash, and they're handy for shopping—online or in person—or handling emergency expenses. You may even earn rewards for using them. However, credit cards can quickly become financial boondoggles if you don't pay off your entire balance each month. If your card has a high interest rate, it will take an eternity to pay it off if you let your balance get out of control. Here's how to use credit cards wisely.

Pay on time. Even if you're only making the minimum payments, it's critical to pay on time. Credit card companies jack up rates and add fees for missed payment deadlines.

Stop using the card. It's virtually impossible to pay off credit card bills when you keep adding to the total balance each month. Switch to cash or a debit card, which is linked to your checking account.

Pay high interest rates first. If you have multiple credit cards with balances, focus on paying off the ones with the highest interest rates first.

Budget. The key to using and paying down credit cards is smart budgeting. Figure out how much you need to spend on necessities, and apply the rest of your income to paying your credit card bills.

79. Building Good Credit

As a young person just beginning to deal with your personal finances, you can build a good credit rating right off the bat. Remember, it's much easier to build good credit than to try to repair bad credit later on. Here's how to build a strong financial foundation.

1. **Pay your bills on time.** Pay every bill—utility bills, phone bills, doctor bills, etc.—on time. This keeps them from going to a collection agency and prevents black marks on your credit report.

2. **Pay your credit card balances each month.** If you don't, you'll hurt your credit score and you may plunge into debt.

3. **Don't charge more than a third of a card's limit.** Using too much of your available credit can hurt your credit score (and make balances hard to pay off).

4. **Don't have too many open credit accounts.** Having too many credit cards will tarnish your record. You need only one or two credit cards, which should be paid off each month.

> ## Use Your Freedom
> You are entitled to one free credit report per year from each of the three major credit-reporting agencies (Experian, TransUnion, Equifax). Checking these regularly, and fixing any discrepancies, will help you maintain a good credit history.

5. **Maintain checking and savings accounts.** Having both is a sign of stability.

80. How to Check Facts

What can and can't you believe? Here's how to verify the legitimacy of things that you hear or read.

1. Check the information against reliable sources, such as encyclopedias, dictionaries, atlases, and reputable Web sites— particularly those of government agencies, foundations, and professional organizations and associations

2. Use Web sites such as Snopes, FactCheck, and The Straight Dope, whose missions are to get to the bottom of urban legends, hard-to-answer questions, and political spin.

3. Be wary of words like "always," "exactly," and "in fact," and investigate claims of total certainty.

4. Ask a reference librarian for help. They can point you toward helpful resources.

5. If possible, go straight to the source. Consult a professional— a scientist, lawyer, teacher, or doctor, for example.

81. How to Spot an Urban Legend

Urban legends, like folklore, are invented stories told to express fears or pass along moral lessons. They often sound so believable that they can be difficult to spot. Here are a few telltale signs.

The story is about "a friend of my uncle" or "a cousin of a friend." Urban legends almost always take the form of an event that has happened to a distant connection of the storyteller.

The teller insists it really happened. Think about it—when you tell somebody about something that happened to you, do you preface it with assurances about its truth?

The story has a moral or an unexpected twist. Urban legends often take the forms of morality tales or "lessons."

You've heard very similar stories before. How many people's cousins' friends could have had the exact same bizarre experience with a McDonald's chicken sandwich?

It's an e-mail chain letter claiming "not to be a hoax." Just about every e-mail chain letter claiming not to be hoax actually *is* one.

82. Know the Difference Between Facts and Opinions

Being able to differentiate between factual statements and opinions is a critical life skill. Today more than ever before, opinion masquerades as fact in print and over the air. Here's an example: "The new school dress code is not supported by 54 percent of the student body and will lead to students rebelling against it." The statement "not supported by 54 percent of the student body" is a fact (if the students were polled), but the statement "will lead to many students rebelling against it" is an opinion—no one knows for sure whether this will occur. Pay attention to language and ask yourself whether statements can be proved. Although certain words, such as "stated," "demonstrated," and "according to," are often clues to the presence of factual statements, they can be attached to opinions to make them seem true. Watch out for descriptions that could be fact but often are opinion. A statement such as "The man was angry," is only fact if the man himself said that was his emotional state—perceptions are opinions, too. Be aware that writers can misuse language and, thus, misrepresent information. Don't accept any statement without questioning, and always check facts.

83. How to Tell if You Have a Cold or the Flu

It's easy to mistake a cold for the flu, or vice versa. Both can bring on headaches, sore throats, and stuffy or runny noses. The flu, however, is accompanied by muscle aches and fever, and it makes you feel sicker than a cold does.

A lab test is the only way to determine which illness you have. Usually it doesn't matter—both illnesses require rest, fluids, and a nutritious diet. Antibiotics are ineffective against both, since neither is a bacterial infection. (Secondary infections, such as bronchitis, are caused by bacteria and may require antibiotic treatment.)

The flu can be treated with prescription antiviral medication, which is most effective when taken within 48 hours of the first symptoms. The best defense against getting the flu is an annual flu shot, which can prevent or decrease the length and severity of the illness.

84. Effective Cold Remedies

On average, adolescents and adults come down with two to four colds per year. There's no cure, so you should simply look for symptom relief. Here's what you need to know.

Drink plenty of fluids, rest, and gargle with salt water. These are simple and very effective.

Stick with ibuprofen or acetaminophen for aches and pains. These can relieve muscle aches caused by colds, as well as sinus pain. However, don't take them in conjunction with a cold medicine that lists one of them as an ingredient.

Look for single-ingredient over-the-counter medicines. Cold symptoms can last up to two weeks, but you won't have all of them at the same time. It's best to use medication that treats only the symptoms you currently have.

Know that a sore throat might signal a more serious infection. A burning, painful sore throat or one that doesn't go away after a few days can be caused by a different infection. See your doctor.

Try natural remedies. Studies have found that honey actually eases a cough better than over-the-counter medicine. Saline nose drops thin mucus in sinuses, opening up the passages and making them easier to clear.

85. When to Use a Walk-in Clinic

If you're ill and can't reach your doctor or lack a health insurance plan, go to a walk-in clinic—which also may be called an immediate- or urgent-care clinic—for efficient, low-cost medical care.

Retail walk-in clinics only treat common conditions, such as strep throat, sinus infections, and minor injuries. If you're not sure whether the clinic treats the condition you have, check its Web site or call ahead. When you arrive at the clinic, you will likely meet with a nurse practitioner (rather than a doctor) who can write a prescription for you, if necessary. Some clinics accept insurance coverage, but call first to find out. Your other option is to pay in cash. Basic procedures—such as flu shots and treatment for minor burns—are relatively inexpensive.

Don't Walk In with These

There are times when you shouldn't go to a walk-in clinic. If you have a high fever (above 103 degrees Fahrenheit), a recurring condition (or one that afflicts you more than four times per year), or a severe pain, get an appointment at a doctor's office or go a hospital emergency room.

86. When to See a Doctor

If you have early symptoms of a cold or flu, you can treat them on your own. If congestion drags on for more than two weeks, however, or if you are vomiting and cannot keep down fluids, make a doctor's appointment. You should see also see a doctor if you have any of the following symptoms: an earache, a cough that lasts for more than two or three weeks, dehydration, persistent fatigue, unexplained weight loss, a seizure, a severe headache, abnormal bleeding or blood in the urine or stool, or problems with vision. You can assess your symptoms before seeing a doctor by using the online symptom checker at WebMD.com.

87. Where to Get Medical Help if You Don't Have a Doctor

Young, healthy people don't often think about their health—or bother to find primary care doctors—until they need to see one. Finding a doctor is even more challenging if you're sick and without insurance. But just because you don't have a permanent doctor doesn't mean you can't get medical assistance. Try these:

Free clinics. Contact your local library or department of health and human services for a list of free health clinics in your area. One caveat: Many free clinics require proof of low income or are appointment only.

Walk-in clinics. Many hospitals have satellite walk-in clinics in city neighborhoods, suburbs, and rural areas. A visit may be followed by a hospital-size bill afterward, however, so ask about charges first.

Pharmacy clinics. Some major pharmacy chains, such as CVS and Walgreens, have low-cost, no-appointment, in-store clinics that are staffed by nurses and doctors. They provide quick diagnosis and treatment for common illnesses such as strep throat and the flu.

88. The Shelf Lives of Seven Common Foods

Green fuzz is a clear indication that cheese has gone bad. But other foods don't give such obvious signs of spoilage. Use the following guide.

1. **Butter.** When refrigerated, one to three months. If frozen, six to nine months.

2. **Eggs.** Raw: Three to five weeks after purchase. Hard-boiled: Use within one week.

3. **Milk.** Refrigerated milk lasts for about one to three weeks, depending on when it was packaged (check the sell-by date). Milk in an aseptic package (the unrefrigerated kind found on store shelves) lasts six months unopened, and seven to fourteen days after opening.

4. **Hamburger.** Ground beef should be used within a day of purchase, but it can be frozen for up to four months.

5. **Lunch meat.** Unopened, packaged lunch meat will last for about two weeks. Once opened, plan on eating it within three to five days.

6. **Ketchup.** This culinary staple will last for a year unopened and six months in the fridge after opening.

7. **Breakfast cereal.** Stored unopened in a pantry, cereal should last for about a year. After it is opened, it lasts for about two to three months.

89. How to Tell if Food Is Spoiled

You're half-starved and the fridge is empty except for a small container of ancient leftovers. Is it safe to eat?

If the food has an odd color or has mold or fungus growing on it, don't eat it. Similarly, swollen, dented, and bulging cans are classic signs of spoilage. Spoiled food will often smell rotten or rancid. You'll know a rotten food odor when you sniff it! Check the expiration date. Foods don't magically go bad after the date marked—and in fact, many foods stay unspoiled well past their expiration dates. But it *is* useful information. If a food seems suspicious and it's past its expiration date, throw it out.

90. When to Replace Four Common Household Items

A great way to save money—and be environmentally conscientious—is to use products until they wear out. But how old is *too* old? Here's a quick guide to replacing five common items.

Toothbrush. Frayed bristles or a little grime means it's time to replace the toothbrush. The American Dental Association recommends getting a new toothbrush every three to four months.

Pillows. After a year, most pillows have absorbed enough hair oil and allergens that they may be hindering your sleep more than helping it. Use a pillow protector (a zippered case that goes on the pillow and under the pillowcase), which can increase its lifespan to two years.

Cosmetics. Makeup that touches the eyes, such as eyeliner and mascara, should be replaced every six months. Other kinds of makeup, such as foundation, can last up to three years.

Contact lens solution. Change open containers every three months to avoid bacterial growth.

FAST FACT

Though most household goods go bad after a few months, there are some that you never have to replace. Rubbing alcohol is one example. Since alcohol kills bacterial microbes, a bottle of the stuff can last for decades.

91. How to Write a Cover Letter

A cover letter offers a glimpse of your personality and reinforces your strong points. A good one will keep your résumé out of the "circular file." Here are the ABCs of cover-letter writing.

Always use an appropriate format. Include your address, the date, and the name, title, and address of the person to whom you are writing on the upper left side of the letter. Follow with a formal salutation ("Dear So-and-So"). Explain your reason for writing and highlight your experience and what makes you special. It should take no more than three paragraphs to get your point across. Use a formal closing ("Respectfully," etc.) and sign the letter in blue ink—it contrasts with the black type on the letter.

Be personal. Send your letter to an actual person. If possible, make a personal connection—mention a mutual friend, organization, or event, or drop the name of a friend who works at the same company.

Confidently state what makes you the right person for the job. Everyone juggles responsibilities, but your experience doing so while working on a transatlantic ocean liner—sans Internet and daily communication with the home office—gives you an edge. Be specific and relate your experience to the position, but don't boast.

92. Acing a Job Interview

The best way to make a good impression at a job interview is to be prepared.

✦ Find out as much as you can about the position, the interviewer, and the company beforehand. Do some online research, ask friends and family if they know anyone who works at the company, and visit the company's Web site to familiarize yourself with its mission/goals. Be ready to talk about your strengths and weaknesses. Prepare anecdotes about your strengths and a way to spin your weaknesses into positives. For example, discuss something that you struggled with but overcame in your last job.

✦ Don't forget the basics: Be on time and dress appropriately.

✦ The interview is also your opportunity to learn more. Ask questions to show that you're interested and to get clarification if you need it.

✦ Don't bring up salary. You can talk numbers after you land the job.

93. How to Finish Strong

Follow-through can be the difference between getting a job and standing in the unemployment line. Ask when a decision may be made and when it might be appropriate to check back. Then do it. Send a brief, genuine, and enthusiastic thank-you note. If it comes down to a choice between you and another candidate, this can make all the difference. If someone referred you to the job, ask him or her to put in a good word about you.

94. How to Cope with Jealousy

When life isn't fair, it's easy to turn green with envy. Occasional jealousy is normal; plotting revenge 24/7 isn't. How can you shake a case of the greens and get on with your life?

- ✦ **Exercise.** Working up a sweat will work off negative feelings.
- ✦ **Do something for someone else.** Helping others will help put your own problems in perspective.
- ✦ **Polish your self-image.** Make a list of ten things you like about yourself.
- ✦ **Write down your goals.** Then try to come up with one or two things you can do to achieve them.

The trick to beating jealousy is to look forward, not back.

95. What to Do if You're in an Abusive Relationship

Are you afraid of your partner's temper? Do you avoid certain topics of conversation with him or her? Is your partner highly critical of your friends and family? Have you stopped socializing or seeing other people? Do you feel like it's your fault when your partner isn't happy?

> **FAST FACT**
>
> One in every five teenagers has experienced an emotionally abusive dating relationship, according to the U.S. Centers for Disease Control and Prevention.

Abusive relationships don't always involve physical violence. Some relationships are psychologically and emotionally abusive.

To leave an abusive relationship, you need a support network. Talk about the situation with a close friend or family member. If you fear the abuse will turn physical, contact the domestic violence unit of your local police department or call social services. If you're a student, college counseling services can help. Keep a journal of the practical steps you take; it will help you sort out your emotions.

If you live with your partner, make sure that you have a safe place to go. If you've signed a lease together, contact your landlord. If you decide to stay and ask your partner to move out, you will have to change the locks on all doors.

If you feel comfortable talking with your partner face-to-face, choose a neutral, public location to tell him or her that it's over. It's okay to have mixed feelings about the situation. You don't have to justify your decision or beg for forgiveness—just state clearly, "I'm taking control of my life and doing what's best for me."

96. How to Start a Fire Without Matches

Warmth is almost as important to the human body as air and water. Knowing how to start a fire without matches could make the difference between life and death.

You need two things to start a fire: tinder and heat. Tinder (the stuff that catches fire) can be anything that's dry and easily combustible—brown pine needles, dried leaves, or old newspapers can work. Heat comes from the sun, and you can use a lens to amplify its intensity. A magnifying glass, an eyeglass, a broken bottle glass, or even ice carved into a lens shape can act as a lens.

> ### Fiction About Friction
>
> In the old movies, people often started fires by rubbing two sticks together. Unless you have absolutely no other option, avoid this friction-based fire-starting technique—it's the most difficult way to get the job done.

Pile the tinder in a flat, wind-sheltered place. If you can dig a small hole, that's even better. Next, generate heat. Angle the lens so that it concentrates the sunlight into a point. and direct it onto the pile of tinder. Eventually, you should see smoke coming from the tinder; blow gently on it to encourage the flame. Once it combusts, add kindling such as small twigs or branches to make the fire larger.

Of course, this only works on a sunny day. If it's cloudy or dark out and there's an automobile nearby, you can get a spark from its battery. Take two pieces of wire and attach each to one of the battery's terminals. Collect some tinder and bring it over to the car. Touch the wires together, right over the tinder—there should be a spark, which will make the tinder smolder. Blow on it and continue as above.

97. How to Stay Afloat in the Water

You don't have to know how to swim to learn how to float! The key to floating is to relax. Tightening and tensing your muscles will make you sink. Practice in shallow water with a friend to get the hang of it before you venture into deeper water.

✦ Spread your legs shoulder-width apart, and put your arms out to the side.

✦ Take a deep breath and hold it.

✦ Relax all your muscles as you lay back in the water.

✦ Achieve a supine position—your legs should be spread apart and your arms still out to the side, almost as if you're sprawled on the bed after a hard day at work. Breathe.

98. Save a Life: Learn CPR

Cardiopulmonary resuscitation, or CPR, restores the circulation of oxygen-rich blood to the brain of someone who is in cardiac arrest. Without it, permanent brain damage or death can occur in fewer than eight minutes. To learn CPR, it's best to take a class. But if you're in a situation that calls for CPR, follow these guidelines.

1. Call 911, then check to see if the person is breathing. Tilt the head back, put your ear next to the mouth, and listen. Gently shake the person and ask if he or she is okay.

2. If something is in the person's mouth, scoop your finger inside to remove it.

3. If the person isn't breathing, tilt the head back, pinch the nose, and cover the mouth with yours. Blow a breath into the person's mouth until you see the chest rise. Repeat. Each breath should take about one second.

4. After two breaths, start chest compressions. Place the heel of one hand into the middle of the person's chest, between the nipples, and cover it with your other hand. Push down on the chest forcefully and quickly, one-and-a-half to two inches. Do this 30 times to achieve a rate of 100 pumps per minute.

5. Continue with breaths and chest compressions until help arrives.

99. How to Use a Compass

To read a compass, first you must find north. No matter what kind of compass you use, one end of the needle—usually the red end—points north, so rotate the compass until the red end lines up with "N." For accurate compass readings, make sure that you keep the magnetic red end lined up with north at all times. If you are reading a map, rotate it so that north on the map lines up with the "N" on the compass.

Lunar Locator

You can use the moon to find the general direction of true north. If the moon rises before sunset, its bright side is in the west; when the moon rises after midnight, its bright side is in the east. Once you've established these directions, you can easily figure out which way is north.

100. Meet Your Stove

You may be avoiding your stove, but the two of you are due for a dinner date. Here are a few things it can do better than your microwave.

Broil a steak. Broiling is cooking under high heat. Some ovens have separate broiler units; others broil within the main oven. There should be a notch on the oven dial marked "broil." Broiling doesn't take long, so don't overdo it. For best results, place the food four to six inches from the source of the heat.

Bake a potato. Baking is cooking in dry heat. Most baking is done between 350 and 475 degrees Fahrenheit. Your potato is done when a fork slides into and out of it easily.

Boil some pasta. Boiling is done in a pot of water on the stovetop. The water should be at least two inches from the rim of the pot. It has reached a rolling boil when bubbles break through the surface. As soon as this happens, add the pasta. Wait for the water to return to a boil, then reduce the heat and simmer.

Sauté vegetables. Also known as pan-frying, sautéing is cooking food in a pan that contains about an inch of liquid, usually oil, liquefied fat, or broth. The burner should be set to low or medium heat.

101. How to Clean the Refrigerator

The easiest way to keep a refrigerator clean is to prevent it from getting too dirty in the first place. Wipe up spills quickly and don't let food sit around until it's gross. Take a couple minutes to do this, and you won't be faced with a disgusting cleaning job a couple times a year. When deep cleaning is called for, however, first empty the fridge. Remove all dishes that contain leftovers, toss old food items, and wipe down jars, making sure to clean their bottoms. Remove vegetable drawers and shelves, wash them with warm soapy water, and let them dry. Use a warm, soapy cloth to wipe out the entire inside of the refrigerator, making sure to clean the inside of the door, door shelves, and the back-of-the-drawer slots. Use a wet cloth to wipe away any soap residue. Empty the drip pan if there is one. Remove the grill from the bottom-front of the refrigerator and pull out the drip pan. Wash the pan with warm, soapy water; use an old toothbrush and a baking-soda-and-water paste if vigorous scrubbing is required. When it is dry, slide the drip pan back in place. Replace racks and drawers. To deodorize the entire fridge, open a box of baking soda and put it in the back on a shelf.

102. How to Clean the Microwave

If the inside of your microwave is beginning to resemble a Jackson Pollock painting, it's time to give it a thorough cleaning. First, remove the glass carousel tray. Then take a damp sponge or paper towel and wipe down the entire inside of the microwave, removing any crumbs. Fill a microwave-safe bowl with several cups of water and two tablespoons of vinegar or lemon juice (though if you have neither, just water will do). Microwave the bowl on high for three to five minutes. Keep the door closed for a few minutes afterwards—the steam will loosen baked-on food and grime. Carefully remove the bowl (it may be hot), then wipe down the inside again. Stubborn food spots can be removed using an old toothbrush and a paste of baking soda and water. Alternately, you can continue heating water and steaming until no baked-on residue remains. Clean the glass carousel tray with warm, soapy water, rinse it, and dry it before putting it back in the microwave.

103. How to Keep the Kitchen Clean

Really cleaning the kitchen—which includes sweeping behind the oven and scrubbing the bottom of the refrigerator drawers—is a lot of work, though it is necessary every once in a while. But before you sweep this advice away, remember that by doing little things each day to keep your kitchen tidy, you won't need to undertake a huge cleaning quite so often. Here are some suggestions.

✦ Don't leave dishes in the sink.
✦ After cooking on the stove (especially if you made a bubbling soup or a messy pasta sauce, for example), wipe the surface—including the area around each burner—with a damp, slightly soapy sponge.
✦ Clean up spills right away.
✦ Wash dish towels before they get a mildewy smell. Wring out your sponges after each use and replace them every month.
✦ Designate a "junk drawer" where you can store odds and ends such as pens, takeout menus, matches, and twist ties.

104. How to Improve Your Knowledge of Geography

Do you know where to find Uzbekistan and Turkmenistan on a world map? Need to brush up on the names of countries, cities, and seas? Improving your knowledge of world geography can help you win at trivia, but more importantly, it will remind you of the vastness and diversity of our world. Here are some fun ways to increase your knowledge of geography:

✦ Tag a globe or atlas with all the places you've been or want to go in the world. Calculate how far these locations are from you.

✦ Memorize all 50 U.S. state capitals. Have a friend or family member quiz you on them.

✦ Go online and play geography games to hone your skills.

✦ Explore unfamiliar countries, as well as the streets and buildings of your own town, on the Web site Google Earth.

✦ Read books such as *Don't Know Much About Geography: Everything You Need to Know About the World but Never Learned*, by Kenneth C. Davis.

105. How to Improve Your Vocabulary

To improve your vocabulary, try some of the following suggestions.

1. Read!

2. If you come across a word you don't know, write it down, then look up its definition as soon as possible. Many online dictionaries now feature audio options that allow you to hear words pronounced correctly.

3. Sign up to receive a daily e-mail with the "Word of the Day" from *Dictionary.com.*

4. Do word searches and crossword puzzles, and play word-oriented board games such as Scrabble.

Eleven Common Misspellings

These words are often spelled incorrectly: Accidentally (often "Accidently"); Cemetery (vs. "Cemetary"); Jewelry (not "Jewellery"); Millennium (often "Millenium"); Occurrence (not "Occurence" or "Occurrance"); "Precede" (instead of "Preceed"); Relevant (often "Relevent" or "Revelent"); Separate (as opposed to "Seperate"); "Twelfth" (vs. "Twelth"); Weird (often "Wierd").

106. How to Be Ignorant Gracefully

It's impossible to know something about everything. This is what to do when other people are discussing a topic about which you know nothing.

Ask questions. This will help you learn about the topic and show that you're interested—and it will keep you from feeling left out.

Don't belittle. Just because you aren't interested in the topic doesn't mean that it's not important.

Don't bluff. Watching somebody hem and haw and pretend to know something is agonizing for everyone.

Steer the conversation. Subtly try to nudge the discussion toward a more familiar topic. Just don't drop a non sequitur.

107. What to Do if You're in a Car Accident

Being in a car accident can leave you rattled, so it's important to know what to do in advance. First, check to see if everyone involved is okay. Call 911 if there are injuries; the operator will call police to the scene. If you don't require emergency assistance, call the police yourself.

If no one is hurt and the accident is minor, move your car to the side of the road if possible. Put on your emergency flashers. Determine if you can safely stay in or with the vehicle. Don't walk around to assess the damage unless you are away from traffic.

Take your insurance card and related papers out of the glove box. Exchange names, driver's license numbers, phone numbers, and insurance company and policy information with the other driver. Write notes about the model, make, and color of the other car, its license plate number, and what you remember about the accident. If you have a cell phone with a camera, take a few photos. Do not be tempted to settle the situation on your own; without a police report, you won't be able to file an insurance claim.

If your car needs to be towed, remove any valuables and personal items. If police don't come to the scene, go to the police station to file a report. Notify your insurance agent as soon as possible.

108. What to Do if Your Car Is Towed

First, stay calm. Look around to see if you missed a restricted- or prohibited-parking sign. Call your local non-emergency police number (*not* 911) and give as much information about the vehicle as possible—its make and model, license

> **FAST FACT**
>
> If your car is a clunker or in disrepair, don't be tempted to let the towing company keep your vehicle. Cars that sit in tow lots rack up "storage" and "abandonment" fees, which will be charged to the registered owner of the vehicle.

plate number, and registration information. The police will give you instructions about how to retrieve your vehicle. If your car was towed due to unpaid parking fines, you'll have to clear those up before it is released. Call the tow lot to find out their hours of operation and how soon you can come to get your car. You'll need a ride to the tow lot and plenty of cash—not all towing companies take credit cards or checks.

109. What to Do if You're Stopped by the Police While Driving

If a police car signals for you to pull over, do so quickly and safely. Pull over as far as possible so the officer has enough room to walk up to your window without having to worry about traffic. Roll down your window, turn off your engine, and place your hands on the steering wheel. Don't reach for your license, insurance card, or vehicle registration until the officer asks to see them. When asked, present them readily. Let the officer speak first—don't ask "So what did I do?" or "What's the problem?" Officers are trained to decide whether they will issue you a ticket or warning *before* they leave their vehicles, so the things that you say in your defense probably won't help and may actually come back to haunt you later in court. Stick to straightforward "yes" and "no" answers. Be calm and cooperative. And remember: What you *don't* say *cannot* be used against you in a court of law.

110. Five Tips for Being a Healthy Vegetarian

Vegetarianism is more popular than ever. If you want to try giving up meat for a while, here are a few things to keep in mind.

Chips and soda don't count. Replace meat with healthy foods. Skip the chips and grab an apple.

Watch your protein. Protein is necessary for the body's muscles to grow and function correctly. Vegetarians need to find alternative protein sources, such as beans, eggs, and soy products.

Eat a balanced diet. A vegetarian's daily diet should include five portions of whole grains, five portions of fruits and vegetables, two to three portions of high-protein foods, two to three portions of dairy products, and limited fats and sugars.

Buy a good vegetarian cookbook. This will help you prepare healthy, tasty meals.

Find other vegetarians. Having a vegetarian community is great for support, and most vegetarians love to share tips on healthy cooking.

111. Fad Diets: What You Need to Know

Not all fad diets are dangerous, but health experts agree that you should avoid a diet with the following characteristics.

Promises rapid returns. It's dangerous to lose more than a pound or two per week—and weight lost this way often comes back quickly.

Promises you don't have to cut out fats or sugars. We all need to eat some fat, but most of the fats and sugars in our diets are little more than empty, waistline-expanding calories. Diets that claim you can lose weight without cutting down on sugars and fats aren't to be trusted.

Uses before-and-after pictures. Anyone familiar with Photoshop knows that this sort of "evidence" is flimsy at best.

Tries to get you to buy its program or products. A true weight-loss program is not brand-specific. Diets that force you to subscribe to seminars or food packages are more interested in profit than public health.

112. Four Healthy Foods and How to Eat Them

It's easy to stick with the foods you know and like, but you're really missing out if you don't venture into new taste territory. Here are four foods that you should try.

Swiss chard. This leafy, red-veined green is loaded with cancer-fighting and vision-improving nutrients. Simply chop off the thick stems and sauté them in water or olive oil for a delicious side dish.

Flaxseed. Flaxseed is loaded with alpha-linolenic acid, which has been shown to improve cerebral cortex function (that means it makes you smarter). Just put a tablespoon of flaxseed oil in your oatmeal or morning smoothie.

Blueberries. Blueberries are loaded with antioxidants, which help to protect you against cancer. Try throwing some blueberries on your cereal or in yogurt, or toss a few atop a scoop of ice cream or frozen yogurt.

Turmeric. This spice, which is commonly used in Indian cooking, has incredible anti-inflammatory properties. It has been used since ancient times to treat digestive and skin conditions. Try it in curries, scrambled eggs, chicken salad, or marinades.

113. How to Register to Vote

Registering to vote is easy, but the requirements vary by state. Many require you to be registered 30 days before an election, so it's essential to understand what you need to do in the state in which you want to vote long before you will be voting.

Each state has a department of elections, which is in charge of voter registration; go to its Web site for requirements and registration information. Other good resources are the League of Women Voters, Rock the Vote, and Project Vote Smart. Local city or village halls, county boards of elections, and libraries can also assist you.

> **FAST FACT**
>
> Six states—Idaho, Maine, Minnesota, New Hampshire, Wisconsin, and Wyoming—have same-day registration. If you're a resident of one of these states, you can show up at the polling place, register to vote, and vote in one trip; just bring identification and proof of your address. One state, North Dakota, allows you to vote without registering.

114. Election Savvy: How to Find Out About Political Candidates

Voting responsibly can be difficult. How do you know which candidate best represents your beliefs? Here's how to find out.

Just ask. Most politicians—especially at the local level—welcome questions and comments from their potential constituents. Find contact information on their Web sites.

Read the newspaper. Keep abreast of current issues and political situations by reading the paper every day. Local newspapers often provide "election guides" that list each candidate's position on major issues in the weeks leading up to a vote.

Watch the debates. You'll get a sense of a candidate from watching him or her in action. Even local politicians will hold debates in the run-ups to elections.

Check online. Web sites, such as OnTheIssues.org, maintain comprehensive databases of candidates' stances on virtually every issue. (These summaries don't substitute for your own critical assessment, however.)

115. How to Get Involved in Local Politics

You can get more involved in your community and effect change by participating in local politics. Check out meetings of local governing bodies, political parties, and independent political organizations. Many national organizations have active local affiliates. If there is a subject about which you feel passionate, such as the environment, look for local groups that are devoted to it. Educate yourself on local issues by reading the newspaper, listening to public radio, and watching news programs. Volunteering is a terrific way to get more involved, meet people, and learn—help out at a community center, at the office of a politician you respect, or with an organization with which you connect. If there is an issue you feel isn't being adequately addressed, write to your elected officials. Organize your own group to support a cause, issue, or candidate about whom you care. At election time, volunteer to work at a polling place. And be sure to vote in local elections.

116. Jury Duty

Any English-speaking U.S. citizen who is at least 18 years of age and doesn't have a disqualifying mental or physical condition or felony record can receive a jury summons. There's a penalty for noncompliance, so follow the instructions in the letter that arrives from the court. Just because you receive a summons in the mail doesn't mean you'll sit on a trial jury, however. You may simply spend the day sitting in a holding room waiting to be called for questioning; be sure to bring something to read or with which to occupy yourself. If you're called into a courtroom, a judge and/or attorneys will ask questions to assess whether you can be fair and impartial. There are many reasons why you might be rejected as a juror; if you appear to have already formed an opinion about the case, for example, you will be dismissed. If you are selected for the jury, you'll see that actual jury duty can involve long, dull periods of waiting.

117. How to Get a Passport

Traveling to any foreign country—even Canada or Mexico—requires a passport. It can take six weeks or more to get one, so plan ahead. You will need proof of U.S. citizenship, such as a birth certificate or expired passport; a picture ID; and two 2×2 passport photos that were taken within six months of your application. You can get specific instructions and an online application form at the U.S. Department of State's Web site. If you're seeking your first passport, you are required to apply in person at a U.S. post office or passport agency. If you are renewing your passport, you can send it to the address on the passport application form. (Make sure to include the fees—both the execution fee and the application fee.) You'll receive your passport in the mail within six weeks. Expedited service, which delivers your new passport within two weeks, is available for a higher fee. There are also several private companies that you can pay to expedite your application.

118. When Do You Need a Visa?

In addition to a passport, you may need a visa to travel to some foreign countries. A visa is a special certificate that is issued by a nation's government. There are many different types of visas, including tourist visas, work visas, student visas, and business visas. Some visas, such as tourist visas, are easier to get than work visas. You'll need to know what type of visa you require before applying for one. Visas are issued by the foreign country to which you'll be traveling. This means you'll have to write to or visit the nation's local consulate or embassy to apply for one. You can also contact the U.S. embassy in the foreign country for visa information requirements.

Not every country requires a visa; many have agreements to allow their residents to travel freely within each other's borders. This list is constantly changing, however, so check the U.S. Department of State's Web site at travel.state.gov for the latest travel updates and visa requirements.

119. How to Pack for a Trip

These tricks will lighten your load and save you money on baggage fees.

✦ **Make a packing list and bring only what you need.** Call ahead to find out what is available for use at the hotel or residence at which you're staying.

✦ **Plan for weather and activities.** If forecasts don't call for rain, don't pack your raincoat. For a work trip, pack business clothes. For sightseeing, pack comfortable shoes.

✦ **Mix and match.** Use one complete outfit as a base, then plan your second outfit using as many pieces from the first as you can for a different look. Continue planning this way for the days you'll be away. Make a list of your outfits to which to refer.

✦ **Save space.** Roll T-shirts, underwear, and other soft items. Put socks inside shoes and arrange each pair of shoes so that the heel of one aligns with the toe of the other. Put shoes, phone chargers, and accessories around suitcase edges.

✦ **Pack plastic.** Put your toiletry bag in a resealable plastic bag and pack a few extra bags for your return. Place these inside your suitcase between rolled items.

✦ **Leave room for souvenirs.** Save space for purchases.

120. Ten Essential Items for Carry-on Luggage

When you have to check your luggage, remember to put these items in your carry-on bag.

1. **Laptop, digital camera, cell phone.** You may want access to these during your flight or upon touchdown.

2. **A change of clothes.** If your luggage gets lost or you miss a transfer, you'll be grateful to have this.

3. **Toiletries.** These are also helpful if you get separated from your luggage—or if you want to brush your teeth or take out your contact lenses on board.

4. **Glasses/contacts lens case.** Ten thousand feet in the air is a bad place to get something in your eye.

5. **Pain reliever/prescription medicine.** Traveling with a headache is difficult. Make sure to pack at least a couple of days' worth of your prescription drugs in your carry-on.

6. **Sweater/sweatshirt.** Airplanes are notorious for being too hot or too cold.

7. **Lip balm.** Air travel dries you out.

8. **Snacks.** Most airlines don't provide free food, and it's expensive to purchase snacks on board.

9. **Travel info.** This includes your itinerary, confirmation numbers for rental cars and/or hotel reservations, and airline boarding passes.

10. **Reading material.** You may want to peruse something a little more stimulating than The SkyMall catalog.

121. Tips for Traveling on Airplanes

Make your next flight a safe and pleasant one for everybody by following these tips.

Stow your carry-on near you. Nobody likes people who stick their carry-on bags into the first open compartment they see. Store yours in a compartment by your row or under your seat.

Drink water. Cabin air is very dry, so stay hydrated before, during, and after your flight.

Chew or swallow. Chewing gum or swallowing frequently helps to open the passageways in the ears, which prevents pain.

Take a stroll. Even young, healthy people can get blood clots in their legs when traveling. Stretch your legs once in a while during a flight.

Turn off your cell phone. Using a cell phone during a flight is potentially dangerous and is incredibly annoying to other passengers.

122. Where to Keep Money While Traveling

Tourists are often targets for pickpockets and thieves. Here's how to keep your money safe while you're traveling.

Wear a money belt. Tourists with visible wallets and dangling purses are prime targets for thieves. Don't keep all of your cash and important documents in them; instead, get a money belt. There are many types of money belts, but the most popular are cloth, worn around the waist—under the clothes—and have zippered pouches large enough for passports, money, and plane tickets.

Cash in a Flash

Once upon a time, using traveler's checks was the only way to bring money on a long trip. Nowadays, cashing a traveler's check can be a pain. Consider using your ATM card to withdraw cash along the way.

Spread your risk. Keep your important documents in your money belt, but also carry some spending cash for the day in your pocket. This way, potential thieves won't see you digging wads of cash out of your money belt, and if you do lose the cash in your pocket, your trip won't be ruined.

Use lockers or safes. If you'll be in one area for a few days, find out if the hostel or hotel in which you're staying has a safe or lockers in which you can store valuables.

123. Eradicate Shower Fungus

Fungus—including the mildew growing on your shower curtain and the mold that blackens your bathtub grout—is unsightly, unhealthy and destructive. With the right chemicals and a little elbow grease, however, you can kill the culprits and make your bathroom sparkling clean.

To kill existing fungus:

1. Coat shower tiles, fixtures, grout, and the drain with store-bought mold-and-mildew remover or a homemade mixture of equal parts bleach and water. Let it sit for ten minutes.

2. Wear rubber gloves and use a scrub brush to scour the entire bathtub or shower stall. Clean shower grout with an old toothbrush to remove black fungus.

3. Rinse the entire shower and tub area with hot water, then hand-dry with a towel to prevent new mold growth.

To prevent new fungus from growing:

1. Use an exhaust fan during and after showering. Open windows and doors afterward.

2. Make it a habit to dry the inside of the shower area after bathing.

3. Spray mold-and-mildew shower cleaner daily after showering, especially if you don't dry the shower area after use.

124. Make Your Own Cleaning Supplies

Most homemade cleaners are more environmentally friendly and less expensive than their store-bought counterparts—and they are just as effective. What's more, they are easy to make and can be stored indefinitely.

All-purpose cleaner. Mix ¾ teaspoon liquid Castile soap, ½ teaspoon tea-tree oil, and 1 tablespoon each Borax and baking soda. Add 2 cups warm water, pour into a spray bottle, and shake until all ingredients have dissolved.

Creamy bathroom scrub. Mix 1 cup baking soda, 2 teaspoons vegetable glycerin (available at health food stores), and enough liquid detergent to make a thick paste. Spread onto a sponge and scrub into the surface. Store in a sealed jar to retain moisture.

Window cleaner. Mix together 4 cups water, ⅜ cup vinegar, and 1 teaspoon liquid detergent into a spray bottle. Shake well.

Wood furniture polish. Mix ½ cup vinegar or fresh lemon juice, 3 teaspoons olive oil, and 2 teaspoons water in a small spray bottle. Shake well; stores for one month.

125. Eliminate Foul Household Odors

Some smells are easy to tackle—take out the garbage or toss out the moldy leftovers and the problem is solved. Other odors, however, can seep into fabric, wood, and plastic, becoming almost impossible to eliminate. Air-freshening sprays will only mask the smells for a short time. Try these odor-eaters instead.

Microwave. Add peppermint oil or lemon juice to a bowl of water and heat until it boils. Let it sit until the water has cooled.

Shoes. Wipe them clean and, if possible, remove the insoles and wash them. Generously sprinkle the insides of shoes with baking soda and let them sit overnight; in the morning, shake out and wipe up the baking soda. Store your shoes with a scented sachet tucked inside the toes.

Carpet. Sprinkle baking soda or carpet freshener on the rug and leave it for at least two hours before vacuuming.

Trash cans. Sprinkle baking soda generously on the bottom of the can, then wet with vinegar. Add enough water to make the mixture sloshy. Let it sit for at least an hour before rinsing.

Soured clothing. Add half a cup of vinegar to the rinse cycle.

126. Eco-Friendly Cleaning Tips

Keeping your dorm room or apartment clean in an eco-friendly way is easy. Use nontoxic, biodegradable products or make your own household cleaners out of ingredients like baking soda, white or apple-cider vinegar, lemon juice, and tea-tree oil. (Look online or see #124 for recipes.) Use old T-shirts or scraps of fabric as reusable rags rather than disposable materials like paper towels. Buy some houseplants to help clean the indoor air. Conserve water by shortening your showers, shutting off the faucet while washing dishes or brushing teeth, and sweeping the floor frequently to minimize the need to mop it with soap and water. Leave your shoes outside the door or put down a mat in front of the entryway so you don't track in dirt and toxins.

127. The Cleaning Power of Vinegar and Baking Soda

Vinegar and baking soda are the wonder twins of household cleaning. Due to its acidic nature, diluted vinegar works just as well as many chemical cleaners. To make a versatile cleaning solution, simply mix one part vinegar with one part water in a spray bottle. Diluted vinegar cleans just about all hard surfaces, including tile, grout, sinks, toilets, tile floors, glass, mirrors, and countertops.

FAST FACT

If you like vinegar's cleaning power but not its smell, add some lemon juice to infuse a citrus scent. Lemon has cleaning and disinfecting properties too.

If vinegar doesn't get the job done, try a baking soda paste. Baking soda is abrasive and can be used to clean everything from stoves to silver. Leave open boxes of baking soda inside refrigerators, closets, and bathrooms to absorb odors. Add half a cup of baking soda to your wash to boost the cleaning power of your detergent and freshen the laundry; then, add another half a cup to the rinse cycle as a fabric softener.

128. Eleven Cleaning Tools Everyone Needs

Cleaning is easier when you have the right tools for the job. Here's what you need.

1. **Broom.** Natural fibers last longer than plastic ones.
2. **Dustpan.** To collect the dirt that you sweep up.
3. **Wet mop.** The kind with the detachable sponge head.

4. **Large plastic bucket.** Two- to three-gallon capacity.

5. **Sponges.** Large and small.

6. **Nonmetal scouring pads.**

7. **Empty plastic squirt bottle.** To fill with homemade or generic cleaning products.

8. **Large plastic garbage bin with lid.**

9. **Toilet brush.**

10. **Scrub brush.**

11. **Microfiber cloths.** For dusting and all-purpose cleaning.

Keep your cleaning tools clean. Rinse out sponges and buckets after use, and store brooms and mops in a dry, well-ventilated space.

129. How to Treat Acne

Acne isn't caused by poor hygiene or a fast-food diet. Since dirt isn't the culprit, it won't help to vigorously scrub your skin. (In fact, harsh treatment actually makes acne worse.) Gently cleanse your skin to remove

FAST FACT

Greasy foods like pizza and french fries can't cause acne. Any oil that produces acne is already in your skin.

excess oil and dead skin cells. Keep your hair away from your face, and try not to touch it. Do not pick at your skin. Try a topical over-the-counter acne medication that contains benzoyl peroxide—which kills bacteria and helps eliminate cellular debris from your pores—or salicylic acid; these medications are helpful for mild acne. If these products don't work, see a dermatologist, who can prescribe more powerful topical or oral medication.

130. How to Get Rid of Cold Sores

Cold sores usually appear around the mouth and lips, and they seem to pop up at the worst times—probably because stress can trigger them. A tingling sensation often precedes their emergence.

Follow these steps to limit their damage.

Keep them clean. Cold sores are prone to infection, especially after they start drying and cracking. Cover a cold sore with a layer of petroleum jelly to keep it protected.

Use over-the-counter medications. Look for over-the-counter medications that contain docosanol, which has been shown to limit replication of the virus that causes cold sores.

Cold sores should clear up on their own after seven to ten days. If you get frequent cold sores or have sores that just won't go away, talk to your doctor. There may be alternative treatments.

131. What to Do When You Have the Runs

Diarrhea is often caused by a virus or bacteria—the runs are your body's way of eliminating the bug from your system, so it's best to let it "run" its course. Most cases last no more than 48 hours.

The most important thing to do when you've got the runs is stay hydrated, since diarrhea causes considerable loss of fluid. Try to drink six eight-ounce glasses of water or caffeine-free soda per day. Fruit juice (noncitrus and pulp-free), fat-free chicken broth, and dry crackers with salt will also help replace sodium and potassium and restore your electrolyte levels. Yogurt with active cultures can help shorten the duration and severity of the illness. Rice, dry toast, and bananas may also be tolerated and helpful.

To relieve abdominal cramps, try gentle stretching or walking for a few minutes while taking deep breaths. Also try massaging your abdomen with small circular movements.

Call a doctor if you have diarrhea for more than three days, fever of 102 degrees Fahrenheit or higher, severe abdominal pain, dizziness, or blood in your stool—or if you're vomiting and can't keep food and liquids down.

132. How to Stop a Nosebleed

Nosebleeds are usually caused by dry air, trauma, or irritations such as from colds or allergies. Lots of blood vessels line the nose, and they lie close to the surface, which makes them easy to injure. During a nosebleed, sit upright and lean forward—not back—to reduce pressure on the blood vessels and prevent blood from trickling down your throat. Let the blood drip out of your nose into a trashcan or onto a cloth. Pinch your nostrils closed for five to ten minutes; this slows blood flow and helps clotting begin. It may also help to apply a cold compress or ice pack across the bridge of your nose. After the bleeding stops, avoid blowing your nose or bending over for at least a couple of hours. If bleeding persists after 20 minutes, call a doctor.

133. How to Care for a Piercing

Getting a piercing can be a fun way to express yourself, but it's not so fun if you get an infection. With proper care, however, you can avoid infection and help the piercing heal correctly. Always wash your hands with soap and water before touching your piercing—it's the easiest way to stay infection-free. Don't touch the piercing or jewelry except to clean it. Different sites require different cleansing methods, but general directions for a skin piercing call for using a cotton swab dipped in warm water to remove any crusted discharge. Several times a day, dip a cotton ball, cotton swab, or piece of gauze in liquid antibacterial cleanser (avoid creams or astringents) and gently clean around the piercing site. Rotate the jewelry so that the cleanser is worked into the opening. Keep clothing from rubbing the piercing, and don't press a phone receiver against an ear that recently has been pierced. If you have any signs of infection—such as pain, swelling, inflammation, or yellow pus—seek medical attention immediately.

Avoid Astringents

Do not apply hydrogen peroxide, rubbing alcohol, or tea-tree oil to a new piercing! Hydrogen peroxide kills white blood cells, which are critical to the healing process, and rubbing alcohol and tea-tree oil dry out the skin, which can prolong the healing time.

134. What to Consider Before Getting a Tattoo

Fashions change. The hairstyle you wore ten years ago probably would look pretty silly today. But what if you had to wear it permanently? That's the reality of getting a tattoo—once you have one, you're pretty much stuck with it for life.

There are also health considerations—infections and other problems related to the tattooing process are not uncommon. If you have a skin condition or other health problem, speak with your doctor before you get a tattoo.

If you decide to get a tattoo, carefully choose the kind you want and where you want it. Remember that not everyone will be interested in seeing your tattoo—employers, for example. A discreet location is advisable.

Be careful when choosing a tattoo studio and an artist. Make sure the studio is licensed and clean, and that it has a good reputation. Some body artists are gifted, and others, well . . . not so much. Read reviews, get opinions, and visit a few tattoo studios before making your choice.

FAST FACT

Some states have laws against getting tattoos on certain body parts, such as the face. The only places on your body that can't be tattooed are your hair, nails (they both grow out), and the enamel of your teeth (it's too hard).

135. Preventing STDs

Here are some scary statistics about sexually transmitted diseases (STDs): One out of every four teens in the United States becomes infected with an STD every year, and half of all sexually active young adults will get an STD. Of course, the best way to avoid an STD is abstinence, but you can reduce your risk by staying informed and practicing safe sex. Always use a latex condom, limit the number of partners with whom you have sex, and make sure to have regular checkups—many STDs do not have any symptoms. The earlier you catch and treat an STD, the better your prognosis. Symptoms to watch for include red sores on the genital area, anus, tongue, or throat; small blisters that turn into scabs on the genital area; soft, flesh-colored warts around the genital area; scaly rash on the palms of your hands and soles of your feet; pain during sex or when urinating; discharge from the penis or vagina; genital itching; swollen glands, fever, body aches, and fatigue; and sore throat (if you are having oral sex). Get private, personal, confidential information about STDs and referrals 24 hours a day, 7 days a week from the Centers for Disease Control and Prevention, 800–CDC–INFO (800–232–4636).

136. How to Take Your Temperature

Your mom's not around to feel your forehead, so you'll have to rely on a thermometer to tell you if you have a fever. Today, most people use digital thermometers. The old-fashioned glass thermometers, while more accurate, contain mercury, which is an environmental toxin. Mercury thermometers have been outlawed in many states.

Don't eat or drink right before you take your temperature, as these activities can change body temperature. Clean the tip of the thermometer with soap and hot water. Turn the thermometer on and wait for the display to light up. Gently place the thermometer under your tongue, as deep inside your mouth as you can. Close your mouth and breathe through your nose. When the thermometer beeps, remove it from your mouth and read the display. Clean the thermometer with soap and water before putting it away.

137. How to Take Your Pulse

To take your radial pulse, turn one hand palm up and press gently on the wrist, just below the thumb, with the middle and index fingers of your other hand. (Do not use your thumb because it has a pulse in it.) Using a clock with a second hand, count the beats for 15 seconds, then multiply that number by four to get your beats per minute. For some, it's easier to find the carotid pulse in the neck. Choose either side and follow the same directions as above.

Your resting pulse is your heart rate after you've been sitting quietly for at least ten minutes. Most healthy people in their late teens have a resting pulse of about 70 beats per minute.

138. The Pitfalls of Procrastinating

Everybody procrastinates once in awhile, but the consequences—sloppy work, missed assignments, enormous stress levels, unhealthy all-nighters—can be severe. Removing distractions is the best way to avoid procrastination. Turn off the TV (even better, go somewhere without one), turn off your instant messaging clients, and turn off your cell phone. Take care of unpleasant tasks first, and reward yourself for completing them. Also, try breaking up tasks into smaller, more manageable pieces.

Blame the BlackBerry

Ninety-five percent of all college students procrastinate occasionally, and the number of chronic procrastinators has risen by more than twenty percent in recent years. Technology is the likely culprit, according to researchers.

139. How to Set Goals

There's an old saying: "Any road will do for those without a destination." This may be fine for characters in Beat novels, but most of us need to plan routes to our ultimate destinations. Here's how.

Be realistic. You're probably not going to play in the NBA, but you might be able to dunk a basketball. Attaining a challenging but achievable goal will give you confidence.

Start small. Break a larger goal into smaller goals. This will eventually let you achieve your heart's desire.

Put it in context. Choose goals that mesh with your personal, academic, or professional life.

140. Motivating Yourself

All the talent in the world is useless without a motivated individual to use it. Here are some tips for becoming—and staying—motivated.

> ### Heed Mr. Twain
>
> Mark Twain once said, "In 20 years, you'll be more disappointed by what you didn't do than by what you did." Remember his words the next time you're reluctant to start something.

First, figure out what it is that motivates you. Know that failure is part of the journey. Many people lose motivation at the first roadblock, but roadblocks can be unexpected gifts—they may force you to find an alternate route to your ultimate goal, and you may learn and see things on that new path that you never would have otherwise.

Motivational experts say that goal-setting is a key to becoming motivated. Starting out with small goals—and achieving them—creates a mind-set of success. This builds momentum, which helps you to sustain your motivation.

141. How to Overcome Self-Doubt

We all feel a little trepidation once in a while, especially when we're undertaking new challenges. Ironically, though, it's self-doubt that often causes failure. Take these steps to overcome your doubt.

Write down your fears. Putting doubts and fears on paper can make them seem more manageable.

Let the past go. You can't change the past, but you can ensure that you won't repeat it.

Prove it wrong. That little voice in your head that says you aren't smart enough or talented enough is just self-doubt talking. Prove it wrong. Accomplish what it said you couldn't.

142. Developing a Work Ethic

A strong work ethic is the foundation for success; here's how to develop one. Plan your day, making a list of attainable goals and tackling them one at a time. Wherever you go, arrive five to ten minutes early; this will help you avoid feeling rushed or flustered. Ask questions and propose solutions to problems. Don't complain (at work or in a study group, for instance); instead, think of how you can improve your situation. Take initiative—it's not enough to plan; you also have to follow through. Be a team player, but keep your focus on your performance or contribution to the group; that's the only thing you can fully control.

143. How to Be a Good Host

Adequate information and advance preparation are the keys to being a good host. If you're throwing a party, find out how many people are coming so you will have enough food and drink. If you have friends coming from out-of-town, clean up your place and dedicate some space to them. Also, find out how long they'll be staying so you can organize meals and plan activities. When you're having people over, finish your preparations with time to spare so you can breathe for a few minutes—or take care of any emergencies that may arise. Don't refuse offers of help if you can use it, and be specific about what you need. When your guests arrive, introduce them to each other if they aren't already acquainted. Know that things may not go exactly according to plan—even Martha Stewart can't control everything!

144. How to Be a Good Houseguest

An invitation to visit your roommate's or girlfriend's family home for the weekend usually means a freshly made bed, a home-cooked meal, and access to a free washer and dryer. Be helpful and use good manners, and you'll be rewarded with an invitation to come back.
+ Bring an inexpensive gift.
+ Offer to help. Little things like setting and/or clearing the table will make an impression.

- Pick up after yourself. Make your bed, don't leave dishes you've used lying around, and keep your clothes in a closet or suitcase.
- Be appreciative and don't complain.
- Send a thank-you note after your visit.

145. Meeting the Parents

If your romantic relationship has developed to the point of "meeting the parents," here are some ways that you can make a great first impression. Ask your significant other to tell you about his or her parents and what topics of conversation or behaviors are appropriate around them. Find out how you should address them. Make an effort to look your best (shave, shower, groom, and dress neatly). Arrive on time, and offer a firm handshake when you are introduced. Talk, but also listen well and answer questions thoroughly and thoughtfully. Use good manners and be on your best behavior, but also be genuine—don't let nerves get in the way of being yourself!

146. The Art of Declining an Invitation

After you move out on your own, invitations that used to be issued via your parents—to weddings, showers, and other major events—will go directly to you. You'll also continue to get invitations from your friends. If you're not able or simply don't want to attend, you must respond with your regrets. Do not ignore the invitation; it's not fair to the host. You don't need to give an explanation; simply say, "I'd love to come, but I have prior commitments." Always be tactful—don't mention that you aren't attending because you can't stand your friend's significant other, for example. Let the

> **RSVP: The "P" is for Promptly**
>
> If you must decline an invitation, do so promptly. Waiting until the last moment inconveniences the host, who may become aggravated with you.

host know that you are grateful for being asked. Saying, "Thank you for thinking of me, but I'm not going to be able to make it," will make the host feel appreciated rather than snubbed.

147. When and How to Write a Thank-You Note

Send thank-you notes for gifts, meals, job leads, help of any kind—from moral support to packing boxes for a move—interviews, or even compliments. A thank-you note lets the giver know how much his or her gift or thoughtfulness meant to you. Your gratitude is a gift, too. Start your note by mentioning the kindness by name, then discuss how you plan to use it or how much it means to you. Include your intention to follow up, if that's appropriate. ("I'll call you at the beginning of next week to see if you have made a decision," or, "Let's make plans to get together next month.") End your note with another "thank you." You can never thank people enough!

148. What to Do with a Gift You Don't Want or Won't Use

It's awkward to receive a gift that you don't like or want. If the gift is from a retail establishment, check the packaging for a gift receipt, which can be used to exchange the item for cash or credit towards a future purchase. If there is no gift receipt, call the retailer and ask about its return policy. A handmade item or one that has no identifiable origin clearly cannot be returned. If you know someone who might like the item, you can regift it or just give it away outright. When regifting, make sure that you first remove cards and any other evidence that it was given to you, then rewrap the item. To avoid future embarrassment, make sure that the regift goes to someone who does not know the original giver. Often, the best policy is to donate the item to charity.

No matter what you do with the gift, you still must write a thank-you note to the giver. "It was so kind of you to think of me," is a polite and noncommittal way to express your gratitude.

149. When Should You Bring a Gift?

Wedding receptions and baby showers are obviously occasions that require you to bring or send a gift. However, gift-giving etiquette for lots of other events—such as dinner parties or weekend visits— isn't so clear-cut. It can be hard to know whether to bring a gift—and,

> **One Gift or Two?**
> Since a wedding shower and the wedding itself are separate events, it is appropriate to give a gift on both occasions.

if so, what kind of gift is appropriate. Bringing a gift is never considered rude, and it is an effective way to show your appreciation for the invitation. If you're going to a dinner party, it's thoughtful to bring a small gift that is selected with the host in mind.

150. How to Balance Your Checking Account

To know how much money you actually have at a given time, you need to keep your checking account balance up-to-date. The current balance that you can retrieve online, via phone, or on your statement does not usually reflect pending transactions. Bank errors can only be addressed within 60 days, so being diligent about your account allows you to report discrepancies in time.

To balance your account, record every single transaction— including every debit card purchase, check, and transaction or bank fee—and deduct it from your balance. Add any deposits and credits to your balance.

Compare the bank's transaction list on your statement to your checkbook register and mark off all those that match. Then add all unrecorded deposits to the ending balance on your statement. Next, subtract all unrecorded expenditures and fees. The result should equal your register balance; if it doesn't, check for duplications, transposed numbers, omissions, and bank errors. Balance your account at least monthly, but if your statement is available online, it doesn't hurt to review it nightly or weekly.

151. Understanding (and Avoiding) Bank Fees

Banks charge for certain services and "slipups." Each bank has its own policies, so ask a teller for written information or to show you where you can find the fees spelled out online. The following are common services for which banks charge.

✦ Withdrawing cash from an ATM not owned by your bank—in addition to the surcharge you pay to the ATM owner.

✦ Printing new checks.

✦ Charging to your debit card, although you may be granted a few free debit card transactions per month.

✦ Bouncing checks. If your bank covers your bounced checks, you must pay an overdraft fee.

✦ Falling below a minimum balance. Some banks charge you a monthly service fee if your account balance dips below a certain amount.

152. Understanding Interest Rates

Almost every financial interaction in which money is lent or borrowed accrues a fee, which is known as interest. Interest is calculated based on an interest rate—a percentage of the borrowed sum. For example, if you deposit $1,000 into a savings account with a 1-percent interest rate, you will earn $10 in interest (1 percent of $1,000) at the end of the year. As you can see, when you're *receiving* interest (through savings accounts, mutual funds, or other investments), you want the interest rate to be higher; when you're *paying* interest (on credit cards, student loans, or purchase plans), you want the interest rate to be lower.

The more frequently interest accrues, the more interest (money!) will be earned—or owed—so pay attention to this when comparing interest rates. If interest accrues annually, that means it is only calculated once per year; if it accrues monthly, the balance on which interest is calculated grows each month. So if you're earning money, you want the interest to be compounded more frequently; if you're paying interest, you want it to be compounded less often.

153. The Pros and Cons of Credit Cards

Using a credit card responsibly will help you to build a good credit history, which will help you when renting an apartment, getting a loan, finding affordable insurance—even getting a good cell phone plan. Credit cards can be lifesavers in emergency situations, and they are convenient to use for purchases, whether in person or online. Paying bills via credit cards can be helpful when money is tight.

The problem with using a credit card is that it can easily lead to debt. Since you're not using cash, you can quickly lose track of how much money you're spending.

Look for a card with low interest rates and try to pay the balance each month. Your bill will skyrocket if you only make minimum payments or pay late. To avoid overspending, charge no more than 30 percent of a card's limit, and keep scrupulous track of your purchases.

154. What to Do if You're in Debt

It's easy to fall into debt, but it's a challenge to get out of it! If you're having debt difficulties, you need to establish a budget. To get help devising a plan, check out some books on money and debt management from your local library. In-person assistance from a credit counselor can also be very helpful—one may be available through your school, place of work, or credit union. Then, contact your creditors, explain your situation, and ask for modification to your payment schedule. Making a payment plan with your creditors is preferable to dealing with debt collectors!

155. How to Order and Read a Credit Report

Your credit report provides banks, landlords, and potential employers with a peek into your credit history, so make sure that nothing suspicious or inaccurate lurks within the fine print. Order a free report at AnnualCreditReport.com (a central site developed by the three national consumer credit reporting companies) and review the information within to ensure its accuracy. Check your identifying information, such as former addresses and names. Review the list of accounts you have opened over the years, from mortgages to credit cards; those listed in the "collections" section have been referred to a collection agency for payment. Check the "public records" file; you want it to be empty. In the "inquiries" section, you'll find a list of those who have requested credit reports about you in the last 30 days. Report any discrepancies—including listed accounts that you did not open and inaccurate balance amounts and payment histories—and dispute them immediately.

> ### Know the Score
> Your credit—or FICO—score is an indication of your risk to lenders. The higher your score, the less likely you are to skip out on payments.

156. How to Change a Tire

Many people call a road-service company to fix a flat tire, but there may be times when you'll have to do it yourself. Here's what to do.

1. Park in a safe place, away from traffic, with flat and firm ground. Turn on your hazard blinkers and set the emergency brake.
2. Get out your jack, spare tire, and tire iron.
3. Using the tire iron, turn the lug nuts counter-clockwise to loosen them. Don't remove them completely just yet!
4. Put the jack beneath the car (check your owner's manual for correct placement). Raise the jack until the flat tire is off the ground.
5. Remove the loosened lug nuts.
6. Remove the flat tire and put on the spare. Replace the lug nuts, tightening them by hand as best you can.

7. Lower the jack. After the car is completely on the ground, remove the jack.

8. Using the tire iron, tighten the lug nuts completely.

157. How and Why to Put Air in a Tire

Having low air pressure in your car's tires can be dangerous, leading to a blowout or an accident. Insufficient air pressure also causes uneven tire wear, tread damage, and poor gas mileage. Buy a tire gauge and use it to routinely check your car's tires; if you find that they need air, here's what you should do.

✦ Find a gas station or car wash with an air compressor. You can also use a portable compressor, if one is available.

✦ Unscrew the cap from the tire valve. Using a tire gauge, check the air pressure in each tire.

✦ Attach the compressor's air hose to the valve and add air in short spurts, checking the pressure after each spurt to prevent overinflation. If you add too much, press the pin in the middle of the valve to release excess air.

> ### Inflation Specs
> The air pressure specifications for your vehicle's tires are posted on a sticker on the driver's side door near the jamb. You can also find this information in your car's manual.

✦ Reattach the valve cap before driving.

158. Why You Need to Change the Oil

There's no more effective way to keep your vehicle in great shape and running like new than to change the oil regularly. Oil changes improve the life of your vehicle's engine and allow it to run smoothly. They are relatively inexpensive and simple procedures—their costs are minimal compared to the serious problems your car will develop if you don't change its oil. When engine parts are not lubricated sufficiently, they can grind, fuse together, or even fail completely.

159. Why You Need to Check Your Brakes

Auto-safety experts say that you should check your brakes at least twice a year. One easy way to do this is to have them examined when you bring your car in for any service, such as an oil change. Heed these signs that your brakes need to be serviced.

> ### FAST FACT
>
> If your car has been sitting in wet weather, the brakes might screech or grind for the first few miles after you start driving. This is normal. If the sounds continue, though, get your brakes checked right away.

"Spongy" braking. If you need to push progressively harder on the brakes to get the car to stop, they may need repair.

Grinding or squealing. Harsh noises that come from the brakes mean the brake pads have worn away and the rotors are grinding. Get them repaired right away.

Occasionally check your brake fluid. A full reservoir with no other brake problems means that you're good to go.

160. How to Jump-start a Car

All you need to revive a dead car battery are jumper cables and another car with a working battery. Follow these directions.

1. Line up the cars so the batteries are close to each other. Open both hoods.

2. Turn both cars off. Clean any corrosion off the dead battery's terminals.

3. Connect one end of the red jumper cable to the (+) terminal of the dead battery; connect the other end to the (+) terminal of the good battery. Connect one end of the black jumper cable to the (−) terminal on the good battery. Attach the other end to an unpainted metal surface (such as the engine block) in the car with the dead battery; *do not* connect this cable to the dead battery itself.

4. Start the car with the good battery and carefully move the black cable to the (−) terminal of the dead battery. Allow it to run for a few minutes, then try to start the dead battery.

5. Remove the cables in the reverse order in which you attached them.

6. Allow the jump-started car to idle for several minutes in order to recharge the battery.

161. How to Hard-boil an Egg

Out of both cash and time? Hard-boiled eggs are nutritious and easy to cook, and they make great snacks when you're on the run. Follow these steps for foolproof hard-boiled eggs.

1. Place eggs in a pot and add enough cold water to cover them by at least an inch.

2. Place the pot on a burner that's set to medium-high heat. When the water comes to a rolling boil, turn off the heat and remove the pot from the burner. Cover the pot and let the eggs sit for 15 minutes. (The whites will get tough if the eggs are overcooked.)

3. Remove the eggs from the pot and place them in a bowl filled with ice cubes and water for about two minutes. If you're not planning to eat them right away, refrigerate the eggs in their shells. They'll keep for up to a week.

4. To peel the eggs, gently tap them all over on a hard surface to create tiny cracks. Start peeling at the wide end. Use water to help remove any small bits of shell.

162. How to Crack a Raw Egg

The pros make it look so easy—they can even do it one-handed! Practice this simple method and you'll soon be breaking eggs with the best of 'em! Tap the egg gently on a hard, flat surface. You don't have to break through the shell; just tap until it's slightly dented. Over a small bowl, press your thumbs into the dent and pull back each side simultaneously, letting the egg white and yolk slide out. If a piece of shell happens to fall in, use a larger piece of shell or a utensil to scoop it out.

163. How to Make a Smoothie

Smoothies can be healthful and satisfying snacks or meals, but like fancy coffee drinks, they can strain your budget if you buy them from cafés or restaurants. To save money, make your own smoothies at home. Start with these simple suggestions—then get creative.

✦ **Strawberry-banana smoothie.** Wash and hull six large strawberries; peel one ripe banana and break into chunks. Combine fruit in a blender with several ice cubes, ¾ cup plain or vanilla yogurt, a splash of orange juice, and 3 tablespoons honey. Blend until smooth.

✦ **Mixed-berry smoothie.** Follow the steps above, but substitute frozen mixed berries (available in the freezer section of the grocery store) for fresh strawberries and eliminate the ice.

✦ **Peanut-butter smoothie.** Combine two sliced bananas (or use frozen bananas), 3 tablespoons creamy peanut butter, ½ cup milk (or soy milk), 2 tablespoons chocolate syrup, and ½ cup vanilla yogurt. Blend until creamy.

164. How to Make Rice

Rice is nutritious and easy to prepare—just use the following instructions as a general guide. The cooking time and the amount of water you use will vary a bit depending on the variety of rice you choose (follow the directions on the package).

✦ Use 1¾ cups of water for every cup of uncooked white rice.

✦ In a saucepan, bring the water to a full boil. Add the rice and half a teaspoon of salt, and stir just enough to combine everything (one stir is best).

✦ When the water returns to a boil, turn the heat to the lowest setting (simmer) and cover the pan with a tight-fitting lid. Don't lift the lid during the cooking process.

- ✦ After 18 minutes, take the pan off the burner and let the rice sit, still covered, for another five to ten minutes to finish cooking.
- ✦ Uncover the pan and fluff the rice with a fork.

Brown rice will take longer—about 45 minutes—to cook and requires 2¼ cups of liquid per cup of rice. For more flavor, try cooking the rice in vegetable, chicken, or beef broth instead of water.

165. How to Make Perfect Pasta

Everyone loves pasta! It's inexpensive and versatile, and it's super-easy to make. Here's how.

Fill a large pot with cold water—about six cups (1½ quarts) for every four ounces of pasta. The water should be at least two inches from the top of the pot. Bring the water to a rolling boil over medium-high heat. Add about one teaspoon of salt for every quart of water.

When the water is at a full boil, add the pasta. Stir or gently push it down so it is completely covered by water. Continue to stir until the water returns to a boil; at that point, lower the heat to medium to prevent the water from boiling over. Give the noodles an occasional stir. Most types of pasta cook in approximately 8 to 12 minutes, but check the package

> ## Little Ears and Mustaches
>
> Pasta comes in more than 500 shapes. *Orecchiette* is rounded like a tiny bowl, and in Italian means "little ears." *Mostaccioli*, or "mustaches," are shaped into short, smooth tubes. If there's an Italian neighborhood in your city, explore a *groceria* for more pasta inspiration.

for specific cooking times. Test individual pieces/strands several minutes before you expect them to be done. When the pasta is tender yet slightly firm to the bite, drain it in a colander, then return it to the pot.

If you're serving pasta with sauce, heat the sauce in a separate pan while the pasta is cooking. Put the drained pasta into the sauce in the pan and gently toss it. Add grated cheese or dried herbs, if desired, and enjoy!

166. How to Make a Simple Salad Dressing

Salad dressing is easy and inexpensive to make—and homemade dressing is a healthy alternative to store-bought varieties that contain lots of fat and/or additives. For a basic vinaigrette, whisk together two tablespoons vinegar (balsamic, white wine, or red wine varieties), salt, and pepper. Add other ingredients that you like, such as minced garlic, Dijon mustard, sugar, dried herbs, and grated parmesan cheese. Pour in six tablespoons of extra-virgin olive oil and whisk briskly (or combine the ingredients in a small jar, screw on the lid tightly, and shake well). Use it immediately or refrigerate and remix it just before eating. This vinaigrette also makes a tasty dip for sliced bread.

167. Soup: A Meal in a Bowl

Soup fills you up for mere pennies. If you have a free afternoon, make a big batch of soup from scratch and freeze the leftovers to have as quick meals when you're busy. Otherwise, store-bought varieties will do, especially if you add your own personal touches. Here are some suggestions that will help you make canned soups your own.

+ Enliven plain tomato soup with herbs, such as fresh or dried basil or oregano. Add sour cream or shredded cheese before serving.

+ Make ramen soup healthier by adding raw or sautéed vegetables (such as mushrooms, carrots, zucchini, and/or scallions). Turn up the heat with red-pepper flakes or a dash of sriracha (the popular Thai condiment that is also known as "rooster sauce").

+ For a quick white-bean chili, combine two cans of white beans (navy or great northern), a jar of salsa, and a small onion (chopped and sautéed). Season it with cumin and/or chili powder, and let it simmer on the stove for 10 to 15 minutes. Top with shredded cheese or slices of avocado.

168. How to Make Coffee

Clean the Machine

For a sparkly clean coffeemaker, place a denture-cleaning tablet in the filter and run fresh water through the machine several times. Or, you can cycle equal parts vinegar and water.

All you need to brew a fine cup of joe is an ordinary coffeemaker and good-quality coffee. If your budget allows, get a coffee grinder; freshly ground beans create a better-tasting beverage. Always start with a clean pot; scrub the inside to remove hard-water deposits and leftover coffee oils, which quickly become rancid. Rinse out the filter basket to remove loose grinds. Run the cold-water tap for a few seconds before filling the pot; if your tap water smells or tastes of chlorine, use filtered or bottled water instead. Pour the water into the reservoir. Put a filter (paper or reusable) into the basket, making sure that it is the right size and shape. Put two tablespoons of coffee into the filter for every six ounces of water in the reservoir. (Adjust subsequent pots to your taste by adding more or less coffee.) Once the coffee is brewed, don't let it sit for hours on the warming element; pour it into a thermal carafe to preserve the fresh taste.

169. How to Make a Cup of Tea

If you can boil water, you can make a good cup of tea—right? Well, it's a little more complicated than that, but not much.

Start with fresh cold water—about six ounces for each cup of tea—and bring it to a boil on the stove. While the water is heating, fill your teacup or a teapot with hot tap water to warm it. Pour out the contents when the boiling water is ready.

Bagged teas are convenient, and many brands produce a perfectly acceptable cup. However, loose tea is not only more "authentic," it also usually tastes better and can be more economical. If you like loose tea, invest in an infuser (a small, inexpensive strainer shaped like a ball) to fill with tea leaves. Use one teaspoon of loose tea or one tea bag for each cup. Pour the boiling water over the tea and steep according to instructions.

If you like, add honey or sugar and milk or cream. A simple squeeze of fresh lemon is tasty, too—just don't combine it with dairy products or your tea will curdle.

FAST FACT

Tea actually has more caffeine per pound than coffee, but you use much less tea per cup. The average cup of black tea has about 27 milligrams of caffeine; coffee scores around 85 milligrams per cup, and a cup of hot chocolate contains a whopping 150 milligrams. Many herbal teas do not contain caffeine.

170. How to Pop Popcorn on the Stove

You don't need a microwave oven or an electric popper to make popcorn. In fact, popping corn on a stovetop is cheaper, and the result is better for you than microwave brands that contain chemicals masquerading as butter. So why not give the stovetop method a try? You'll need vegetable oil, popcorn kernels, a large pot with a lid, butter or margarine, and salt. Pour enough oil into the pan to cover the bottom. Set the burner to medium-high heat. Drop in a few popcorn kernels and cover the pan. When the kernels start popping, add a single layer of kernels and put the lid back on. Using oven mitts or pot holders, continually lift and shake the pan gently so the kernels don't burn. When the popping slows, take the pan off the burner and remove the lid. Dump the popcorn into a bowl. If you want buttered popcorn, melt some butter or margarine in the still-hot pan; pour it over the popcorn and add salt to taste.

171. How to Sauté Vegetables

Fresh vegetables are easy to prepare if you know how to sauté. This quick, simple cooking method uses high heat to unlock the flavors of foods without leeching out their nutritional benefits.

Use a wide, shallow pan with a sturdy handle, butter or oil, and vegetables chopped into half-inch pieces. Add the butter or oil—or substitute vegetable or chicken broth for

a more healthful sauté—to the pan and heat on medium until it is hot (but not smoking). Carefully add the vegetables to the pan; they should sizzle right away. Stir to coat them with the liquid, then let them cook for three or four minutes. Sprinkle the veggies with your favorite herbs or with simple salt and pepper. You can also add a squeeze of fresh lemon or orange juice or a splash of balsamic or wine vinegar. Stir once more to combine, then serve over brown rice or pasta, or use as a side dish.

172. How to Make a Hamburger on the Stove

You may be wishing for a flame-grilled hamburger, but cooking outdoors isn't always possible. Use this easy method to make a hamburger in the comfort of your kitchen.

Season approximately six ounces of ground chuck with salt and pepper, and shape it into a patty (½- to ¾-inch thick). For flavor, you can add other ingredients, such as minced onion, Worcestershire sauce, minced garlic or garlic powder, and other dried spices.

Preheat a frying pan, putting it on a burner that's set to medium; let it get good and hot. Put the burger in the pan (it should sizzle) and leave it alone for three or four minutes. Flip it over with a spatula and continue frying for another couple of minutes. Insert a food thermometer into the center of the burger to test for doneness. (To ensure your safety, cook hamburgers to at least 155 degrees, until the juices run clear and the meat is no longer pink; that will kill potentially harmful bacteria.)

173. How to Fix a Leaky Faucet

They don't call it "water torture" for nothing: The sound of a leaky faucet can drive you crazy. Here's how to fix a leak and maintain your sanity. A leak often occurs when a faucet's washer becomes hardened or worn. First, shut off the water supply (look for a shut-off valve under the sink). Next, plug the drain securely so you don't lose any parts. Unscrew the handle from the faucet. Remove all the faucet parts and examine them for damage. Most likely, you'll need to remove the old washer and replace it with a new one. Visit a hardware or home-repair store to ensure that you get an exact replacement for the old washer. Put the faucet parts back together (including the new washer), turn the water on, and check for any leakage. Some faucets leak due to poor construction, and if you find that's the case, you might need to replace the entire faucet.

174. How to Stop a Running Toilet

A running toilet is annoying and it wastes water. Try these quick tricks, one at a time, to remedy the situation.

✦ If jiggling the handle solves the problem temporarily, adjust the chain length inside the toilet tank.

✦ Gently tighten the arm of the float.

✦ Test the flapper seal (the black ring at the bottom of the toilet tank). Push it down with your fingers; if the water stops, you will need to replace it.

✦ Gently pull the valve arm, which extends from the tube connected to the bottom of the toilet, up as far as it will go.

If none of these fixes works, the contraption inside the tank—called a ball-cock—might need to be replaced.

175. How to Turn Off the Water

Knowing how to turn off the water may help you to prevent a flooded home. First, identify the location of the leak and attempt to turn off the water at the source. Sinks have two stop-valves (one for hot water and one for cold) underneath. In kitchens, the under-sink valves also control water to dishwashers. Toilets have a stop-valve on their back walls, near the floor. Washing machines have two valves on their backs. If shutting these off doesn't work, you'll need to turn off your main water valve. Look for it on the pipe that brings cold water into your house. In cold climates, look for this valve inside; in warm climates, outside. The valve may also be attached to the cold-water pipe that runs into your water heater. To shut down water to your house entirely, find your water meter, which is usually located in the yard near the street, and turn off the valve that's located there.

176. How to Unclog a Drain

Hair is the most common drain-clogging culprit. You don't have to use caustic chemicals to clean the drain, however. An inexpensive flexible "snake," otherwise known as a drain or closet auger, is more effective. You can find one at a hardware or plumbing-supply store. To use it, remove the drain stopper, feed the snake into the drain as far as it will go, spin it around, then pull straight up. Continue doing this until you have removed as much hair as possible.

If you don't have a snake, you can make your own drain cleaner. Pour half a cup of baking soda down the drain, followed by half a cup of vinegar. Let the mixture sit for four hours before running water. If the clog is caused by grease, pour half a cup of salt down the drain, followed by half a cup of baking soda. Chase them with a pot of boiling water. Leave overnight, then run some water in the morning.

177. How to Unclog a Toilet

Unclogging a toilet is unpleasant, but given the cost of hiring a plumber, it's worth investing in a good plunger and learning how to remove obstructions. Lay a few old towels around the toilet in case it overflows. Raise the lid and position the plunger over the hole at the bottom of the toilet. If the water level is higher than midway up the plunger, you may have to scoop out excess water. Wiggle the plunger around to allow any trapped air to escape, then fit it into the hole and plunge up and down to lock it in place. Begin pumping the plunger using forceful strokes, keeping it as upright as possible; it can take up to 20 pumps to open a clog. If plunging doesn't work, try feeding a sewer snake into the drain to remove the clog.

178. "Righty Tighty, Lefty Loosey" and Other Quick Tips

Chances are there are at least a few gaps in your practical knowledge. Here are a few "life tips" that will make your day-to-day existence a little bit easier.

Righty tighty, lefty loosey. This phrase refers to screws, nuts and bolts—twist clockwise to tighten and counterclockwise to loosen. There are exceptions, though, so don't break your wrist trying to turn a screw that won't budge.

Starve a fever, feed a cold. Research has shown there may be some legitimacy to this adage. Still, experts agree that proper nutrition is a key to getting over any health problem.

Go with the grain. This is good advice when it comes to shaving, tearing newspaper, and cutting wood. It's bad advice when cutting meat, though—cutting with the muscle fibers will lead to tough, stringy meat.

179. How to Give Advice

Before you dispense advice, make sure it is welcome—even if you believe that you know exactly how to solve someone else's problem. Ask yourself if your urge to give advice arises from self-interest or from a genuine desire to provide wise counsel. If you are asked for advice, listen carefully to the description of the problem or issue. Try to empathize. Take time to thoughtfully formulate what you want to say. Keep your advice brief and straightforward. Make every effort to avoid giving advice that you wouldn't take yourself. Follow up to see if there is anything else you can do. Don't be disappointed if the person who sought your advice ends up taking another course of action.

180. How to Give Driving Directions

Clarity and detail are the essential components in an explanation of how to efficiently get from point A to point B. Mention landmarks in addition to street names to help those who are unfamiliar with the area. Incorporate the directions "left" and "right," as well as the cardinal directions (north, south, east, and west). Try to estimate the distances between points, being as realistic as possible. It's helpful to offer "warning" signs—a landmark, say, or particular street—that will indicate that the driver has gone too far. A hand-drawn, well-labeled map is a helpful visual aid. Finally, if you're not sure how to get somewhere, don't give incomplete or—even worse—wrong directions; instead, direct the driver to a nearby rest stop, gas station, store, or restaurant where he or she can ask for help.

181. How to Tell a Great Story

A great story may only be as great as the way it's told. Here are some tips that will help make your storytelling captivating. Make sure that the content is compelling and appropriate to your audience. Start strong with a catchy opening to hook your listeners. Watch them for verbal and nonverbal signs of interest and adapt the story accordingly. Avoid saying "um" as much as possible. Know where you are going with your story. Establish a clear beginning, middle, and end, and be sure to maintain momentum. Don't ramble—make it short! Practice so you are relaxed and confident. Humor, dramatic pauses, gestures, and sensory detail all enhance a story.

182. Finding Time to Exercise

You know that exercise is good for you, but how can you find the time to hit the gym when you barely have time to eat? Here are a few easy ways to fit exercise into your daily routine.

Take the stairs. Whenever you have a choice, take the stairs. Even better, go up and down a flight of stairs an extra time or two throughout the day.

Walk—better, *run*—the dog. Crank up the speed when you take your dog outside.

Flex. Simply tightening your abs or flexing your leg muscles while working at your desk is an easy way to stimulate and benefit your muscles.

Don't hold the handrails. If you ride buses or subways, you can strengthen your core and improve your balance by standing without holding onto support rails or overhead straps. You'll be surprised by how hard you have to flex your abs and legs to stay upright!

183. The Importance of Cardiovascular Exercise

Inactivity can be perilous to your health, contributing to problems that range from heart disease to obesity. Here are a few more reasons why you should work out your heart.

Mood. Studies have shown that regular cardiovascular exercise stimulates brain chemicals that regulate and boost your mood, helping to stave off chronic depression.

Weight. Burning calories through regular cardiovascular exercise is the best way to lose weight.

Insomnia. Try exercising for at least 30 minutes a day—a good cardio workout has been shown to help people fall asleep faster and sleep deeper. Just make sure that your workout isn't too close to bedtime, because your body and brain stay stimulated for some time after you exercise.

Illness. Regular cardio workouts improve lung and heart functions, and they strengthen your blood vessels. These exercises may also help to prevent other diseases, such as diabetes and osteoporosis.

184. The Importance of Strength Training

Regardless of your age or body type, strength training is an important part of a healthful lifestyle. Here are just a few of its benefits.

Better self-esteem. Building up your muscles and losing flab will make you look great and feel better about yourself.

Stronger heart. Strength training at least twice a week helps to prevent heart disease.

Revved-up metabolism. At rest, regularly exercised muscles burn up to 15 times more calories than fat does.

Lower risk of cancer. People who regularly participate in weight training are able to fight off cancer-causing free radicals more efficiently than those who don't.

> ### Get Ripped, Not Ripped Off
>
> Only strength training builds muscle. Products that promise to build muscle without exercise are bogus. Save your money.

185. Four Low-Impact Exercises for the Beginner

Low-impact activities, which are easy on joints and bones, can be just as beneficial as high-impact exercises such as running—without the wear and tear on your body. Try these low-impact exercises to improve your fitness.

Swimming. Studies have shown that swimming laps strengthens your heart, helps control weight, and tones muscles. It also reduces symptoms of chronic illnesses such as asthma and arthritis.

Step aerobics. Step-aerobic routines get your heart pumping hard. Rent or buy a step-aerobic video and exercise in the comfort of your own home.

Cycling. Most gyms have stationary bikes, and once you feel comfortable using one, you can intensify your effort by taking a spinning class (intense cycling to music).

Cross-country skiing. This gives you a great full-body workout while elevating your heart rate.

186. Make the Most of Your Gym Membership

The enthusiasm that accompanies a new gym membership often wanes after a few weeks. Avoid losing your motivation by following these tips.

Choose the right gym. Every facility has its own character. Visit a few gyms to get a feel for different kinds of environments and to determine which one is comfortable for you.

Use the services and staff. Use the free classes, fitness assessments, complimentary personal training sessions—everything that's offered. Staff can help you maximize your workout and explain how to use the exercise equipment.

Set small goals. Many people give up exercising because they set unrealistic goals and see few immediate results. You're not going to lose 30 pounds in the first two weeks, so set manageable goals and work steadily toward them.

187. Yoga: Why You Need It

Yoga is soaring in popularity, and it's good for you—it vastly improves flexibility, core strength, and muscle strength. It benefits people who have heart conditions, anxiety, depression, insomnia, and asthma, according to the National Institutes of Health. Other studies indicate that yoga also helps patients who suffer from arthritis and multiple sclerosis.

Yoga is more than just stretching and bending. Holding physical poses (*asanas*) is a part of the routine, but yoga also seeks to provide physical, mental, and spiritual unity. There are many schools of yoga, all of which take different approaches to attaining this goal.

188. How to Dance When You Have Two Left Feet

You can have fun on the dance floor if you learn to do the mambo—one of the world's most basic dance steps. It can be performed to pretty much any beat, except perhaps a waltz or a jig.

1. Stand with your feet about shoulder-width apart. Smile—it will help you relax.

2. Step forward with your right foot, placing it almost directly in front of your left foot as if you were walking on a balance beam.

3. Shift your weight onto your right foot. Rock forward very gently, then rock backward to your left foot.

4. Place your right foot behind your left foot.

5. Rock backward onto your right foot, then forward onto your left.

6. Repeat. Essentially, you're moving your right foot back and forth while your left foot steps in place.

Start slow. Keep your steps small. Bend your knees just a tiny bit. Let your arms swing a little as you move.

Once you get used to the basic movement, you can switch feet, move sideways, switch directions, and even pivot.

189. Street Smarts

Having street smarts means knowing how to keep yourself safe when you're out and about. It means always having your antennae up—being aware of your surroundings. Don't wear headphones when you're walking or jogging alone. Stick to well-lit streets and walk with purpose. Don't look distracted or uncertain or draw attention to yourself. Don't take shortcuts through alleys, parks, or isolated areas. Wear your purse close to your body, and don't carry a lot of cash in it. Stash a credit card or money in an inside pocket or shoe. Become familiar with the neighborhoods in which you live and work, and check out the locations of the local police and fire stations, as well as stores and restaurants that are open late. Trust your instincts and use common sense when navigating unfamiliar territory. Wear clothing and shoes that allow you to move quickly and easily.

190. Basic Self-Defense

The best self-defense is to avoid risky situations. If you are confronted by an attacker, however, here's what to do.

✦ **Run away only if you have somewhere to go.** If running is not your best option, scream, yell, act crazy, and try to call 911. As a last resort, physically fight with the attacker. Convince him or her that you are not worth the trouble.

✦ **Have a weapon and know how to use it.** You might have mace in your pocket, but if you don't know how to aim and spray under duress, it's not going to do you any good. Keep a hard object (such as a car key) in your hand and use it.

✦ **Use your body as a weapon.** Sign up for a self-defense class and get comfortable with gouging, poking, biting, kicking, punching, and head-butting.

191. Mall Safety

You've got street smarts, but do you have mall smarts? Here are some tips that will help you stay safe while shopping.

> ### Fight Back
>
> If someone tries to push you into a car, bite, kick, scream, and flail about as if your life depends on it; in most cases, it does. Your chances of escaping unharmed dramatically decrease once you've left your original location.

✦ Note the entrance you use to enter the mall and the location of your car so you don't have to wander around the parking lot after you're done shopping. Use specific landmarks to jog your memory.

✦ At night, take a friend, park in a well-lit space, and lock all your car doors. Wait to exit with other shoppers when you're ready to leave.

- If a stranger approaches you, turn and walk into a store or over to a group of people. Ask a police officer or store personnel to escort you to your car.
- Pay attention to the people around you and don't talk on your cell phone.
- If someone bumps into you, immediately check your purse, pockets, and shopping bags to make sure that you haven't been robbed.
- Don't carry a lot of bags. You need to have at least one hand free at all times.

192. How to Get a Safe Ride Home

Whether you've had a couple of drinks and don't want to get behind the wheel or you don't feel safe traveling on your own, here's what you should do if you need a ride home.

Use a prepaid taxi card. Many cab companies will accept these as payment, which means that you can get a ride home even if you don't have cash to pay a fare and tip. Buy one to keep in your wallet for emergencies.

Call a friend or relative. Carry phone numbers of people you can call in case you need an emergency ride.

Call a community safe-ride service. Many communities have these. For a small fee, the organization will send a driver to pick you up and take you home safely. Some services will send two drivers: one to take you and one to take your car, so you don't have to return the next day.

Ask the bartender. Some bars and nightclubs participate in services that provide rides for customers who have overindulged.

193. Four Things to Do on the First Day of a Job

You'll probably be a bundle of nerves on the first day of a new job. Follow these tips to make your debut a successful one.

Arrive early, stay late. It doesn't look good to show up late on your first day. Likewise, people notice if a new coworker is clocking out on the dot.

Introduce yourself. Introduce yourself as you meet people throughout the day. A friendly demeanor is appreciated by coworkers.

Keep suggestions to a minimum. Even if you know of a better way to do something, wait to make suggestions until you've been on the job for a few days. Don't talk about how things were done at your previous job(s).

Ask questions. It's better to ask for help than to do something the wrong way. However, try not to pester the boss every five minutes either. Use your discretion, and keep a running list of questions that you can ask all at once.

194. How to Wow Your Boss

Everybody starts out on the bottom rung of the workplace ladder. To move up, you need to impress those above you. Here are a few tips.

Take initiative. Volunteer for tasks, especially the assignments nobody else wants. And if you have ideas for making the workplace more efficient or productive, offer them up. Let it be known that you want to take on more responsibility.

Admit mistakes. Nothing is less impressive to a boss than somebody who is always passing the buck. Take responsibility; admit your mistakes and explain what you'll do to avoid repeating them in the future.

Ask for guidance. An employee who asks questions about how to better do his or her job comes across as an employee who cares about that job. Just be mindful of using too much of your supervisor's time.

Stay positive. Negativity breeds negativity, and nobody likes to work in a negative environment.

195. Free Speech and the Workplace

Consult your employee manual for guidelines and policies that pertain to expressing your opinion. For example, your employer likely prohibits you from using office e-mail to send messages with political or religious content. U.S. law gives employers most of the power and discretion in matters of freedom of expression, so be aware that everything you say is up for scrutiny. This includes what you say outside the workplace too. Many employers monitor what employees write about on blogs and social-networking sites; if your words or online image don't portray the company in a positive light, you may be reprimanded or even fired. You *do* have the right to complain about discrimination or harassment in the workplace, however. Unionized workers and those with contracts have more protections.

196. How to Fill Out the W4 Form

The way that you fill out your W4 form—the "Withholding Allowance Certificate"—can affect your weekly paycheck. The W4 is used by your employer and the IRS to determine how much money to withhold from your paycheck for taxes each pay period. The amount you take home is determined by the number of "allowances" you claim—the more you claim, the less money is withheld.

Your annual tax liability is independent of how many allowances you claim. If you declare too many allowances, you could owe big money at the end of the year; if you declare too few allowances, every paycheck will be smaller but your annual tax refund will be bigger.

The IRS provides a worksheet to help you figure out how many allowances you can claim. Most young adults only claim themselves, but if you're married or have dependents, you may claim more. For more information, check out the IRS's Web site.

No Deduction

There's an advantage to claiming no allowances on your W4 form. Money will be withheld from your paycheck at the highest tax rate, which helps to ensure that you won't owe anything at tax time.

197. Understanding Your Paycheck

When you opened your first paycheck, were you stunned by the difference between your gross pay and your net pay? Here are the factors that account for the disparity.

Federal deductions. There are generally three federal deductions: The federal income tax is the amount withheld based on the number of allowances you claim in your W4; the Social Security tax, 6.2 percent of your gross pay, is withheld to fund the Social Security program; and the Medicare tax, 1.45 percent of your gross pay, is withheld to fund the Medicare health care program. Social Security and Medicare are collectively referred to as "FICA"—the Federal Insurance Contribution Act.

State deductions. All but seven states withhold income tax at various rates.

Employer deductions. If you pay for part of your health insurance, for example, your employer will deduct your portion of the premium from your paycheck.

198. What to Consider Before Renting a Sublet

Renting a sublet apartment can be an economical and efficient way to transition to a new city. Sublets are often offered for short terms and may be furnished, which makes moving much easier. If you're considering a sublet, first be sure that the landlord allows subletting. Many don't, so contact the landlord for confirmation before signing a sublease, putting down a deposit, or paying rent up front. Check for cleanliness before signing or moving in; dirty apartments may be infested with bugs, which make terrible roommates. Take photographs of the apartment just before you move in so you have proof of its condition in case the tenant or landlord claims that you damaged something during your occupancy. Make sure that you know whom to contact if there is a problem with the apartment. This is especially important if the tenant from whom you're renting will be out of the country or difficult to reach during your stay.

199. What to Consider Before Subletting an Apartment

Just because you've signed a 12-month lease doesn't necessarily mean you're tethered to the apartment for a year—it depends on the lease. If it allows you to sublet, you can rent your apartment to someone else for the remainder of the time that's left on your lease.

The main thing to remember about subletting is that you are still responsible for the condition of the apartment. Give careful consideration to the person who wants to rent the apartment. Will this person pay the rent on time and keep the place clean?

Always get written permission to sublet an apartment from your landlord. Consider drawing up a sublease similar to the lease you signed with your landlord, or even getting the rent up front. Remember that if anything goes wrong with the apartment, your tenant will call you, not your landlord. And if your tenant fails to pay the rent or draws complaints from the neighbors, your landlord is going to hold you responsible.

200. Moving Tips

Moving is often expensive and a lot of work, but with a little advance planning, you can minimize stress and move cheaply and efficiently. First of all, don't wait to pack until the night before you're scheduled to move! It will take longer than you think. Get boxes from a local bookstore or a business that uses a lot of copy paper; these are more likely to be bug-free than those that you get from the grocery store. Use free shopper's guides or newspapers as packing materials. Label each box to make unpacking easier. If you don't need a moving van, ask friends or family members for help in exchange for pizza or a favor from you (e.g., babysitting or lawn mowing). If you're unable to round up a moving crew, try Craigslist; check out the "Labor/Move" listings in the "Services" section.

201. How to Paint a Room

A fresh coat of paint can give a room a whole new look. You'll need paint (one gallon covers about 400 square feet), an old sheet or tarp (to cover the floor), an old rag (kept damp for wiping up any spilled or spattered paint), an angled paintbrush (for cutting in along corners and around trim),

How's the Hue?

Paint colors look different at home than they do under store lighting. Tape color swatches up in the room you want to paint to see how they look before you make a final color decision.

old clothes that you can get messy, a chair or stepladder, painter's tape, a tray, and a roller. Cover the floor with the sheet/tarp and remove dust and cobwebs from the walls. Tape around outlets, light switches, moldings, and the ceiling. Stir the paint, dip in the angled brush, and cut in a narrow band of paint (approximately two to three inches wide) along all taped areas. Pour some paint into the tray, saturate the roller with it, and apply it to the walls in long, even strokes. Keep the roller moving. Let the first coat dry, then determine if you need a second coat. When the last coat is dry, peel off the painter's tape and wash out the brushes.

202. How to Hang Posters Without Destroying Walls

Posters add color and personality to your living space, but using tacks or other mounting hardware to hang them is a quick, easy way to lose your security deposit.

Home Art Gallery

If you have a drop-tile ceiling, you can use the frame to hang posters. Just attach wires to the posters' backs and hang them from the frame for a gallery-like feeling.

For unframed posters, buy special "poster strips" or "glue dots" that are designed for poster-hanging at a home-goods or office-supply store. If these don't work, you can try poster putty, though it may leave a greasy film on both your posters and the walls. For cinder-block walls, you can use a hot-glue gun, though getting the glue off the poster after it's removed can be difficult.

For heavier, framed artwork, you'll need to use picture-hanging hooks or other mounting hardware. Talk to your landlord before you put holes in the wall, as some will charge you for repairs after you move out.

203. How to Hang a Picture Straight

You've found the coolest print at the museum gift shop, and now you want to hang it in your bedroom. Unless it's by M.C. Escher, you're going to want it hung straight and centered. To center the picture, measure the length of the wall with a tape measure and mark the halfway point with a pencil. Hold the frame at the height at which you want it to hang—ideally, the picture should be at eye level; mark the top of the frame with a pencil. The hook or wire on a picture frame is usually located a couple of inches below the top of the frame; mark this spot with a pencil. Hammer in the picture hook or the nail at the spot you marked for it. Attach the frame to the hook—to make sure that it's level, you can either eyeball it or use a carpenter's level.

204. What to Consider Before Signing Up for Cable

There's nothing wrong with relaxing in front of the television after a hard day, but can you afford a cable channel package? Take a hard look at your budget and consider that TV is free on the Internet. Many major networks stream their shows on their Web sites, and aggregator sites like Hulu offer everything from documentaries to the latest episodes of hit shows online for free. Many sporting events can be found online too. Investigate satellite TV rates;

The Bottom Line

Make sure that you ask what the total monthly cost of your cable bill is going to be before you sign up. That $30-a-month special rate might not include additional fees for HD service, cable-box rental, and/or local taxes.

satellite companies may offer competitive prices, but you need to make sure it's okay with your landlord to install a satellite dish before signing a contract. Decide how many channels you really need so you can choose the right package. Always try to negotiate the price; the one that's posted on the provider's Web site is not the only option. Companies often run promotions that offer low rates for the first six months or year of service; in fact, when you move to a new place, you'll probably be inundated with such offers. If not, call and ask what deals are available.

205. What to Do When You're Locked Out of the House

Keys have a way of not being in your pocket when you're standing outside your locked door. You want in—but how? Help is just a phone call away. First, call a roommate if you have one. If you've had the foresight to give a spare key to a friend, relative, or neighbor, contact that person. The landlord should be able to let you in, but he or she may charge a hefty "lock-out" fee. If no one is available, call a locksmith. However, even if you're in a rush, choose a locksmith carefully—make sure he or she is licensed and bonded, and get an estimate before agreeing to any work. This can be a costly way to gain entrance to your abode.

> **Don't Call the Cops**
>
> Unless you're in danger, being locked out of the house is not a situation in which you should call the police or fire department.

206. How to Create Closet Space Without a Closet

Many dorm rooms and apartments have limited or no closet space. Get around this problem with a few space-creating tricks.

✦ There's prime storage real estate beneath dressers and beds. Plastic storage bins fit perfectly and will stay discreetly out of sight.

- Get a free-standing closet. There are many varieties available at home-goods stores.
- A bookshelf is great for folded clothes and other sundries. (Use bins to contain them.) You can even hang a sheet, curtain, or veil of beads over the front to disguise it.

> **Lock 'em Up**
>
> If there's a locked storage unit in your building, use it to keep out-of-season clothes in sealed plastic containers.

- Milk crates are modular and easy to stack, making for good storage. Don't waste your money on the knockoff milk crates for sale at home-goods stores—you can often find the real thing at a nearby restaurant (or the alley behind it) for free.

207. Easy Soundproofing Tricks

If you love to crank up your music late at night, it's time to sound-proof your room. Here are some quick and easy soundproofing methods.

- Seal holes or cracks where air comes through with caulk or insulation foam. Wherever air travels, sound travels.
- Cover windows with plastic, heavy curtains, or blankets, and put temporary magnetic covers over all air vents.
- Weather-strip doors to fill in gaps and crevices.
- If the room's floor is linoleum, tile, or wood, cover it with rugs or pieces of carpet to help mute sound. Put carpet pads or foam underneath for an even better sound barrier.
- Cover walls, floors, and ceiling with acoustic absorption mat (a lightweight, polyethylene foam). You can also hang blankets or tapestries on walls to dampen sound.

208. How to Burglar-proof Your House

Use these deterrents to help a burglar choose some other place to hit.

Think like a thief. Look for vulnerabilities such as windows that are slightly ajar and doors that are easy to break into.

Conceal your stuff. Burglars often peek inside windows to case places. Cover windows with nontransparent shades or curtains. Keep important papers and jewelry hidden in inconspicuous places.

Install several layers of defense. Breaking through multiple locks, deadbolts, door chains, alarm systems, etc., takes too much time and work.

Get a dog. A barking dog attracts attention and can scare burglars away.

Fake your presence. Leave the television or radio on and set a few lights with electronic timers.

Mark electronic equipment and computers. Scratch your driver's license number visibly on the backs of all electronic equipment and computers. Thieves can't easily hawk goods that appear to be stolen.

209. How to Patch a Nail Hole

If you know how to patch nail holes successfully, you have a better chance of recouping your entire security deposit. The secret is to disguise the hole, not perform an all-out repair. If the hole is less than half an inch wide, use fine sandpaper to carefully remove rough spots. Fill the hole with spackling compound using a toothpick, spackling knife, or your finger. Smooth the surface with your finger so it is flush with the wall. Dab any bits of compound off the wall with a soft cloth. When the compound is dry, sand lightly if needed, then use a small brush to paint over the spot with the exact color of the rest of the wall. Feather your paint strokes so the edge of the wet paint blends with the surrounding dry paint. If you don't have the exact color, go lighter—it's less likely to show than a darker color.

> ### A "Hole" Lot of Fillers
>
> Try these substitutions for spackling compound: a thick mixture of baking soda and glue, modeling clay, caulk, or wood filler. Toothpaste can work too, but it lacks the longevity of other fillers.

210. How to Organize a Closet

A neat, organized closet reduces frustration and allows you to use your wardrobe more effectively.

◆ Start by noting what you have. Tailoring your closet redo to your specific needs is the key to getting organized. If you have more shirts and pants than dresses, for example, creating upper and lower hanging racks will optimize space.

◆ Put a small dresser inside your closet for storage if you have room. Use the dresser top for jewelry.

◆ Use baskets, boxes, and bins to group like items such as ties and socks.

◆ Hang a shoe bag or rack on the back of the closet door to store shoes and scarves.

Shelve It

For ultimate organization, purchase and install a shelving system. Know your closet's dimensions (width, height, depth) and your clothing needs, so you can purchase the configuration that works best for you.

◆ Install hooks for hanging belts and jewelry.

◆ Get rid of anything that is dated, worn, or doesn't fit. Don't waste precious space on clothing that you never wear.

211. How to Iron a Shirt

You can get away with laundered permanent-press shirts for casual occasions, but an ironed shirt is essential for job interviews—and when you want to look your best.

First, read the care instructions on the shirt's tag and set the iron to the recommended temperature. (If you use too high a temperature, you can melt or burn the shirt.) While the iron is heating, spray water or sizing all over the shirt. Water will help ease wrinkles; sizing does the same while adding body.

Start with the collar. Flip the collar up and press the underside, using the tip of the iron to smooth wrinkles. Keep the iron moving to distribute heat and prevent scorchmarks. Turn the collar down and iron gently on the fold.

Next, iron the body of the shirt. Slide the shirt's shoulder over the ironing board's pointed end. Press from the top to the bottom, then shift the shirt until a new wrinkled area is exposed. Iron between buttons—not on them—using the tip of the iron. Anchor the other shoulder at the top of the ironing board and press.

Press the sleeves last. Lay one sleeve flat with the seam on one side and press to create a crease on the outside of the arm. Repeat with the other sleeve.

212. How to Crease a Pair of Pants

Here's how to create knife-edge creases on your pants.

1. Put your pants on a firm, flat surface such as an ironing board or a kitchen counter that's covered with a layer of towels.

2. Turn your iron to the steam setting.

3. Grip the pants by the cuff and hold them upside down so the seams align. This will help you locate the natural fold along the front of the pants.

4. To straighten out the pants for ironing, lay them on the surface, making sure they are completely flat. Use your fingers to gently press along the front crease.

5. Lay a clean, damp cloth over one leg and press with the iron. Apply extra pressure along the fold to help with creasing. Iron the outside of the leg, then lift it up so you can iron the inside of the other leg.

6. Flip the pants over and repeat. Finish by ironing the waistband and pleats.

213. How and Why to Polish Your Shoes

A shoeshine can make worn shoes look new, and it can protect leather against the elements. Shine your shoes after purchasing them; a good base coat will protect them from dirt and wear. Polish them again when they appear dirty or dull. To begin, you'll need clean, soft cloths, a shoeshine brush, and shoe polish that matches the color of your shoes. Remove the laces, then clean off dirt with a warm, damp rag. Dry the shoes with a clean cloth. Using another clean cloth, apply polish evenly to the entire shoe. Let it sit for five minutes, then shine it using short, gentle, circular strokes. Add a second coat of polish, then buff the shoes with the brush. Bring the shine to the surface by lightly rubbing another cloth over the shoe. If you need more coverage or want a shinier result, continue to apply coats of polish until you achieve the look you desire.

214. How to Buy a Man's Suit

It's important to own an all-purpose suit so you're ready for any occasion. Keep these things in mind when shopping for one.

> ### Size Matters
> Have a professional tailor take your measurements. You may be a different size than you think.

Jacket style. A two-button, single-breasted suit jacket is a classic choice, fits nearly any body type, and is always appropriate. Three- and four-button jackets are good for taller men; double-breasted jackets add girth to slim figures.

Jacket fit. Shoulder seams should align with the top edge of your shoulder. The sleeve should stop at the wristbone to allow shirt cuffs to show, and the jacket should hang to the middle of your hips.

Pants style. Flat-front pants are slimming; pleats are considered a bit dressier and provide extra room for movement.

Pants fit. Pants should fit comfortably around the waist but allow for some movement. They should be long enough to cover your socks and fold slightly on top of your shoes when you walk.

Color. A dark suit—black, charcoal gray, or navy—will be most versatile.

215. Understanding Dress Codes

Confused about what to wear to a "resort casual" function or a "black tie" event? This guide will help you avoid a fashion *faux pas*.

Black tie. Men: black tuxedo, black bow tie, black shoes and socks, cummerbund. Women: evening gown (floor length).

White tie. Men: black tailcoat, matching trousers, formal shirt (white pleated), white tie and vest, black shoes and socks. Women: evening dress (floor length).

Semi-formal. Men: dark suit. Women: cocktail dress or elegant separates.

Cocktail. Men: dark suit. Women: cocktail dress or dressy pantsuit or separates.

Business casual. Men: sport coat or blazer, matching pants or khakis. Women: dress, skirt and top, pants and top, or suit or pantsuit.

Resort casual. Men: Sport coat, collared golf shirt or button-down shirt, khakis. Women: casual dress, skirt or pants, no jeans.

216. Bargain-Shopping Tips

Bargain-shopping can be a lot of fun—what's not to like about paying less? There are a number of creative ways to save.

Check online. Many retailers use Web sites like Facebook and Twitter to keep customers up-to-date on sales. You can also compare prices online with a variety of price-aggregator sites.

Ask for a price adjustment. If you buy something at full price and the item goes on sale a couple of days later, many stores will compensate you for the price difference (usually within seven to ten days of your purchase).

> ### In the Clear
> Learn the clearance schedules for your favorite stores. That way you won't miss the best deals.

Use your student discount. If you're in school, you may be eligible for special rates on movie tickets, electronics, clothing, and more.

Time it right. Sales are often associated with certain holidays (Presidents' Day, Memorial Day, the day after Thanksgiving, etc.) and with various store events (closeouts, anniversaries, inventories, etc.). Being mindful of these occasions can help you get more bang for your buck.

217. Five Things You Can Buy Used

Some things you need or want can be purchased used, which can save you lots of cash. Consumer experts recommend buying the following items used.

Textbooks. Buy used books online or from the college or university bookstore—just be sure to get the right edition.

CDs and DVDs. You can wait a couple of months for a new release and get a used copy for significantly less than a new one.

Board games. A used board game is as good as new if it has all its pieces. Thrift shops often have them for just a couple of dollars.

Tools (nonpower). Basic tools like hammers and screwdrivers can be purchased used, but don't buy used power tools, as you don't know how much wear and tear their motors have experienced.

Some kinds of furniture. Beds should be bought new, but other items—such as desks, dining tables, and chairs—can be had for cheap at yard sales and through Web sites like Craigslist.

218. Five Things You Should Never Buy Used

Scouring yard sales and thrift stores for used items is a great way to live on the cheap, but the following items should only be purchased new.

Underwear. Even if it's been washed a hundred times, do you really want to wear somebody else's old underwear?

Shoes. Shoes mold themselves to the feet and gait of their wearer. Buy used shoes only if you're sure that they've been worn just once or twice.

Car seats. Older car seats may have been recalled and won't

> ### As Good as New
> Refurbished electronic equipment—items that have been restored to like-new condition at the factory or by a factory-authorized dealer—are often good deals and will frequently come with warranties.

have the most up-to-date safety features. What's more, a used seat may have sustained invisible damage that compromises its ability to protect your child.

Helmets. There's no way to guarantee that the protective padding of a used helmet will get the job done when it's needed.

Mattresses/pillows. Before buying a used mattress, think about the different activities that take place in a bed. Then walk away.

219. How to Compare Prices

Here's an essential bit of shopping wisdom: The lowest-price item on the shelf is not necessarily the cheapest. To determine the best value, find the product with the lowest "price-per-unit" cost—this tells you how much each ounce, pound, quart, gallon, or other unit of measurement of that particular product costs. Using the price-per-unit costs, you can compare different brands and sizes. The cost per unit can almost always be found on the item's shelf label, but if you can't find it, it's easy to calculate it yourself.

> ### When Big Isn't Better
>
> It's not always best to buy the cheapest-per-unit item. Although larger sizes are often cheaper per unit, if you're not going to use the entire product before it expires, your savings will be wasted.

Suppose you're comparing two bags of rice: a three-pound bag that costs $4.69, and a five-pound bag that costs $6.99. You might be tempted to grab the lower-price item, but by comparing the cost per pound, you'll see that the more expensive product is the better value. ($4.69/3 = $1.56 per pound; $6.99/5 = $1.40 per pound).

220. Save Money by Shopping at Ethnic Groceries

If you live in an urban area—or any area that has a strong ethnic presence—you can save big money at ethnic groceries, especially on staples like noodles and rice. Ethnic groceries cater to immigrant populations, so their prices for cuisine-specific items are often considerably lower than those at the supermarket. At Asian groceries, for example, you can find bulk bags of rice for about a third of the cost of brand-name converted rice. Check out spices, vegetables, and frozen foods at these stores for more deals.

Not *everything* at an ethnic grocery is cheaper than at your average chain supermarket, however. In fact, many typical American brands and foods cost considerably more. Stick to buying staples and off-brand items at ethnic groceries, and make a separate trip to the supermarket for your Oreos.

221. Making the Most of Your Coupons

Clipping coupons might seem like something only old people do, but you'll see the light the first time you use one. Coupons can save you big money, but they can also tempt you to buy products that you don't need. Buy only what's on your list, and look for the cheapest product, even if you don't have a coupon for it. For even greater savings, use coupons on sale items. Using coupons can take a bit of organization—they don't do you much good expiring in your kitchen drawer. Devise your own system or get an expandable coupon folder or organizer to help you sort coupons into categories and store them. Just make sure to take your coupons with you when you shop.

222. How to Avoid Grocery Stores' Psychological Tricks

More than $300 billion of annual grocery purchases are impulse buys that are influenced by clever marketing and psychological tricks. Use the following tips to avoid falling into the overspending trap.

When a sale isn't a sale. Not everything in the store flyer is on sale. Supermarkets often advertise expensive items next to sale items in their flyers to give the illusion of a bargain.

Look high and low. The most expensive name-brand items are placed at eye-level. Check out the top and bottom shelves to find cheaper versions of the same things.

> **Hold Your Nose**
>
> Rotisserie ovens and bakeries are placed near store entrances to engage your sense of smell, which prompts you to buy more. Resist this urge by eating before you shop.

Beware the end caps. End caps, those displays at the outer ends of each aisle, are prime real estate that can boost an item's sales by more than 30 percent. End caps are often used for items that the store is trying to get rid of or might be near their expiration dates.

223. "Shop the Perimeter" and Other Grocery-Shopping Tips

While we'd all love to go out to lunch every day and order pizza every night, it's a sad fact that this isn't feasible; sooner or later, you're going to have to face the grocery store. You can keep the pain to a minimum by employing these strategies.

Buy generics. Most generic products are at least as good as name brands, according to *Consumer Reports*—and they can save you big money.

Shop the perimeter. The perimeter of the store is where grocers usually keep the healthiest products, such as produce, dairy, and fish. Stick to the perimeter to shop healthy and stay trim.

Eat first. When you're hungry, everything looks good. The next thing you know, you've spent $100 on Little Debbie snacks.

Make a list. Sticking to your list is key to a budget-friendly shopping trip—and it will save you from waking up to realize that you have no milk for your cereal.

224. Saving on Snacks

Snack purchases can really take a toll on your budget. You can save money without depriving yourself with these tips.

Make your own. You pay—big-time—for prepackaged snacks purchased at the local convenience store. Make your own—there are hundreds of recipes on the Internet for everything from trail mix to homemade Cracker Jack. It's easy and it's cheap!

Buy in bulk. Health-food stores and large supermarket chains sell loose snacks in bins. You can purchase everything from dried fruit to chocolate-covered raisins in bulk, and doing so is relatively inexpensive.

Buy generic. The main difference between brand-name snacks and generic varieties is usually the name on the label—and the price. Nobody cares what brand your candy corn is—as long as there's plenty of it.

225. When to Buy Generics

In 2005, *Consumer Reports* compared 65 generic products to their name-brand counterparts and found virtually no difference between many of them—except the price. Many store-brand items are actually made by name-brand manufacturers, yet these products—sometimes the *exact* same items—are sold for far less.

One of the best ways to save money is with generic over-the-counter medications. These drugs have to pass stringent tests in order to be sold in the United States. This means that the drugstore-brand acetaminophen that costs half as much as Tylenol will get rid of your headache just as quickly as its name-brand counterparts.

Another category in which you can save a lot of money with generics—without sacrificing quality—is basics such as sugar, flour, salt, butter, and eggs. Their tastes will be virtually identical to those of name-brand items, and they're all held to the same FDA standards for quality and production.

The generic versions of basic toiletries—such as shaving cream and hand soap—are also just as good as the premium brands.

226. How to Find a Doctor

Moving away from home often means having to find new doctors. If you're covered by health insurance, check with your insurance company, since your options will be limited to those doctors within your network; the insurance company can provide you with a list of eligible doctors in your area. Ask friends and colleagues who have been living in the area for a while if they can recommend a doctor, especially if they are familiar with your network. You can also check online—many community-generated Web sites have listings and reviews of doctors and medical facilities for major cities. (Remember that these reviews are opinions, not facts.) Also, check the "DoctorFinder" section of the American Medical Association's Web site; the AMA maintains basic records on all the certified doctors in the United States.

227. Four Questions to Ask Your Doctor Before Leaving the Office

A visit with your doctor should be a dialogue—after all, it is your body and your health. Here are a few questions to ask at your next appointment.

1. **How will this prescription interact with the other things I take?** When mentioning medications you take, be sure to include any herbal and vitamin supplements, which can interact with pharmaceuticals.

2. **What should I do if the symptoms don't improve?** Always find out when you should follow up with the doctor.

> **Be Prepared**
>
> Before your appointment, make a list of any unusual bodily changes or symptoms you've been experiencing, no matter how small or insignificant they seem, and be sure to go over them with your doctor. This will help your doctor get a better idea of your condition.

3. **Are there other treatment options?** There are almost always alternative treatment plans available.

4. **What do these tests involve and what are the risks?** Most
    doctors will explain any tests they order. If yours doesn't,
    ask—you have a right to know what is going to happen to your
    body.

228. When to Make Health Appointments

How often do you need to visit your doctors? Here are some general
guidelines for a healthy adult. If you have ongoing health problems,
speak to your doctor about your situation to determine which spe-
cialists you need to see and how often you need to see them.

Primary care doctor. It's important to have an annual checkup,
which can help to identify and prevent serious illnesses.

Dentist. Two visits yearly. However, if you have very strong and
healthy teeth, you may only need to go once per year.

Dermatologist. Annual visits, especially if you spend a lot of time
in the sun or have experienced severe sunburn in the past—these
factors increase your risk of skin cancer.

Gynecologist. Women should go for a pap smear every two years,
beginning at around age 20—or three years after becoming sexually
active, whichever comes first. A pap smear is the best way to catch
early-stage cervical cancer.

Ophthalmologist or optometrist. Young adults without vision
problems should go every three to five years; those who need vision
correction or who have other ocular issues should go every one to
two years.

229. Finding Affordable Dental Care

Finding affordable dental care doesn't have to be like pulling teeth.
If you're looking for a dentist, start by asking trusted friends, family members, and colleagues for recommendations. You can also
request a referral from your doctor or pharmacist, or check the
American Dental Association's member directory. (Local and state

dental societies are also resources for referrals.) If possible, visit a few different dental clinics to find one that's right for you. When calling or checking out various clinics, inquire about payment and insurance plans, as well as any additional fees. (Make sure to do this *prior* to treatment.) For help with payment, contact your state dental society and ask about dental assistance programs. You can also seek more affordable care at dental school clinics.

230. Where to Find Contraceptives

If you're sexually active and need help finding contraceptives, here are some suggestions.

1. Talk to a gynecologist or other health professional. Ask about the side effects that are associated with different forms of birth control and which ones protect against sexually transmitted diseases.

2. Talk to a parent, counselor, or other trusted adult and ask for help in obtaining protection.

3. Visit a family-planning clinic, such as Planned Parenthood, for advice about preventive care and contraceptives.

4. Research your options online, but be sure to consult reputable medical sources. Not all the information on the Web is reputable.

> **FAST FACT**
> What kind of contraceptive is right for you? Your choice of contraceptive depends on personal factors like your age, health, lifestyle choices, and number of sexual partners.

5. Asking for help is a way of taking responsibility for your health and well-being. Don't let embarrassment get in the way.

231. Once You Hit "Send," You Can't Take It Back

It's easy to dash off an e-mail without thinking it through. Here are four tips that will help to ensure you don't suffer from e-mail regret.

- ◆ **Check the basics.** Make sure that you haven't screwed up the obvious. Double-check the address and choose the appropriate salutation and closing—you don't want to accidentally sign an e-mail to your boss with "Love."

- ◆ **Is it ironic?** Literary subtleties such as sarcasm and irony usually don't translate well in an e-mail message—in fact, they often come off as rude.

> **Actually, Yes You Can**
> Some e-mail services, such as Gmail, have introduced an "undo send" feature, which gives you a few seconds after hitting the "send" button to ponder whether you *really* want to deliver that message.

- ◆ **Edit.** Like any other form of writing, editing a first draft is important. Don't hit "send" without revising, especially if the message addresses professional, academic, or personal subjects.

- ◆ **Sleep on it.** We tend to say things that we don't really mean when we're sad, angry, or otherwise agitated. This is why it's critical to save such messages for a day before sending them. Chances are, you can make your communication more tactful.

232. Texting Etiquette

Maintaining contact with people is the primary purpose of sending text messages on your mobile device, but constantly tapping on your keyboard can be a big distraction and wastes time. Follow these rules of etiquette to become more efficient at work and play.

Don't multitask. Typing or reading texts when your attention should be elsewhere is potentially dangerous and often downright rude. If you need to check your messages for important lab results or info about your mother's delayed flight, let those who you are with know that ahead of time.

Be judicious. Texts can be traced, recalled, and forwarded, which means that they remain "out there" long after the emotions that triggered them have passed. If you've caught someone's eye, though, discreet texting can make you seem friendly and approachable.

Use the telephone for important exchanges. Phone calls trump texting when it comes to asking someone for a date or confirming a job interview.

Consider your recipient(s). If you are conversing with someone who may not understand "text-speak," drop the "omg's" and "lol's," and spell out your messages clearly.

233. Telephone Etiquette

Between instant messaging, texting, and Twittering, does anybody really use the telephone anymore? Of course, plenty of people do. But even if the phone is going the way of the dodo, it doesn't mean that telephone etiquette should do so as well. When you're on the phone, be sure to speak loudly and clearly: Mumbling in the general vicinity of the mouthpiece is a good way to have your message misunderstood. If you can't stay focused on the conversation—you're more interested in what's happening on TV or you're trying to figure out dinner plans with your roommates, for example—ask if you can call the person back at another time. Keep your voice down in public places—or don't use the phone at all; remember that you're not the only person on the subway, in the restaurant, or at the grocery store. Other people don't want to hear about your private life.

234. How to Console a Crying Friend

It can be hard to know what to do when a friend is upset and crying. Use your own experience to guide you. A hug and a hand placed lovingly on the back will let your friend know that you're there and that you care. His or her response will help you gauge whether you should do more, back off, or keep doing what you're doing. Try to say something encouraging if you think that your words will be well received. Speak slowly and gently, being careful not to offer judgment or unsolicited advice. If you feel clueless about how to help, it doesn't hurt to ask. Don't give your friend an "attitude adjustment," even if you think he or she needs one; wait until calm has returned and the tears have dried up—and until you can speak tactfully. If your friend seems distraught and beyond consoling, advise him or her to consult a counselor or therapist.

235. How to Handle Rejection

Rejection stings, no question about it. As much as it hurts, though, try to remind yourself that it is part of life and can present an opportunity to learn about yourself. Consider that the rejection may be more of a reflection of the rejecter than it is of you. It's all too easy to believe rejection is an indication that you're not worthy. Resist this interpretation—instead, affirm who you are and identify your positive traits. Go easy on yourself, and seek support from friends and family. Finally, let the rejection go. Look ahead to acceptance and opportunity!

236. How to Get Over Heartbreak

There's no magic way to mend a broken heart or bounce back from a breakup. Friends and loved ones will offer all kinds of advice and encouragement, but you may not be able to accept it at first. Give yourself some time to mourn the loss of the relationship, then stop wallowing and get back out into the world. Even if you're not quite up for social events, you need new experiences and new things to think about. Go somewhere you've always wanted to go; try a new hobby or plan a vacation. And lastly, go easy on yourself. It will take some time to retrain yourself to no longer replay the happier moments of your relationship on an endless mental loop. Time will bring relief—it just takes patience and perseverance.

237. Saying Goodbye

"Only in the agony of parting do we look into the depths of love," wrote English novelist George Eliot. There's much truth to this statement. Often, we take special people and relationships for granted— until we realize that they might not be around forever. It's only then that we reflect on how they have shaped and inspired us. When you must say goodbye to people—friends who are moving away, your parents when you move out of the house, an ill grandparent who doesn't have long to live—let them know how important they are to you. Share some specific ways in which they have touched you. Say the things that you've been meaning to say but never have. Take comfort in the fact that these special people will stay with you—in your memories, in the lessons they've instilled, and in the way that your life has been enriched just by knowing them.

238. How to Dump Your Significant Other

When you decide that it's time to end a relationship, do it with grace and tact—and don't do it in anger. This can be easier said than done, so here are some strategies to help you make as clean a break as possible.

1. Plan exactly what you are going to say, as well as when and how you are going to say it. Explain your reasons for ending the relationship in a straightforward but sensitive manner.

2. Do it in person. You owe it to your significant other to communicate face-to-face.

3. Give him or her time to process the information.

4. Hold back. The other person might become upset or angry, but you should stay calm and resist the urge to resort to name-calling or verbal abuse.

5. If you want to stay friends, accept that this probably won't (and shouldn't) happen right away. You will eventually have to work out what a friendship might be like, if your ex agrees.

239. How to Establish a Lifeline

No one ever plans to be in an emergency situation, which is exactly why you should prepare for one in advance. One way to do this is to establish a lifeline—a person you call in an emergency. Your lifeline could be a parent, a grandparent, a friend, a sibling—anyone you feel you can count on. Make sure the person you choose is reliable, relatively calm under pressure, and easy to contact. And be sure to ask for permission; using someone as a lifeline might involve listing his or her name and number on medical forms, school applications, and various release forms. If your chosen person is comfortable with all this, discuss what your plan of action would be if you found yourself in trouble.

240. How to Wow Your Professor

You'll need to do a little more than show up to stand out in your college classes. Here's how to make sure you get an "A" for participation (which can be a significant percentage of your grade).

> **Back Off**
>
> There's a fine line between participating in and dominating a class. Be sure to let other students offer their opinions and answers too.

Act interested. Put away your electronic devices and pay attention. An alert, focused student is every professor's dream.

Engage. Ask questions and answer questions—just make sure that they are relevant.

Use office hours. Visit the professor during office hours to discuss the week's material. Interacting via e-mail is acceptable too.

Refer to previous class material. Referencing material and discussions from earlier in the semester shows that you really have a handle on the class.

Give thanks. If the professor gives you helpful comments on a paper or agrees to give an extension on a deadline, let him or her know that you are grateful.

241. How to Avoid Plagiarism

In college, plagiarism—using someone else's words or ideas without attribution—will cost you dearly, regardless of whether it was intentional or accidental. Guard against it by following these guidelines.

✦ **Cite your sources.** Even if you're explaining another author's ideas in your own words, you'll need to give credit for the original idea to that author.

- **Use quotation marks.** If you use a sentence that somebody else wrote, put quotation marks around it and credit the original author.
- **Check your work online.** There are numerous sites—such as Copyscape—that will run inputted text across the entire Web looking for matches. It's always a good idea to run your paper through one of these sites to make sure that you don't inadvertently use somebody else's words.

> **Not the Easy Way Out**
>
> Don't purchase a research paper online unless you want to get expelled. It's unethical to take credit for someone else's work, and most professors can spot a Web-bought paper from a mile away.

242. The Benefits of an Internship

One of the best career moves you'll ever make is taking an internship. You'll learn more about a particular profession than you will in a classroom, and you'll develop skills, experience, and contacts that will help you land a job later on. Many internships are unpaid (although some offer a modest stipend), but if you can forgo the income now, it will pay dividends later. Your internship may also be eligible for academic credit, so talk to your advisor to learn how to apply for and use it. During your internship, ask thoughtful questions and show that you are motivated. Even if you're stuck making copies or doing a lot of data entry, you can still make a good impression and catch the eyes of potential employers. Before your internship ends, ask your supervisor to write you a reference that you can use for future jobs or school applications.

> **Finding an Internship**
>
> Check with your school's career services office, as well as on Internet job sites, which often have internship listings. Browse the Web sites of companies you'd love to work for; they often have links to information about internships.

243. How to Take a Gap Year Without Falling into a Hole

A "gap year" is a year taken off from studying—usually after high school and before college—for travel, work, or volunteering. The key to having a successful gap year experience is knowing what you want to accomplish and then planning ahead. Determine what your budget will allow and what your financial and educational objectives are. Are you trying to save money for college? Build your portfolio or resume? Explore the world? Web sites such as GapYear.com and YearOutGroup.org provide links to many opportunities. You might consider serving in AmeriCorps, which offers placements ranging from literacy tutoring to environmental cleanup, or participating in the City Year program, which partners with urban schools and after-school programs. You can even teach English in a foreign country or go on an extended backpacking trip. The possibilities are endless!

244. Is an Online Class Right for You?

Many colleges and universities offer online courses as an alternative to traditional classroom-based education. Online courses have a number of advantages. If you're shy in the classroom, you may find the relative anonymity of posting from your computer to be liberating. Online classes give you more flexibility, since you can work on your studies at any time of the day or night and anywhere you have a computer and Web access. In some ways, though, online classes demand more of students. Unlike traditional courses, which meet two or three times per week, online courses may require you to log in and participate—by posting comments and questions—more frequently. You may be tempted to put off class preparation because you don't have to go to a classroom or deal with your professor in person, but procrastination is a recipe for disaster. If you do decide to take an online class, allow some additional time at the beginning of the semester to get comfortable with the technology.

245. The Scoop on Online Degrees

Advertisements for online universities are everywhere, but are these colleges as good as traditional brick-and-mortar schools? The answer is: sort of. Just a few years ago, online degrees were considered to be second-rate, offered by fly-by-night "universities" with inferior faculty members teaching subpar students. But since then, many traditional universities—including esteemed institutions such as Stanford—have begun to offer their own online degrees. Since this happened, online education's reputation has improved. That being said, it's important to recognize that, fair or not, many employers regard online degrees with some suspicion. If you decide to go the online route, be sure to choose an institution that is accredited. You can check accreditation through the U.S. Department of Education, which maintains a database on its Web site.

FAST FACT

The perceived value of an online education depends largely on the student's field of study. In technical fields, such as information technology and Web programming, online degrees are more widely accepted.

246. What to Consider Before Taking Herbal Supplements

Herbal supplements are so popular that Americans spend almost $15 billion a year on them. Here's some important advice to consider before you take any herbal remedies.

+ **Talk to your doctor first.** This is especially important if you take medication, are pregnant, or are preparing for surgery. Many herbs interact with pharmaceuticals and anesthetics; this can cause unpleasant or dangerous side effects.

+ **Take one at a time.** Buy single-herb supplements so you know exactly what—and how much of it—you're getting.

- ✦ **Look for the seal.** Several independent organizations certify herbal supplements, ensuring that they have met quality-control standards. Make sure the herbs you buy have been approved by one of these groups.
- ✦ **Check the country of origin.** Some foreign-made herbal supplements have been found to contain toxic ingredients. All supplements made in the United States, however, are subject to FDA regulations.

> ## Reliable Information
>
> For a comprehensive rundown of almost every herb available, including relevant scientific research, visit the National Center for Complementary and Alternative Medicine's Web site at nccam.nih.gov.

247. Recognizing the Side Effects of Prescription Drugs

Prescription drugs can cause unpleasant side effects. Usually these are minor, but they can be serious—which is why you need to know how to recognize them. Pharmacies provide a list of possible side effects with each prescription; take the time to read about these symptoms. Many Web sites, such as Drugs.com, provide comprehensive information about drugs and their side effects. Keep track of how you feel after you begin taking a medication so your doctor can figure out if you are experiencing side effects. Be sure to jot down any new symptoms you have, no matter how trivial they may seem. If you suspect that your prescription is causing side effects, call your doctor right away. It may not be anything to worry about, but it's better to let a professional make that determination.

248. Medicines That Don't Mix

When you pick up a prescription, make sure that you read and understand everything on the drug's label and information insert. (Ask the pharmacist for clarification if you're unsure about anything.) Always take the medication exactly according to the directions—for example, if the drug should be taken with food, don't just stir it into your meal, as this may alter its effectiveness. Avoid taking vitamins at the same time that you take medication. Be sure not to take supplements and painkillers together, as the contents of many supplements are not always made clear (different regulations are applied to them). Other things that don't mix include blood pressure medicine and oral nasal decongestants, Tylenol and alcohol, and alcohol and cold medicines. Generally speaking, it's best to avoid alcohol when you're on medication. Also, many antibiotics will interfere with oral contraceptives. If you're unsure about what you can and cannot mix, consult a doctor.

249. How to Read the Labels on Over-the-Counter Medications

When you're sick, it's tempting to grab the first multisymptom remedy that you find, but you need to take your time and read the labels before you take anything. Here's a guide to the terms you'll find on these labels.

Active ingredient. The first section tells you what the active ingredient is and what it does.

Uses. This lists the symptoms that the drug treats. Be sure that the symptoms you're experiencing appear here.

Warnings. Read this section carefully, as it will alert you to conditions under which you shouldn't take the drug, possible side effects, and when to see your doctor if you experience anything unusual.

> ### Overdose Warning
>
> Taking more than one drug with the same active ingredient is dangerous. Read the drug labels on all over-the-counter and prescription medications that you're taking and compare ingredients.

Directions. This is where you find the dosing schedule. Note how often you can take the drug and how many doses you should take in a 24-hour period.

Storage. Follow these directions carefully, as improper storage can reduce the effectiveness of the medication.

Inactive ingredients. These are important to note, especially if you're allergic to certain additives, such as lactose.

250. Home Remedies That Really Work

Whether it's taking Vitamin C supplements or drinking honey-lemon tea, everyone uses home remedies for minor health issues. Do any of these treatments really work, or are their benefits all in your head? There is little scientific evidence to support the usefulness of most of our cherished home remedies, but here are a few that you can count on.

✦ **Chicken soup.** If you have a respiratory infection, eating chicken soup can help to relieve your congestion by accelerating the movement of mucus through the nose—and it acts as an anti-inflammatory agent.

✦ **Saline nasal spray.** This helps to clear congested nasal passages and sinuses.

✦ **Milk of magnesia.** Apply this to canker sores.

✦ **Oatmeal.** Add finely ground oatmeal to a bath to soothe irritated skin.

✦ **Aloe.** A bit of the slimy stuff helps to heal minor burns.

251. Vitamins Aren't Substitutes for Food

The best sources of vitamins and minerals are whole, nutritious foods. Vitamin supplements cannot replace the benefits that you get from food, but they can complement your diet if it is lacking in certain nutrients. You may benefit from a supplement if you eat fewer than 1,600 calories a day, are a vegetarian, suffer from an illness that interferes with nutrient absorption, or are pregnant or nursing. The best type of

> **Bulk Up**
>
> Consider taking a fiber supplement if your diet is lacking in whole grains, beans, and fruits and vegetables. You should get between 20 and 35 grams of fiber a day.

supplement to take is one that provides 100 percent of the recommended daily value of all the vitamins and minerals. (Calcium is an exception because the required dose would make a pill too large to swallow. Your body can only absorb 500 milligrams of calcium at one time, so break up your calcium intake throughout the day.)

252. How to Have Good Bones

Your teens and twenties are when you need to build the strong bones that will support you for the rest of your life. This is because girls will reach 90 percent of their peak bone mass by age 18 and boys will do so by age 20; maximum bone mass is reached by age 30. Getting enough calcium in your diet is one way to ensure that you will have strong bones. In fact, calcium deficiency in young people is responsible for a 5- to 10-percent reduction in peak mass later in life, which puts bones at risk for fractures. If you don't get enough calcium in your diet (through milk, yogurt, broccoli, beans, and tofu), be sure to take supplements. (In addition to calcium, you need to get enough Vitamin D, which is essential for calcium absorption.) You can also build strong bones by being physically active; get at least 30 minutes of weight-bearing exercise—such as walking, running, or playing basketball—every day.

253. How to Extinguish a Kitchen Fire

If your cooking sparks more than your appetite, extinguish the fire quickly, before it spreads.

PASS the Fire

To use a fire extinguisher, remember the acronym **PASS**: **Pull** the pin on the top, **Aim** at the base of the fire, **Squeeze** the lever slowly, and **Sweep** from side to side over the fire until it is out.

1. Turn off the burner, then determine the type of fire: grease, paper, or electrical. Call 911 if you have any doubt about your ability to put it out.

2. Use a fire extinguisher if you have one. If you're dealing with a paper fire, use baking soda or a soaked cloth to smother it. You can toss small burning objects into the sink under running water.

Smother grease fires by placing a lid on the pot; fire that's outside a pot can also be smothered with a baking sheet or baking soda. *Never use water on a grease fire.*

3. If your clothes catch on fire, stop, drop, and roll. Attend to burns only after the fire is extinguished.

254. What to Have On Hand for Emergencies

Emergencies happen, and when they do, it's important to be prepared. Here are some items that are helpful to have in case of an emergency; keep them together in an emergency kit so you don't have to scramble to find them.

- Flashlight
- Matches
- Candles
- First-aid kit (containing sterile gloves, gauze, tweezers, scissors, bandages, antiseptic spray, pain-relieving drugs, antiseptic wipes, an ice pack, antibiotic ointment, etc.)
- Small radio (a hand-crank radio is ideal)
- Four gallons of distilled or purified water
- Sleeping bag or blanket
- Basic tool kit (containing a hammer, nails, a Phillips-head screwdriver, a flathead screwdriver, a tape measure, and a crescent wrench)
- Energy bars or other nonperishable food
- Extra batteries
- List of emergency phone numbers

255. Fire Safety

Here are some simple precautions you can take to prevent a fire in your home—and to protect yourself in case one breaks out.

Use smoke alarms. They are cheap and easy to install—yet two-thirds of fire deaths occur in homes that don't have them. Place one on the ceiling of each floor and both outside and inside bedrooms. Test them monthly and replace their batteries yearly.

Be prepared. Keep fire extinguishers within reach and know how to use them.

Eliminate fire hazards. Look for overloaded electrical outlets, damaged appliance cords, space heaters that are too close to objects, and light switches that are hot to the touch.

Have a plan. Prepare at least two escape routes from various places in the house. Practice your escape plan at night with no lights on—and crawl, since you'll need to stay below the smoke.

256. Candle with Care

Candles are inexpensive items that add ambience to any room, but you need to be careful when burning them. Never place candles near flammable objects. (This includes curtains.) But how close is too close? The National Fire Protection Association recommends a minimum of 12 inches as a safe distance, while The Home Safety Council (apparently a more protective lot) suggests a minimum of three feet. The candleholder is an important but often overlooked aspect of candle burning. The holder should be sturdy and rest on a stable surface, away from flying elbows or dangling hair. Don't let the candle burn down to a nub—if the candleholder is at all flammable, it could catch fire. Never leave a candle burning when you go to sleep. Finally, be sure to always extinguish candles before you leave a room or building—you don't want to come home to an unpleasant surprise.

257. Is It Really an Emergency? When to Call 911

When is an emergency a 911 emergency? Here are a few tips that will help you decide.

Health emergencies. Life-threatening emergencies such as heart attacks, strokes, anaphylactic shock, drug overdoses, or loss of consciousness all warrant calls to 911. You can also call 911 for other injuries (like broken legs) if moving the injured person could make the situation worse.

Fire and police emergencies. Seeing smoke or fire almost always warrants a call to 911, and the same goes for witnessing any crime in progress. Also, call if you suspect an intruder is in your home or is trying to break into it.

Don't call 911 to ask about power outages, weather conditions, or a cat that's stuck on the roof—these are what police and fire nonemergency numbers are for.

258. What to Do if You're in a Bicycle Accident

If you're in a bike accident, you should basically do the same things that you'd do after a car accident. First, check yourself for injuries and call 911. If the driver hasn't fled, get his or her name, license number, phone number, and car insurance information. Write down the make and model of the car and its license plate number. If there are witnesses, get their names and contact information. If you have a cell phone with a camera, take photographs to record the scene.

Carry I.D.

Keep a card with your name, phone number, and emergency contact information in your pocket. Also, always bring your cell phone in case of emergency.

Don't refuse medical care at the scene, no matter how minor your injuries may seem. Don't sign any medical authorizations or releases of claims, and don't speak to any insurance adjusters who represent the driver; these conversations can happen after you regain your composure and are out of danger.

If police don't respond to the 911 call, go to the police station to file a report.

Keep any soiled clothes and damaged equipment as evidence. See a physician if you have any pain after the accident; sometimes more serious problems can occur if injuries are left untreated. Have your bike checked—and repaired, if necessary—at a bike shop.

259. What to Do if You Have Car Trouble Away from Home

Staying safe is your first priority when you have car trouble. Turn on your hazards and, if possible, move your car to a well-lit area away from traffic. If you don't have a cell phone, raise the hood of your car to let people know that you need help. If you have something white in the car, attach it to the antenna or hang it out a window. Flag down a police car or state trooper if one is nearby. If you have a phone and belong to a motor club such as AAA, call for roadside assistance; otherwise, call information and ask to be put through to local authorities or for the phone number of the nearest open garage. Ask how long it will take for help to arrive and write that information down along with a reference number, if one is provided. Stay with your vehicle, if possible. If you are unable to obtain immediate emergency assistance, lock your vehicle and call a friend or a taxi. Do not accept a ride from a stranger; instead, ask him or her to send help for you.

260. What to Do if You Run Out of Gas

You ignored the fuel gauge when it registered "E," and now your car is making a chugging sound and you feel it losing acceleration. Don't panic. Carefully steer the car to safety—whether that's the side of the road, an exit ramp, or a nearby parking lot. If you're not moving when you run out of gas, put on your hazards, shift your car to neutral, and push it to the side of the road. Next, call for help—contact your motor club (if you belong to one) or a friend or family member. If you can't reach anyone, call the number that your state has reserved for stranded motorists or, if you don't know it, a garage or tow service. If you don't have a phone, you'll have to find a gas station, where you'll be able to to buy a gas can, fill it with gas, and bring it back to your car.

261. How to Maneuver a Car Out of a Skid

If you find yourself in a skid, the very first thing you should do is take your foot off the gas pedal—accelerating will only make the skid worse. However, you don't want to slam on the brakes. If you have antilock brakes, press down firmly and steadily on the brake pedal; if you don't have antilock brakes, gently pump the brake pedal until the car slows down. Meanwhile, steer your car into the skid—if your rear wheels are skidding to the right, turn your steering wheel to the right, and vice versa. Be careful, though: Turning into a skid can sometimes cause a car to "fishtail" and slide in the opposite direction. You may need to steer in both directions a few times to get back on track.

262. Freeing a Car That's Stuck in the Snow

Sure, the wintry scene outside looks beautiful—until your car is completely snowbound! First, clear the snow off the car and from around the tires; use a shovel if you have one, or grab any tool that's handy. If the snow is piled up to the chassis, dig that out too. Tires can't grab onto snow and ice, which means that you'll have to create your own traction to get on the road. A mixture of sand and salt works—the salt will melt the ice and the sand will provide a tractable surface.

Snow Prepared

If you live in a cold-weather climate, buy some small, collapsible shovels and a bag of rock salt, and keep them in your trunk.

(Kitty litter, sandpaper, and car mats also work.) Put the car into a low gear, then gently press the accelerator to try to get the wheels moving. Alternate between "drive" and "reverse" to gain space and momentum. Many people try to get out of the snow by slamming on the gas, but this actually makes the problem worse—the friction from the spinning tires melts the snow underneath, creating a ravine from which it is even harder to escape.

263. How to Deice the Windshield

The easiest way to get rid of the ice on your windshield is to turn on the car's defroster and wait while it does its job. If you don't have time or hate the thought of wasting precious gas, scrape away at the ice on the outside while the defroster is working from the inside. Keep an ice scraper in your car; in a pinch, you can use the edge of a credit card to remove the ice. You can also apply a de-icing solution to speed up removal. If you plan ahead, you may be able to avoid having ice on your windshield altogether by placing a tarp over your car at night (unless a heavy snow is predicted). A homemade ice-prevention solution might also do the trick. To make it, mix three parts vinegar with one part water in a spray bottle. Saturate your windshield before you go to bed at night, and in the morning, you should wake up to a clear, ice-free windshield.

264. How to Break a Habit

There are few things that are more difficult than breaking a habit. Here are some strategies that will help you develop willpower and patience.

Make it mean something. Give yourself a reason to break your habit that means more than the habit itself.

Give yourself a timetable. It takes at least 30 days for a new behavior to become a habit, so it's going to take at least 30 days to reprogram yourself and eliminate one.

Reward yourself. Set small goals and reward yourself for achieving them.

Stay away from bad influences. It takes a very strong person to be around a vice he or she is trying to kick and not give in.

Fill the void with a new habit. If you like to shop but have vowed to stay on a budget, fill the time with something that's fun but free. As you break one habit, you'll be creating another to take its place.

265. How to Manage Your Time

Everyone has 24 hours in a day, so why do some people have time to spare while others don't? The answer is time management. Figure out where your time goes by creating a master schedule—a chart with a column for each day of the week and a row for each hour of the day. Write down the events that occur each week that cannot be changed, then add activities—like studying—that should be done daily. Add personal activities, but do so judiciously. A few additional time-management tips:

- Tackle one activity at a time.
- Carry a digital or paper calendar to prevent double-booking.
- Set goals and schedule the time to achieve them.
- Keep a very short daily to-do list.
- Post reminders around your house or in your car.
- Tackle the most difficult tasks first; reward yourself when they're done.

266. The Benefits of Establishing a Routine

Having a routine will bring order to your life and help you deal with stress. Basic routines help you to accomplish daily tasks—you'll be less likely to forget to take your vitamins or to make your bed if you do the same things in the same order every day, for example—and they free you to concentrate on other things. Psychologists say that having a routine can actually enhance your well-being and boost your immune system. Creating rituals as part of your routine will help you to establish a reliable—and comforting—pattern. A ritual can be as simple as having a cup of coffee at your side when you turn on your computer, or it can be a more elaborate set of preparations for going to sleep at night. It takes about six weeks to establish a routine, so practice one daily to make it stick.

267. Five Ways to Slow Down

Some people love having a jam-packed schedule; others prefer a good amount of downtime. Regardless of your feelings about being busy, there are times when it's simply a reality—at the end of a semester, for example, or when you're facing a deadline at work. Here are some ways you can slow down and avoid stressing yourself out.

1. Take some deep breaths. Concentrating on your breathing is a proven way to calm nerves and refocus.

2. Make a gratitude list. This isn't as time-consuming as it sounds, and it will help you to put things in perspective. It might even improve your mood.

3. Take five minutes, put on your headphones, and listen to a favorite song.

4. Do five to ten minutes of basic stretching exercises or yoga at your desk or in your bedroom.

5. Go for a walk or a run. Engaging in aerobic exercise, even for a short time, will improve your physical and mental health.

268. What You Need to Know About Multitasking

Instant messaging. Checking Facebook. Eating dinner. Listening to music. Working on a paper. In our busy, hyper-connected world, it seems as though we *have* to multitask to keep up with everything we need to do. But productivity experts question the value of multitasking. In a recent study of college students, researchers found that multitaskers were the least organized, had the shortest attention spans, and were the least efficient. In fact, combinations such as texting and driving are actually very dangerous. Some multitasking—such as throwing in a load of laundry while you're writing a paper—is an efficient use of time. But for the most part, doing one thing at a time will actually make you more productive— and less dangerous to yourself and others!

269. How to Set a Table

Table-setting rules were developed to help diners find the right utensils easily—not to make you crazy! The following tips will help make table-setting simple.

+ The acronym "FORKS" can help you remember basic place-ment. Working from left to right, "F" is for "fork," "O" represents the shape of the plate, "K" is for "knife," and "S" is for "spoon." The "R?" Well, follow the pattern we've given, and you'll feel a sense of relief!

+ If you're setting a separate salad fork, it sits to the left of the dinner fork (salads are often served before the main course, so it's the one you'd reach for first). Soup spoons follow the same logic: They go to the right of the teaspoon.

+ The napkin can be placed on the plate (try to fold it creatively— consult the Internet for design ideas). You can also lay the napkin under or to the left of the fork.

+ The blade of the knife should always face the plate.

+ The salad plate goes to the left of the fork; the bread plate goes above the fork.

+ Glasses—including wine glasses—should be placed above the knife and spoon on the right.

270. How to Hand Wash Dishes

If you don't have a dishwasher, you'll have to wash your dishes by hand. It's no big deal; just follow these steps.

+ Scrape the dishes. Get rid of remaining food by scraping it into a trashcan or the garbage disposal.

+ Fill the sink. Use hot water (but not so hot that you can't immerse your hands in it). Add liquid detergent—just a few squirts should produce sufficient suds.

- Put the dishes into the water. Begin with silverware (it will sink and soak), then gently add delicate, lightly soiled items such as glasses and fragile bowls and plates. Let them soak for a couple of minutes.

- Fill a separate tub with very hot, clear water; you'll need this for rinsing.

- Wash and rinse. Wash each piece with a dishrag or sponge, then transfer it to the tub of clean water.

- For heavily soiled pots and pans, drain and refill the sink with fresh hot water, then soak the items before washing them.

- Hand dry the pieces with a clean towel or let them air-dry on a rack.

> ### Waste Not
> Some people wash and rinse dishes under running water. This works, but it uses considerably more water and energy to heat that water, which makes it a much less energy-efficient and more costly solution.

271. How to Load a Dishwasher

This task is as easy as 1–2–3.

1. **Scrape food off the dishes first.** This helps to keep the dishwasher clog-free—and you won't have to rewash dishes that are caked with dried-on food.

2. **Load properly.** Place all plastics in the top rack, as some types can melt if they are set in the bottom rack, which is closer to the heating mechanism. Put small items in the utensil basket so they don't fall to the bottom of the dishwasher. Knives should be positioned point-down in the basket; place all other utensils point-up to maximize cleaning. Heavier items go in the bottom rack; fragile and smaller items go in the top rack.

> ### FAST FACT
> It's best to hand wash Teflon-coated cookware, good knives, and fragile stemware.

3. **Space evenly.** Avoid overloading the dishwasher and space items evenly to help prevent chipping or breaking from vibrations during the wash cycle. This also allows water to circulate properly so all your dishes and flatware will get clean.

272. Inexpensive Ideas for Dates

The next time you want to impress a date but don't have the cash for a fancy dinner, consider one of these creative but inexpensive options.

Embrace the great outdoors. Walk on a beach, hike a trail, take a leisurely bike ride, watch a sunset, or explore the architecture of your city. For food, pack a picnic (bread, fruit, cheese, and wine).

Take a dance class. Community centers offer inexpensive lessons, and the first one is often free. Dancing is a nice way to get up close and personal with your date.

Go out for breakfast or a sandwich. These meals are much less expensive and more relaxed than a formal dinner.

Check out free festivals. Many cities have something going on every weekend—art fairs, concerts . . . even chili cook-offs!

Dinner and a show—at home. Spend the evening cooking together. Choose a couple of good movies (or a season's worth of a favorite TV show) and watch them while dining on the couch.

273. How to Enjoy the Arts Without Going Broke

The best things in life aren't always free—especially if you want to enjoy the finest arts that your city has to offer. However, there are many ways to get a taste of culture without breaking your budget.

✦ Many art museums have free hours on certain days (check Web sites or call ticket offices for information). Some public libraries offer museum passes to their patrons; just ask at the circulation desk. Students often get discounts at cultural institutions, so don't leave home without your school ID.

- Reduced-price or "rush" tickets to plays and concerts go on sale the day of the show. Call the box office for information.

- Work as an usher—you'll get to see performances for free.

- Dress rehearsals may be open to the public for free or a nominal fee.

- Art galleries have free openings, bookstores host readings, and libraries screen films. Many public parks present outdoor concerts and theatrical performances (when the weather permits). Consult your local listings, and you'll quickly cultivate quite a cultural feast!

274. How to Give Gifts Without Spending a Dime

Short on cash? Fortunately, there are a lots of lovely gifts you can give that won't cost you a cent. Here are some ideas.

- Take care of a task that the recipient dreads doing, such as weeding a garden or cleaning out a closet.

- Give the gift of time. Offer to babysit or pet-sit.

- Be creative. Write a poem, paint a picture, compose an original song, make a mix tape, or assemble a photo collage.

- Visit Web sites such as Freecycle.org or the "free" section of Craigslist to find lots of cool stuff to give—and unique ways to give it.

275. Six Reasons to Use the Library

The library is one of the best resources in any community. And, you know—it's free.

1. **Workshops.** Most libraries have workshops about everything from how to file your taxes to how to write your memoirs.

2. **Free Internet.** Can't afford $50 a month for cable Internet service? Take a trip to the library for free Internet access, as well as word-processing and printing services.

3. **Personal research assistance.** Need to write a paper and have no idea where to start? The reference librarian will likely be able to help you out.

4. **Get music and movies—legally.** Check out that new CD or your favorite director's latest film from the library for free or for a nominal charge.

5. **Books!** Even if your local library doesn't have the book you're looking for, it can probably get it through an inter-library lending network.

6. **Access to research databases.** Your library subscribes to research databases, as well as periodicals, journals, and newspapers. Your card gives you access to these for free.

276. What to Do When Someone Tells an Offensive Joke

In an ideal world, when someone tells a joke that's in bad taste, you'd say, "I find that joke offensive, and this is why…." If you can't quite manage this, try these approaches.

Don't even snicker. If you're in a situation that causes you to feel uneasy about reacting negatively to an offensive joke, don't laugh. At the very least, act confused or disinterested. Laughter—whether genuine or not—merely encourages the joke-teller.

Explain yourself in private. Sometimes, people aren't aware that they've told an offensive joke, so there's no reason to embarrass them in front of others. Approaching the joke-teller in private will give you a better chance to explain the *faux pas*—chances are, he or she will be less defensive if the conversation is between just the two of you. In a calm, reasoned way, state your position and identify what about the joke made you uncomfortable.

No Laughing Matter

Offensive jokes promote more than just bad taste. According to research conducted at the University of Granada, men who hear sexist jokes are more likely to tolerate violence against women.

277. How to Stay Cool Without Air Conditioning

Living may be easy in the summertime, but it's also hot. Even if you have air conditioning, cranking it 24/7 is neither cost-effective nor an environmentally sound way to stay comfortable. Here are a few low-cost strategies that will help you stay cool while saving cash.

First of all, get the air around you moving. This can be done with a few well-placed fans. If you have windows on opposite sides of a room, try putting a fan in one window blowing in and a fan in the opposite window blowing out; this will create a cooling wind tunnel. This technique works especially well at night, when the temperature drops. In the morning, when the mercury rises, close the blinds to maintain that evening coolness for a while longer.

> ## Chill Wisely
>
> If everybody bought "Energy Star"–qualified air conditioners, more than 1.3 billion pounds of greenhouse gases would be eliminated, according to the Environmental Protection Agency.

Topical methods can help too: Take a cold shower, put a cool wet rag on your forehead and neck, or soak your feet in a basin of cool water.

If the heat becomes unbearable, find someplace that has air conditioning—such as a library, movie theater, coffee shop, or mall—and hang out there for a while.

278. Using Space Heaters Safely

One of the disadvantages of dorm and apartment life is that, quite often, you have no control over the thermostat, which can lead to some pretty chilly winter days. A common solution is to use a space heater—a small, portable heating device. While they are handy for warming up small areas, space heaters need to be used carefully. Here are a few tips that will help you stay warm without causing a fire.

Never buy used. Used space heaters might be damaged, and damaged space heaters can be fire hazards.

Look for the seal. Stamps and seals from organizations such as Underwriters Laboratories mean that the product has been rigorously tested for safety.

Keep away. Keep space heaters on flat surfaces at least three feet away from furniture, curtains, and other flammable objects.

Turn it off. When you leave the room, turn off and unplug your space heater.

Don't use extension cords. Unless absolutely necessary, don't use extension cords with space heaters; they can't handle the power that a space heater uses.

279. How to Draft-proof Doors and Windows

Up to 25 percent of our homes' heated and cooled air escapes through cracks around doors and windows. Save yourself a few bucks by draft-proofing your home. To test for moving air, light a match and hold it up to door and window frames; a flickering flame indicates airflow.

Install weather stripping.
Installing weather stripping around your windows and doors is the best way to prevent drafts. Clean the jamb or sill so the weather stripping will stick when it's applied. Measure the area you want to fill, then cut a piece to fit; push the long, rounded edge into the lip to secure.

Ask the Experts

Most energy companies will send a technician to your home to conduct a free energy audit, which identifies problem areas and offers weatherproofing advice.

Use caulk in cracks. Caulk is a wet plastic that dries in place to seal cracks. Clear caulk can be used anywhere. Using a caulk gun (available at a home-supply store), apply around windows and along gaps between bricks, wood, and metal. If needed, smooth the caulk into place with your finger.

Hang curtains. Thick curtains insulate your home from cold that seeps through windows. (Pulling down shades will also work.)

280. The Shocking Facts About Electrical Safety

Electrical accidents kill almost 500 Americans in their homes each year—and extension cords cause nearly 4,000 injuries. Use only heavy-duty extension cords for major appliances such as portable heaters. The safest extension cords are the three-prong variety, which should only be plugged into three-prong outlets; removing the third prong can cause an electrical fire. Light switches should always be covered with a switch plate. If the switch feels hot to the touch, turn it off and have it checked by an electrician. Always use light bulbs that do not exceed the wattage suggested for your lamp; using a bulb with too much wattage can cause a fire. Never handle or operate electrical appliances with wet hands or while wearing wet clothes because water conducts electricity and can cause a shock. (Be especially careful with electrical appliances in the bathroom.) Pay attention to your appliance cords—frayed cords are major safety hazards.

> ### Get Grounded
> Three-prong plugs are called "grounding plugs." The extra prong is the "ground"—a term for a wire that connects the electric circuit to the earth. Grounding wires are important parts of electrical safety.

281. How to Reset a Circuit Breaker

Stormy weather, faulty wiring, or the act of illuminating hundreds of Christmas lights at once can plunge your home into darkness.

Usually, though, restoring the power is as easy as resetting the circuit breaker.

Your power box is a gray or beige box that's mounted on an outside wall or set into an interior closet wall—or it may be in the basement. Locate the box, then unplug your appliances and turn off the lights wherever you have lost power. Inside the box is a series of black switches; each should be labeled with the name of a room. Look for the main breaker—a double switch that's usually located at the top of the box. Reset this breaker first by flipping it firmly to the "Off" position, then back to the "On" position.

If you're still in the dark, look for a single "branch" breaker in the box that corresponds to the room without power. If it is set halfway between "On" and "Off" or is completely off, turn the main breaker to "Off," then flip the branch breaker to "Off." To restore power, switch the main breaker to "On," then switch the branch breaker to "On." If this doesn't work, it's time to call the power company.

282. Tips for Indoor Lighting

Renters don't have control over permanent lighting fixtures, but you can make your living space cozy and comfortable by employing other lighting strategies.

✦ **Consider the room.** The kitchen and the bathroom need lots of light for maximum visibility. The bedroom, however, calls for a softer light.

✦ **Consider the bulb.** Different types of bulbs give off different kinds of light. Check the packaging or ask for advice at the hardware store.

Let It Glow

Throw up a few strands of white or colored lights to add a festive, fuzzy glow to your living space. If your space is always cold, they'll also add a few degrees to the room temperature.

- **Flameless candles.** If you like the flicker and warm glow of candlelight but worry about the fire hazards, check out "flameless candles."
- **Use the corners.** Putting lamps in the corners of rooms helps illuminate the entire space and makes the room appear larger.
- **Up and down.** Angled floor and wall lamps can add dramatic lighting accents to any room. If your living area has exposed brick walls, consider lighting them from below. Artwork, on the other hand, looks best when lit from above.

283. How to Choose a Lightbulb That Has the Correct Wattage

Replacing a lightbulb can seem overwhelming when you're confronted with the array of choices you find in a store's lighting aisle. Avoid being the punch line to a "How many teenagers does it take to change a lightbulb?" joke by following these guidelines.

Read the socket. Most of the time, the socket of a lamp or light fixture will tell you which bulb to use. If it doesn't, bring the old bulb to the store and ask for help. Always err on the side of caution—too much wattage can be a fire hazard.

Use the lowest wattage necessary. Even if the socket is designed to hold a 120-watt bulb, do you really need that much light? An extra-bright bulb can ruin the ambience of a room and spike your electric bill.

Dimmer switches. If you have dimmer switches or three-way lamps, make sure that the bulbs you choose are compatible with them. Check the packaging; if you're still unsure, ask for help at the hardware store.

> ### FAST FACT
> It's a good idea to replace traditional incandescent bulbs with compact fluorescent (CFL) varieties. CFL bulbs use far less energy—each will save you about $30 in electric bills over the course of its lifetime—and are far better for the environment.

284. How to Avoid Awkward Silences

You're with someone you don't know very well and your mind goes utterly blank. Yes, it's the dreaded "awkward silence." What in the world is there to talk about? Try these topics.

The immediate surroundings. If you're at a party, comment on the music that's playing—it might lead to a discussion of music in general. If you're at a restaurant, a comment about the food might lead to a conversation about gastronomy.

The news of the day. Current events are great conversation starters—just be careful about touching on sensitive subjects, like politics and religion.

Be Friendly

A sour, unfriendly disposition makes an awkward silence worse than it intrinsically is. Smiling, making eye contact, and being friendly will encourage the other person to open up, too.

The other person. Let's face it—most people like to talk about themselves. A simple, straightforward inquiry can open conversational avenues that you can explore all evening.

The awkward silence. Acknowledging the awkward silence can be a light-hearted way to break the ice. Just be careful, however, as it might make you or the other person even more self-conscious.

285. How to Talk to Customer Service

"Your call may be monitored for quality assurance." "All our operators are busy at the moment. Please hold." Sound familiar? If so, you've probably tried to reach a customer service representative. Being placed on hold or trying to explain a problem to an auto-mated operator can be frustrating, but if you have an issue with your phone bill, insurance plan, Internet service, bank statement, etc., you'll

Getting Through

Try calling customer service during off-peak hours—Tuesdays through Thursdays. Avoid Mondays, Fridays, and the midday lunch period.

need to give customer service a call. Here are some tips that will help you get great results.

1. Stay calm and be polite.

2. Ask for the representative's name, write it down, and use it when addressing him or her in your conversation. Ask for his or her direct phone number, in case your call is cut off.

3. Keep things lighthearted. This way, the rep will be more likely to champion your cause or address your issue.

4. If your customer service rep isn't helpful, ask if there is someone else with whom you can speak.

5. Say "thank you" for the assistance at the end of the call.

286. How to Make a Complaint to a Business or Service

When you need to stand up for your rights as a consumer, it's important to do so in a professional, mature way. Here are the steps you should take.

File It Formally

If you're really unhappy with a business, you can lodge a complaint with an authority. The Federal Trade Commission offers an online complaint form, as does your local Better Business Bureau.

✦ **Identify the problem.** Before complaining, figure out exactly what went wrong.

✦ **Decide on the resolution you want.** Do you want a refund? An apology? A voucher toward future services? Making a complaint with a goal in mind increases the likelihood of a successful resolution.

✦ **Get organized.** Look through your receipts and documentation to make sure that the problem didn't actually originate on your end; be sure to read the fine print.

✦ **Contact the business or service provider.** Most businesses have a dedicated customer service phone number or e-mail address. If you're at the place of business, ask to speak with the manager.

- ✦ **Stay calm.** Kill them with kindness. Getting angry isn't going to get you anywhere. Never, ever use profanity.
- ✦ **You have the power.** As a consumer, you hold the ultimate power in the relationship—the ability to take your business elsewhere.

287. The Art of Complaining

Nobody likes whiners, but that doesn't mean you shouldn't speak up if something isn't going as expected. Here are some tips that will help you make sure your complaints are heard.

Have a better idea. Speak up when you don't like something, but don't just complain—offer a solution. People will be more apt to listen to your gripes if you present an alternative.

> **Save Your Breath**
>
> It does no good to complain about something that can't be changed. As Mark Twain is reported to have said, "Everybody complains about the weather, but nobody does anything about it."

Choose the right time to complain. Don't air a litany of pet peeves in the middle of class or right before a meeting; choose a quiet time to express your concerns. Even better, find the time to meet with somebody who can fix the problem.

Acknowledge the good with the bad. Simply pointing out what's wrong with a situation won't win you any points with your audience. Acknowledging what is going *right* will make your objections sound more reasonable.

288. Knowing When to Bite Your Tongue

Knowing when to give voice to your opinions and when to keep them to yourself is an important life skill. Here are some times when you should bite your tongue.

When your opinion isn't educated. If you don't know anything about the topic that's being discussed, don't argue with people over it.

When you simply want to be right.
If your only goal is to prove somebody else wrong or to prove yourself
right, hold your tongue. If you're
right, it will come out eventually.

When it might be dangerous.
Speaking your mind is important, but

exercise caution if you sense that airing your opinion could lead to
physical violence.

When you just want to hurt somebody else's feelings. Will your
words do more than just make somebody else feel bad about him-
or herself? If the answer is no, keep quiet.

289. What to Do if You Have a Disability Nobody Can See

If you have a disability that isn't obvious—such as a learning disability or a nonapparent medical condition—even people who see you
every day are unlikely to recognize it. Whether you decide to make
others aware of your disability is primarily a matter of personal
preference. If you've only recently been diagnosed with a significant
condition, you may not be comfortable talking about it. However,
you'll eventually need to share this information with certain people.
If you have a learning disability, for example, alerting school authorities will allow them to make classroom accommodations for you. If
you have a condition like epilepsy, letting friends know about it will
help them to react appropriately and quickly if you have a seizure
in their presence. If you decide to disclose your disability, choose
a quiet time when you can speak intimately—and be prepared to
educate others about your condition.

290. Social Etiquette for People with Special Diets

If you have a special diet—perhaps you're vegetarian or vegan,
or you have a gluten allergy—alert the hosts when they issue an

invitation to you. At the same time, be sure to tell them that you don't expect or want them to prepare special dishes for you. Instead, offer to bring something to share. If you don't have the opportunity to let your hosts know about your dietary concerns ahead of time, it's fine to say "No, thank you," if you're offered a dish that doesn't comply with your diet; no explanations are necessary.

If you plan to eat out, research your dining options ahead of time so you know if there's something for you on the menu. If there are few options, ask if the kitchen can make a modification or two to an item that's on the menu. Unless their dishes are prepared in advance, most kitchens can make some accommodations.

291. How to Choose Which Tax Form to File

FAST FACT

Each 1040 form comes with a checklist to help you decide if you should file using that form. If you still have questions about which form you should use, call the IRS's toll-free number.

Everyone who files taxes needs to file one of the "1040" forms (why the IRS chose that number is one of many tax mysteries). Figuring out *which* 1040 form you should file is the first step to paying Uncle Sam his dues.

1040EZ. The 1040EZ form is a simplified version of the 1040. This is the tax form that many young adults use. The advantage of the 1040EZ is its simplicity—it only takes about 15 minutes to fill out. At the same time, this simplicity is its disadvantage—the 1040EZ doesn't allow you to take deductions and credits to which you may be entitled.

1040A. The 1040A is slightly more complicated than the 1040EZ, but it is still much simpler than the standard 1040. If you think that you qualify for education or retirement credits but don't have a very complicated financial situation, consider filing the 1040A.

1040. The standard 1040 form is much more complicated than the other forms we've described, but it is required if you have self-employment income or real-estate investments, or plan to itemize your deductions.

292. How to Fill Out a 1040EZ Form

For most people who are just starting out in the workforce, tax season is a snap. This is because they can file the 1040EZ—that's right, the easy form. You can download this form from the IRS's Web site or pick it up from most municipal offices, including your local library. You'll also need your W2—the form your employer supplies that states

how much money you earned for the year and how much tax was withheld. The 1040EZ comes with step-by-step instructions; follow them carefully, even if you've filed the 1040EZ before. (The IRS is notorious for changing the rules.) Don't forget to sign the bottom before you submit the form; every year, thousands of tax returns are rejected because taxpayers forget to sign them.

293. How to Get Free Tax Help

Is tax time approaching? Do you have any clue where to begin? If your answer is no, you're not alone. Every year, millions of Americans pay big bucks to accountants for help with their taxes. This year, save your money by getting some free help from these sources.

The Internal Revenue Service (IRS). Nobody knows more about taxes than the IRS, and its Web site offers tons of free information, free tax publications, and toll-free numbers to call with specific questions.

Online user forums. There are dozens of Web sites devoted to taxes, and almost all of them have discussion forums in which you can post questions and get replies from other users. Just be aware that not everybody on these forums knows what they're talking about. Your best bet is to seek answers at the large tax software sites, like TurboTax.com.

The public library. You can pick up tax forms at just about every public library, and many libraries have free tax seminars and workshops in the weeks leading up to the April 15th filing deadline. Ask your local librarian for help finding tax resources in your community.

294. Understanding Itemized vs. Standard Deductions

The Internal Revenue Service gives taxpayers breaks by offering them deductions. These deductions are subtracted from the taxpayer's total income for the year; the taxpayer then pays taxes based on the new, adjusted total. You have two deduction options: the standard deduction (a set amount to which every taxpayer is entitled) and itemized deductions (which are based on expenses, such as medical or school costs). You're allowed only one type of deduction, so figure out which will reduce your tax bill the most.

For the vast majority of young adults, the standard deduction is the best bet. That's because most young people won't spend a lot of money on health care, business travel expenses, or mortgage interest—the most common itemized deductions. In general, if you rent, don't own property, and don't have many unreimbursed work expenses, the standard deduction is your best option. If you own a home, though, or have had major medical expenses in the past year, consider itemizing.

FAST FACT

There is a difference between tax *deductions* and tax *credits*. Deductions are amounts that are subtracted from your taxable income; credits, on the other hand, are subtracted from your tax due.

295. Understanding Your Health Insurance

Health insurance is a safety net for times when you are ill or injured. Depending on your coverage, health insurance also helps to pay for some preventative care, such as annual check-ups or dental exams. Here are some important health-insurance-related terms that you need to know.

✦ **Co-insurance** is the amount that you pay for insurance. It is usually deducted from each paycheck you receive. This amount varies from the entire cost of medical insurance to only a percentage of the total.

✦ **Co-payment** is a flat fee that you pay every time you receive a medical service.

✦ A **deductible** is the amount that you must pay out-of-pocket before insurance covers certain medical expenses.

✦ A **Flexible Spending account** allows you to place a specific amount of money from each paycheck into a tax-free account for medical use only.

✦ **Out-of-pocket expenses** are what you owe after your deductible and insurance benefits have been applied to your bill.

✦ A **premium** is the amount of money you or your employer must pay for your health insurance coverage.

296. Keeping Track of Medical Expenses

When it comes time to deal with health insurance claims, having a good record of what you spent at the doctor's office will allow you to catch errors. Every time you pay a medical bill—whether it's for a prescription or for a doctor's visit co-pay—put the receipt in a file or folder that's dedicated to health-related expenses. If you're feeling really organized, start a spreadsheet that lists the date, service, and amount paid. When you receive an Explanation of Benefits (EOB)— the document that's issued by your health insurance company after a claim is filed by your medical provider—check it and save it in your file. The EOB lists the doctor, service provided, and total cost; it will also list how much you've paid, how much the insurance company will cover, and how much of the bill is your responsibility. Your doctor will send you a bill for the expenses that are not covered by the insurance company. Compare it to the EOB and to your own records; if everything is correct, pay it promptly.

297. How to Fight for a Health Insurance Claim

If your health insurance claim is denied, you may receive a shocking medical bill. Here's what to do if you find yourself in this bind.

1. **Check your records.** Pull out your receipts and make sure that the information on the insurance claim matches your records.

2. **Proofread the claim.** A typo on the claim and/or the use of the wrong code are the reasons for a huge percentage of denied claims. Even something as simple as a missing middle initial can trigger a rejection.

3. **Call the insurance company.** Ask why the claim was denied. Write down the explanation, as well as the name of the person with whom you spoke.

4. **Call the doctor's office.** Explain the situation and why the insurance company rejected the claim. The doctor may be willing to resubmit the claim with different wording or codes.

5. **Appeal.** Contact your insurance company to ask about the appeal process. Be persistent—sometimes denials have to be appealed three or four times before they are reversed.

> ### They're on Your Side
>
> If you're really struggling with a denied insurance claim, contact the Patient Advocate Foundation (PatientAdvocate.org), which helps individuals fight for their health insurance rights.

298. Maintaining Health Records

Your health records are probably scattered among the many different doctors who you've seen in your life. Consolidating this information will make it easier to find answers to your health questions if there's an emergency or you change doctors. One way to keep track of health records is to gather the information and put hard copies in a file folder; this should include prescription records, a list of known allergies, immunization records, doctors' contact information, and records of tests that you've undergone.

FAST FACT

Make sure that the PHR provider you choose is run by a reputable company that complies with the Health Insurance Portability and Accountability Act, which protects the privacy of your health records.

Recently, though, the health-care industry has developed electronic health records systems, which are known as Personal Health Records (PHRs). These online records maintain all the same information you'd store in your file folder, and they are linked to your pharmacy, hospital, and doctors. They are automatically updated and easily accessed, so you won't have to lug around a file folder of medical records from doctor to doctor. Ask your doctor about which strategy is right for you.

299. Know Your Family's Medical History

Knowing your family's medical history will help you and your primary care doctor determine appropriate preventative care—and it can be invaluable when diagnosing symptoms and medical conditions. You may be inspired to change some unhealthy habits after you discover potential genetic vulnerabilities. The following conditions tend to run in families: cancer, osteoporosis, diabetes, mental illness, cardiovascular disease, arthritis, and obesity. When tracking your family's medical history, try to include at least three generations with both horizontal (sisters, brothers, cousins) and vertical (grandparents, aunts, uncles) relationships. Make note of the lifestyle habits of family members, if possible, and at what ages they were diagnosed with various diseases.

300. Understanding Living Wills

A living will is a legal document that states your wishes regarding end-of-life care in case you become incapacitated due to injury or illness. It outlines the types of life-sustaining measures you do and do not want to be performed on your behalf, such as tube feeding, resuscitation, and respiration and ventilation treatments. Living wills are also called "health care directives." An attorney can draw up a living will, or you can find standardized forms on the Internet. Make sure that your immediate family members and physicians are aware that you have a living will and either have a copy or know where to find one. When you create a living will, you may want to designate a medical power of attorney, which allows someone else to make health-care decisions for you if you cannot make them for yourself. It is important to choose someone who will honor your wishes despite pressure from family and friends to do otherwise. You can also create addenda that contain additional directives or wishes, including funeral plans, other types of treatments that you would welcome or decline, and your desire to be an organ donor.

301. How to Read Nutrition Facts Labels

Nutrition Facts labels pack a lot of valuable information into a small space on a product's package. Reading and understanding these labels is essential to choosing healthful foods. Here are some steps—suggested by the U.S. Food and Drug Administration—that will lead you to enlightenment.

1. Start with the serving size, which is located at the top of the label. It tells you the size of a serving and how many servings

the package contains. The
details that follow later, which
are listed as "amount per serving," are based on this.

2. Check the calories. Remember—
this number is calories *per serving*. (That's 130 calories for *one*
chocolate chip cookie—not the
entire package!)

3. Check the amounts of Total Fat,
Cholesterol, and Sodium (these are under "% Daily Value"), and
try to limit your intake of them.

4. Check the amounts of the other nutrients—Vitamins A and C,
Dietary Fiber, Calcium, and Iron—and make sure you're getting
enough of them. On the right, you'll see the quantity listed as a
percentage of your daily intake.

302. A Guide to Natural Foods

In recent years, there's been a surge of interest in organic and other
natural foods, and an accompanying surge in terminology. Here's a
quick guide to help you during your next grocery shopping trip.

100% Organic. This means that there are no synthetic products
used in the growing of the food.

Organic. This means that at least 95 percent of the products used in
the food's production are natural.

Pesticide-free. These products are
not treated with pesticides, which
can end up in your body.

Hormone-free. These meat and
milk products haven't been treated
with hormones, which some
believe are health hazards.

Antibiotic-free. These meat and
milk products come from animals

that haven't been treated with antibiotics, which can end up in your food. Many scientists believe antibiotic residue in food is a cause of the drug-resistant strains of superbugs with which we are now contending.

Free-range. This means that the animals that are used are not cooped up in small cages or spaces, but allowed to roam more naturally.

Grass-fed. Conventional cattle are force-fed grains to make them meatier. However, cows don't naturally eat grain; they eat grass.

303. When to Buy Organic Foods

It only takes a second to notice that organic products are considerably more expensive than their conventionally grown counterparts. If your funds are limited, here are the foods that you should still try to buy organic.

> ## Thick-skinned
> It's safe to buy conventional versions of fruits with tough, inedible skins, such as bananas, mangoes, avocadoes, and pineapples. The tough rinds absorb most of the pesticides, leaving the fruit inside largely chemical-free.

Fruits with edible skins. Conventionally grown fruits are sprayed with pesticides because many are susceptible to fungus and insect damage. Unfortunately, fruits and vegetables absorb pesticides, which get into your body when you eat them. Apples are the worst of these offenders.

Potatoes. Potatoes are even worse than fruits because washing them won't remove pesticides. As potatoes grow, they absorb all the pesticides and herbicides in the soil.

Milk. Many brands of conventional milk contain a hormone called recombinant bovine growth hormone, which has been linked to cancer.

Beef. Conventional beef is loaded with hormones and antibiotics, which go right into your system when you eat it.

304. Understanding Expiration Dates

If you have troubling interpret-
ing expiration date information
on food products, it's not without
reason—there is no uniform system
for dating food in the United States.
The federal government requires
product dating only on infant for-
mula and some baby foods. About
20 states require food labeling of

> ### "Eggs-act" Date
>
> Always purchase eggs
> before the sell-by or use-by
> date. For best quality, use
> them within three to five
> weeks of the day that you
> purchased them.

some sort. The following are the types of labels that are most frequently used and what they generally mean.

Use-by. This is the closest thing to an expiration date that you'll find
on many packages. Food (and medicine) should not be consumed
after the use-by date, after which nutritional quality, freshness, and
effectiveness are jeopardized.

Sell-by. This tells the grocery store when to remove a product from
its shelves. Milk usually has a sell-by date because exposure to light
and temperature variation affect its freshness. Milk might be fresh
for up to a week after the sell-by date, but it can also spoil a day or
two before it.

Best if used by/before. Use this date as a guide to getting the best
quality and flavor from your foods.

305. How to Buy Fresh Vegetables

Sometimes it's obvious when a vegetable isn't fresh; mushrooms
that are covered with fuzz, for example, have clearly seen better
days. But sometimes it's more difficult to tell if the produce you're
scrutinizing is fresh. Here are some guidelines that will help you
choose the best of the best in the produce aisle.

1. Shop for seasonal vegetables. Corn is expensive in February
   because it has to be imported.

2. Use your senses—primarily smell, sight, and touch. Sniff the
   vegetables to see if they smell fresh. Examine them for bright

color, pristine green leaves, and firm, healthy skins. Take a pass on veggies that have bruises or cuts, or show signs of wilting or being overripe.

3. Try to buy food that is raised locally. The closer the food is to your store, the shorter the time from harvest to your table. This means fresher, tastier produce.

306. How to Select Seven Common Fruits and Vegetables

Let's face it—you can't live on frozen pizza alone. But the produce aisle can be a mysterious and intimidating place, with people knocking, weighing, smelling, and listening to the fruits and vegetables. Become an expert on choosing produce by following this guide.

1. **Cucumbers.** A good cucumber has a rich green color and is firm throughout. Avoid cukes with yellowish tints or those that feel soft or look withered.

2. **Tomatoes.** A ripe tomato has a deep, bright red color and a very slight softness to it. Firmer is okay—it just means it's unripe. Avoid very soft, overripe tomatoes.

3. **Peaches.** The best peaches are golden-pink and firm but yield slightly to the touch. Ignore wrinkled peaches or those with mushy spots.

4. **Grapefruit.** You'll want grapefruit that is firm, glossy, round, and of a nice weight. Avoid grapefruits that are soft or misshapen.

FAST FACT

Tired of waiting for your fruit to ripen? Put it in a brown paper bag—it will ripen more quickly. Speed up the process even more by sticking an apple or banana in with it. Just don't forget about it!

5. **Carrots.** Select carrots that are well-shaped and firm, and have a bright color. Don't buy them if they're soft or have a greenish hue near the top.

6. **Onions.** Firm, dry onions are best. Skip those that are sprouting or that have wet or mushy spots.

7. **Apples.** Firm, brightly colored apples are the best. Avoid mushy or spongy apples, which may be rotting.

307. Healthier Food Substitutions

Do you fear the infamous "freshman fifteen" or worry that you'll be tempted to subsist entirely on french fries and pints of chocolate ice cream after you leave home? Never fear—you can enjoy some of your favorite foods and still have a healthful diet by using low-fat, whole-grain alternatives. Instead of butter or margarine, try using a vegetable-oil spread (such as Smart Balance or Earth Balance), which tastes great but does not have any trans fats. Buy whole-grain bread, flour, and pasta, which have more nutrients and fiber than their bleached counterparts. Eat fresh fruit instead of fruit that's canned in heavy syrup. (If you must buy canned fruit, choose the kind that's canned in its own juices.) Use reduced-calorie dressing or low-fat vinaigrette for salads. Drink fat-free or reduced-fat milk rather than whole milk. If you drink coffee, replace cream or half-and-half with fat-free dairy products. Add flaxseeds to salads and cereal, and nutritional yeast (which is full of protein and vitamins) to popcorn, stir-frys, and pasta sauces.

308. Is It Okay to Date Someone I Work With?

Many companies discourage workplace relationships, but despite this, they happen all the time. If you're thinking about dating someone from work, consider the following pros and cons.

Pros. You probably already know a lot about the person, since you see him or her every day. This means that you can skip over some of the getting-to-know-you stuff most new relationships require. You probably already have mutual work friends, and working together can give you the opportunity to carpool and even spend lunch breaks together. When the two of you talk about work, you will know exactly what the other person is talking about.

Cons. If the relationship goes sour, it may be difficult to see your ex every day and to share mutual work friends, let alone maintain a professional working relationship. Even if you stay together and make it work, you might tire of spending so much time together, and you may also find yourselves thinking too much about work when you're at home.

If you decide to move forward with an office romance, be sure to check company policies about dating coworkers. Be professional, be discreet, and set some boundaries with your new love interest.

309. Dealing with Difficult Coworkers

Every workplace has difficult coworkers—the gossip, the whiner, the pathological liar, and the tyrant among them—but that doesn't make dealing with them any easier. Here are some strategies that will help you cope.

+ Make lists of the problem person's positive and negative qualities. Try to be objective.

+ Think about your role. Do you encourage or enable your coworker's behavior? If you do, that's something you can alter.

+ Act like a professional at all times. You won't regret it.

+ Take action. Either talk to the coworker yourself or discuss the problem with his or her manager. If you decide to attempt a conversation yourself, schedule a time to talk as soon as possible so the situation won't intensify. Use the positive traits you listed earlier to help keep the conversation cordial and prevent it from feeling like a personal attack.

+ Avoid counterproductive activities like gossiping or spreading rumors about the coworker.

+ If your coworker is noncompliant or doesn't change his or her behavior, ask to meet with a manager or supervisor to discuss the issue.

310. Recognizing a Reasonable Wage

When economic times are tough, *any* job seems better than no job. And while this is true, it's also important to be paid what you deserve.

Compare your salary to others in the same industry. If you're offered a job at a bookstore, compare the rate of pay that's offered to the wages paid at other bookstores—not with those earned at grocery stores or law firms.

Figure out your living wage. The wage that's required to pay rent, utilities and food bills is known as the living wage. Identify the living wage for your area before taking the first low-paying job that comes along.

> ### State Rates
>
> The federal government sets a national minimum wage, but each state is free to pass its own minimum-wage laws as well. Don't forget to consider this if you're moving to another state.

Consider the job. Jobs that require more advanced skills generally pay more money, so if you're applying for a job as a parking lot attendant, for example, don't expect a six-figure salary offer.

Don't be afraid to keep looking. Even if you feel as though you have to accept a low-paying job, there are probably better-paying jobs out there. Make an effort to find something that will pay you more.

311. How to Negotiate Contract Wages

If you have skills and experience, don't sell yourself short— especially if you're doing freelance or contract work. Here are some tips that will help you negotiate fair wages.

Recognize the value of your work. No matter what sort of job you're taking on—whether it's babysitting, painting a house, or walking dogs—you're filling an important need for someone and should be compensated appropriately.

Identify a reasonable rate. Ask around to find out what other people who are doing similar work are earning. Many online job sites have active discussion boards where people like you talk about how much to charge for freelance or contract work. If you have no experience, your starting rate will be considerably lower than that of someone with a long résumé.

State your wage demands politely but firmly. Present your wage requirements with confidence; this implies that you are asking for your usual rates.

Give and take. Remember, negotiations aren't one-way streets. Be prepared to lower your wage requirements if need be.

312. Working for Tips

Tipped jobs appeal to young people for many reasons, not the least of which is that they are sources of quick cash. Here are some things to keep in mind before you take a job for tips.

✦ **Your income won't be fixed.** The incomes of tipped employees fluctuate wildly (although you might be able to estimate your weekly earnings). This makes it hard to budget or plan for big expenses.

✦ **Cash burns a hole in your pocket.** Walking out of a shift with a pocketful of cash can be dangerous, especially if you and your coworkers like to socialize after work. Just because you have cash doesn't mean that you should spend it.

✦ **You'll earn less than minimum wage.** The government assumes that tipped employees will earn at least minimum wage through their tips, so it allows them to be paid an hourly rate that's far below the national minimum wage. This means that you'll get a small paycheck or none at all.

✦ **Consider the schedule.** Many tipped employees—especially deliverypeople and restaurant employees—work late nights, weekends, and holidays.

> **Taxes on Tips**
>
> The IRS has specific guidelines by which tipped employees are to report their earnings. Ask your employer if you have questions about how to claim tips on your income taxes.

313. Self-employment Basics

If you dream about someday being your own boss, you can turn that dream into reality with planning, organization, and discipline. It's important to be aware of the ways in which self-employment differs from working for a company. For example, if you're self-employed, you are considered to be an independent contractor, so taxes aren't usually deducted from the payments you receive. At tax time, you'll have to pay more to the government—but at the same time, you can write off various business expenses (provided that you keep great records and save your receipts). Think carefully about your ability to be disciplined, and make sure that you know how you will manage your time. Will you work five days a week, more or less? Where will you set up your office? To promote your skills and services, create a Web site and print business cards (you can order them on the Internet). Cash flow will be an issue when you first start out—and possibly once your business gets going—so set aside some extra money, if possible, in case you hit a financial dry spell.

> ### Web Resources
>
> There are some great online tools for the self-employed. Check out the Hourly Rate Calculator at FreelanceSwitch.com (click on the Resources tab to find it). For time-management help, try the tips and tools at Lifehacker.com.

314. How to Avoid Work-at-Home Scams

Those ads that say you can make $1,000 a day working from home are awfully tempting—who *wouldn't* want to make a ton of money without leaving the couch? Unfortunately, these schemes make money for only one person—the scammer. The Web has made it much easier for con artists to find naïve people to fleece. Here's how to protect yourself.

✦ **Don't send money.** Most work-at-home scammers make money by selling "kits" or "start-up materials." Have you ever heard of a legitimate business that asks you to pay it to apply for a job?

✦ **Avoid jobs that ask you to pack or ship from home.** The ad says that you'll be repacking legitimate products from a shipping company and sending them overseas—the company just needs your address and bank account info for payment. What you're really going to be doing is repacking stolen goods and sending them to cyber-criminals. Oh, and your bank account? Drained.

✦ **Research the company.** Many Web sites, such as Scam.com, have lots of resources and active communities that can help you determine if an offer is a scam. You can also check with your local Better Business Bureau.

315. How to Earn Money Fast

Your savings account was depleted by an unexpected car repair. You maxed out your credit card with holiday shopping. The month stretches farther than your paycheck. If you can identify with any of these financial crises, you should know that there are some ways you can earn some quick cash. Make flyers, put a message on Facebook, and e-mail your friends to spread the word.

✦ **Run errands.** Time is money, and some people are more than willing to pay others in order to save time on menial tasks.

✦ **Hold a yard sale.** Advertising and location are key.

✦ **Babysit.** Sitters are well-compensated for their efforts. If you have experience, you're more likely to be hired.

✦ **Give lessons.** Are you bilingual or computer savvy, or do you play a musical instrument? Tutors make good money and work flexible hours.

✦ **Do yard work.** Weeding, raking, and mowing lawns can be temporary fixes or ongoing moneymakers, as can shoveling snow.

- ✦ **Sell stuff.** Online auctions, Craigslist, and classifieds are some forums in which you can sell your handmade goods or things that you don't use.
- ✦ **Rent out a room.** If you have the space and don't mind taking on a roommate, renting out a room is an easy way to make cash that you can count on monthly.

316. What to Do if You Lose Your Job

If you are laid off from your job, be proactive so you can stay on solid financial footing.

- ✦ If you were receiving health insurance, find out how to continue your benefits via the federal act called COBRA.
- ✦ Find out if you are eligible to receive unemployment benefits. Consider the following questions: *While you were working, did money come out of your paycheck for unemployment? Were you fired or laid off? Are you willing and able to work again?* If you answered "yes" to all these questions, you qualify.
- ✦ Refigure your budget. Analyze your expenses to find where you can save. You may need to cut back on things like entertainment, eating out, and other "luxuries."
- ✦ Consider other ways to earn money, such as taking on a part-time job or temp work, doing freelance projects, selling things online, or starting an at-home business.

317. Networking

Networking is a fancy word that means, "maximizing your contacts." Whether you're looking for a job or a date, your friends, family, professors, professional contacts, and acquaintances are almost always your best and fastest sources for information and leads. You just need to know how to use your network efficiently and successfully.

Just ask. You may feel uncomfortable asking for help, but it is often the only way to get the information you need. Be polite, and if your contact comes through, take the time to thank him or her.

Maintain your network. Even if you don't have a current need, you certainly will have one in the future. Keep in touch and strengthen relationships with others by periodically going out, sending e-mail messages, or touching base by phone. To create new relationships, attend professional functions and participate in neighborhood events.

Reciprocate. Be generous with who and what you know. Offer to make an introduction or uncover information for a friend. People are always eager to repay favors—your generosity just might be returned when you need it most.

318. When to Stay Home Sick

Nobody likes to get sick and miss an important class or a day of work, but dedicated employees and motivated students know that they should stay home for the following reasons.

You are contagious. Spreading your illness to the rest of the class or office is far worse than missing a day.

You might be disruptive. Ever try to study or work while somebody is hacking and sneezing at the desk next to you?

You are useless. What's worse—calling off work and resting at home, or dragging yourself into work only to be utterly inept all day? If you guessed the latter, you're correct.

Your body needs rest. Instead of pushing yourself, give your body the rest it needs; otherwise, you're just prolonging the illness.

FAST FACT

According to a Commonwealth Fund study published in 2003, nearly 500 million days of work were lost because people went to work sick but weren't able to focus.

319. How to Quit a Job

There is protocol for quitting a job, just as there is for applying for and accepting employment. Don't follow the movie and TV versions of quitting (you know—the scenes in which a disillusioned employee storms up to the boss, yells "I quit!" then promptly exits the office, slamming the door on the way out); they're entertaining to watch and contemplate, but they are always inappropriate. If you decide to leave your job, take a less dramatic—but much classier— approach by following these guidelines.

✦ Give as much notice as possible, but always at least two weeks' worth.

✦ Submit an official resignation letter (you can find examples online) that states clearly and tactfully that you are resigning and the date on which it is effective.

✦ Even if you dislike your place of work, don't burn any bridges; instead, thank your boss for the opportunities that you've been given. You might need to ask him or her for a reference in the future.

✦ Try to make the transition for your replacement as easy and organized as possible. For example, leave any relevant files or training materials out and try to put your desk and files in order.

320. How to Catch a Mouse

If a mouse sneaks into your home, you can use spring-loaded mousetraps, sticky mousetraps, and poison pellets to try to get rid of it. Unfortunately, these methods aren't always effective, and there are other, more humane alternatives to consider—those that don't actually kill the mouse. For example, you can fill a deep bowl with peanut butter and place it where the mouse is likely to step (securing it in place with duct tape), or in a deep sink. (Another option is to coat the bowl with vegetable shortening so the mouse slides in without being able to escape.) If you know the room in which the mouse is hanging out, seal up all the entryways with towels or cardboard, then scare the mouse into the open by making loud noises (i.e., banging on pots and pans). When it emerges, catch it in a container with a lid or cover it with a towel, then release it outside.

321. How to Get Rid of Cockroaches

If you've never had to deal with cockroaches, consider yourself lucky. These vile creatures are some of the most resilient living things in the world. If you suspect that you have a cockroach infestation, lay out sticky traps to find out how many of the pests there are and where they are gathering. Cockroaches feed at night on any food they can find (from human food to pet food), so if you notice them feeding during the day, you probably have a lot of roaches, as this indicates that there is not enough food to go around at night. To get rid of a large population, use a desiccant such as boric acid; if the roaches touch it, it will dehydrate them by draining their exoskeletons of moisture. If you need to get rid of just a few roaches, you can use roach baits (which also use boric acid). These solutions should help keep cockroaches from bugging you!

322. How to Get Rid of Ants

While an ant infestation is a common household problem, it doesn't have to be. The best way to deal with ants is to prevent them from coming inside. Start by sealing up potential entry points, such as unsealed windows and uneven doors. Talk to your landlord about applying caulk or other household sealing products. Inside the living space, be sure to keep countertops clean—be especially scrupulous about removing sugary substances, which are primary ant attractions. Keep unrefrigerated foods in airtight containers.

If it's too late for prevention, there are a number of ways to kill ants. Consider natural methods first—in fact, simply spraying ants with soapy water kills them. Spraying them with window cleaner is also effective. If there are children or pets in the house (or if you just don't like chemicals), these are great alternatives.

Of course, you can always go straight to the chemicals,

> **Leave No Trace**
>
> Ants communicate with the rest of their colony by leaving pheromone trails to follow. Wash countertops and windowsills daily with soap and water to erase these invisible ant tracks.

as long as you use them safely. Ant bait that contains borax or boric acid works especially well. Ants will carry the poison back to their nest, destroying the problem at its source.

323. How to Deal with Other Household Pests

If you run across these household pests, take action so they don't set up camp indefinitely in your home.

Silverfish. Able to live for a year without food, silverfish munch on wallpaper paste, bindings, and paper. Cloves and strong-smelling soaps act as deterrents. Silverfish love moisture, so try a dehumidifier to dry the air in your home. Granular and dust baits also work.

Water Bugs. Also known as Oriental cockroaches, these are the dirtiest of the home-invading bugs and are often found in crawl spaces, near water pipes, and under appliances that have water sources (such as washing machines and refrigerators). To prevent an infestation, seal cracks in the building's foundation and in windows and doors. Keep your living space scrupulously clean so the bugs have no food source. Cap drains and fix leaks.

> ### Bug Off!
>
> Rescind your invitation to bugs by reducing the number of moist, dark, and warm areas in your home. Keep food stored in sealed containers, repair water leaks, vacuum and sweep at least weekly, and seal cracks around windows, baseboards, and doors. If you have a full-blown infestation, call a professional.

324. How to Obtain a Copy of Your Birth Certificate

Your birth certificate allows you to legally establish your identity. It's important to have an official copy of it; you'll need it to obtain other official documents—such as a driver's license, social security number, or passport—or to join the military. Some universities, international companies, and government agencies require a copy of your birth certificate for admission or employment.

Unfortunately, there is no federal clearinghouse that stores and distributes these documents. Births are recorded locally, so you'll need to request a copy from the office of vital records in the state or U.S. territory in which you were born. You can find the address of each state's records agency at the Web site of the Centers for Disease Control and Prevention; search for "Where to Write for Vital Records." You may be charged a nominal fee to obtain an authorized, certified (with state seal stamp) copy of your birth certificate.

To complete the application, you will be asked to provide the following information: full name; gender; parents' names, including your mother's maiden name; the month, day, and year of your birth; the place of birth (city, state, and hospital, if you know it); and your telephone number with area code.

325. Prevent Identity Theft

Identity theft can take years to unravel and resolve. There is no way to stop identity theft, but here are some precautions you should take to reduce your risk.

- ✦ **Shred everything.** All a prospective identity thief has to do is go through your trash, complete a discarded credit card application, and *voila!* Instant credit.

- ✦ **Keep records and personal information in a secure place.** This will make your information hard to obtain, and keeping everything together makes it easy to contact companies if you notice that something is awry.

- ✦ **Safeguard your mail.** Pay your bills online or drop them off at the post office.

Keep an Eye Out

Check bank and credit card statements at least once a month to spot suspicious transactions. Also, request a credit report annually—newly opened credit card accounts that you know nothing about are huge red flags.

- **Never answer an e-mail from your bank.** These invariably represent a type of scam called "phishing" and are meant to trick you into providing personal information about your bank accounts. Call your bank or go to its Web site; if the request is legitimate, it will be noted on your account.
- **Carry as little information in your wallet as possible.** Remove your Social Security card and any unneeded credit cards.
- **Use a credit card instead of a debit card when shopping online.** Credit card companies offer better protections.

326. Memorize Your Social Security Number

Your Social Security number (SSN)—the nine-digit number that's been issued to you by the U.S. Government—is perhaps the most important number in your life. Take some time to memorize it so you don't have to carry the card around with you. (If it's not in your wallet, it's not at risk of being stolen.) You'll need to use your SSN in a variety of situations: filling out tax forms, starting a new job, opening a bank account or applying for a loan, enrolling in school, and more. There are other occasions when you'll be asked to verify your SSN for identity purposes, but often, this is just a request—not a requirement. Employers and creditors may require your number, but try to avoid providing it to others who ask for it. (Just ask, "Is that necessary?") This will help to protect your privacy and safeguard you against identity theft.

327. What to Keep in Your Wallet

Jamming your wallet full of receipts, business cards, and other miscellaneous junk could lead to identity theft if you lose any important items. Follow this simple guide to keep your wallet slim and safe.

What to keep in:

- **Personal identification.** Keep a form of personal identification on hand, such as a driver's license, state ID, student ID, or green card; you never know when you might need it.

- **Cash.** You should always have a few bucks on you for emergencies, and because not everybody takes debit or credit cards.
- **Credit/debit card.** You'll need plastic for emergencies, but don't carry too many cards; limit yourself to the ones that you use most often.
- **Insurance card.** If you're in an accident and need to go to the hospital, you'll need proof of insurance to save hassles later.

What to keep out:

- **Social Security card.** There's hardly any reason to have your Social Security card on you. Losing it is a great way to have your identity stolen, and it's a pain to replace.
- **Birth certificate.** A driver's license provides the same identification just as legitimately.

FAST FACT

Almost 90 percent of lost wallets that contain a baby picture are mailed back to their owners, according to a 2009 study. So even if you don't have any kids, you might consider throwing a couple baby pictures into your wallet, just to be safe.

---

328. What to Do When You Lose Your Wallet

Whether your wallet has been stolen or you've simply left it at the coffee shop, there are a few steps you should take immediately after you realize you've lost it.

1. **Call your credit card company to cancel your card.** Tell the representative the last purchase that you remember making with your card so you don't have to pay for fraudulent transactions made thereafter.

2. **Call the bank to cancel your ATM card.** Do this as soon as possible—many banks have escalating liability charges depending on how quickly you report a lost card.

3. **Call the credit reporting agencies.** You only need to call one of the three major credit agencies (Experian, TransUnion, or Equifax) to have a temporary alert placed on your identity; the agencies share this information with each other. This alert prevents anybody from opening a line of credit in your name.

4. **Get a new driver's license.** Losing your wallet makes for a bad week; getting pulled over without a license will make it terrible. Do this as soon as you can.

5. **File a police report.** It helps to have a police report on file in case unusual transactions start showing up in your name.

> ## Social Insecurity
>
> If your Social Security card gets stolen, you'll need to replace it. You can get a free replacement card by filling out Form SS-5, which is available from the Social Security Administration's Web site. Don't lose your card too often, though—you're only entitled to ten free replacements in your lifetime.

329. How to Get a Document Notarized

Many documents, such as deeds, affidavits, and powers of attorney, need to be witnessed by a notary public. A notary is a person who's certified by a state government to administer oaths and ensure that everything appears to be legitimate when an important document is signed. The notary authenticates a letter or legal document by providing his or her signature and seal. When visiting a notary, you will be asked for some form of current identification with a photograph, signature, and physical description, such as a driver's license,

> ### FAST FACT
>
> To find a notary, look online at NotaryPublic.com or ASNNotary.org (the Web site of The American Society of Notaries, which features a notary locator).

passport, or military ID. The notary has to witness the signing of the document, so don't sign it beforehand. You can find a notary at municipal and other government offices, banks and credit unions, local schools, and currency exchanges. There may be a nominal charge for notary services.

330. Don't Let Too Much Sun Shine In

Nothing beats fresh air and sunshine, and the sun is a good source of vitamin D, which boosts your mood and immune system. Unfortunately, sun exposure also has significant risks. To stay healthy, heed the following advice.

Know your rays. The rays of sunshine that you worship are actually a form of radiation, which are identified as ultraviolet (UV) rays A and B. UVA rays slowly damage skin cells and cause premature aging in the form of wrinkled and sagging skin. UVB rays often cause immediate damage to the skin in the form of painful sunburns—or even that great-looking tan. More significantly, they also cause most forms of skin cancer.

Protect yourself. You don't have to shun the sun in order to avoid skin cancer. Wear a water-resistant sunscreen with a sun protection factor (SPF) of at least 30 (be especially careful during the peak exposure hours of noon to 2 P.M.). Reapply every two hours and after swimming. Other sun-smart measures include wearing a hat, long pants, and long sleeves if you have to be outside between 10 A.M. and 4 P.M.

FAST FACT

Take the guesswork out of SPF with this simple equation:

(SPF number) × (the length of time it takes a person to burn) = amount of coverage time

For example, if you apply SPF 15 and it takes you ten minutes to burn, your coverage time is 150 minutes.

331. How to Check for Skin Cancer

Skin cancer is one of the most common forms of cancer. It's critical to catch it early, when it is still treatable and curable.

Be aware of:

✦ Spots—moles, bumps, or other growths—that bother you and don't heal after two to three months, areas where pigment has spread to surrounding skin, and any changes to existing moles.

✦ Redness or swelling beyond the border of a spot.

✦ Moles or sun spots that become itchy, tender, or painful, or that start to swell, scale, ooze, or bleed on the surface.

Examine all your "parts":

✦ Stand naked in front of a mirror and look at your body from different angles. Examine your face, lips, eyes, ears, and inside your mouth (using a flashlight). Check under your breasts and arms, as well as any other folds in your skin. Look between your toes and fingers. Part your hair and check your scalp.

✦ Using a handheld mirror, check the back of your neck, genitals, buttocks, and back.

Have a doctor immediately check anything you find that is unusual or suspicious.

332. How to Treat a Sunburn

With all the sun protection products that are available today, there is no reason you should get a sunburn. Just slather on sunscreen that has an SPF of at least 30 every time you venture outdoors—even if it's cloudy (in fact, cloud cover offers little protection from the sun). But let's say you skipped the sunscreen and got burned. Here's how to ease your discomfort.

1. Take a cool bath or lay a damp towel on the affected skin.

2. Apply aloe vera or a nongreasy moisturizing cream.

3. Drink plenty of water to rehydrate.

4. If blisters form, leave them alone—breaking them will inhibit healing.

5. Most importantly, stay out of the sun until your skin heals. If the sunburn doesn't begin to fade in a few days or is accompanied by a high fever or extreme pain, consult a doctor.

333. How to Deal with Body Odor

Advertising would have you think that body odor threatens civilization as much as nuclear war. In fact, you can't even detect most types of body odor, nor can anyone else.

You have two kinds of sweat glands, but only one of them—the apocrine glands—contributes to body odor. These glands are primarily located in your armpits and genital areas, and each one empties into a hair follicle. When you exercise or are nervous or under stress, apocrine glands secrete a combination of water, proteins, lipids, and sebaceous oils. When this combo mixes with bacteria on the surface of your skin, you'll detect that certain smell.

The best ways to fend off offensive body odor are to shower or bathe daily, wear clean cotton underwear, and do your laundry. If you don't have easy access to a washer and dryer, hand-wash the items that you can in the sink and air out clothes such as jeans, sweaters, and outerwear.

Deodorants and antiperspirants can help. Some deodorants contain mildly acidic compounds that control odor by drying your skin. Antiperspirants contain aluminum salts that prevent sweating. A little dab of either will control odor for hours.

334. Coping with Depression

Everyone feels down occasionally, but if your blues drag on, you may be depressed. Clinical depression has a wide range of symptoms; some people feel that their senses are dulled while others may be tense and anxious. If you've experienced some of the following symptoms during the last two weeks, you could be dealing with depression.

+ Had trouble sleeping or felt constantly tired no matter how much you sleep.

+ Lost your appetite or started eating too much (i.e., binging).

+ Found it difficult to concentrate.

+ Avoided friends and activities that you normally enjoy.

+ Felt hopeless.

+ Felt that your life was worthless.

+ Thought of suicide.

Don't hesitate to get help. If you have health insurance, ask about coverage for counseling or talk directly to your doctor. If you're in college, use the school's health service. If you're uninsured and out of school, a walk-in clinic can refer you to free or low-cost counseling and connect you to support groups. Call your state's Department of Health and Human Services or a local hospital to get a list of clinics near you.

> **Call!**
>
> If you're thinking about suicide, call someone immediately. The National Suicide Prevention Hotline is available 24/7 to answer your call at 1–800–SUICIDE (1–800–784–2433).

335. How to Tell if a Friend Needs Professional Help

Being an observant friend can help you to identify behavioral changes that might signal trouble. Has he or she lost interest in school, friends, or family? Has your friend lost a significant amount of weight or become more secretive or increasingly stressed? Is he or she constantly fatigued? These can be signs of anxiety or depression, an eating disorder, or an addiction. First, mention the changes you've noticed and ask if there's anything you can do to help. If your

friend denies having a problem or declines your offer but
the self-destructive behavior
continues or intensifies, talk
to a trusted adult (a counselor,
school nurse, or social worker)
about your concerns. If you
think that your friend may be
suicidal, get immediate help by
calling a suicide-prevention or
crisis-intervention hotline.

> ### Staging an Intervention
>
> **To find an addiction therapist to help stage an intervention, contact a local alcohol treatment center. If it doesn't offer such services, contact the Nationwide Intervention Assistance program.**

336. How to Listen

Being a good listener pays dividends in every aspect of life. This critical skill benefits relationships and makes you a better student and employee. If you listen well, you will make good impressions, avoid misunderstandings, and more easily retain information. If you have difficulty staying focused during conversations, try these tips.

+ Take a deep breath and keep quiet for a few minutes.

+ Tune out distractions, making sure that you stick with the conversation.

+ Let the other person know that you are listening by making eye contact, nodding your head, and/or responding with an occasional verbal cue, such as, "Uh huh."

+ Resist the temptation to relate everything back to your personal experience or to prepare immediate rebuttals.

When you listen actively, you seek to understand your conversational partner, so ask for clarification when necessary.

337. Confronting a Friend

Confronting a friend is a difficult thing to do, especially if you shy away from conflict. If something bothers you about your friend's choices or behavior—or about your relationship—you owe it to him or her to speak up about it (rather than gossiping or growing progressively more upset). Carefully consider what you are going to say in advance. Pick a time to talk that works for both of you. Start by explaining that you want to address the matter because you truly care. In a straightforward but calm manner, say what is bothering you. Speak in "I feel" statements. Give your friend the opportunity to respond and ask questions, then try to collaborate on a solution. Your friend may feel some resentment toward you; being confronted is hard, too! But keep lines of communication open, and make it clear that you are invested in preserving and strengthening the friendship.

338. Warning Signs of Suicide

Most depressed people are not suicidal, but most suicidal people *are* depressed. In fact, 90 percent of those who can be classified as "suicidal" have one or more psychiatric disorders. In most cases, the symptoms are recognizable and treatable. If you believe that a friend or family member may be suicidal, look for these warning signs.

+ Talking or writing about dying or suicide
+ Exploring ways to kill oneself such as pills, weapons, and poisons
+ Threatening to hurt or kill oneself
+ Withdrawing from friends and family
+ Increased use of alcohol or drugs
+ Unexpected impulsiveness, recklessness, rage, or anger
+ Major depression that has dragged on

Between 50 and 75 percent of people who commit suicide give some kind of warning, so take your suspicions seriously. Listen to and empathize with the person and let him or her know that he or she is not alone, but also seek professional help. If need be, help the person get to a doctor or psychiatric facility; if immediate intervention is required, call 911. Like any other disease, only professionals are qualified to intervene; you can, however, provide support and love throughout the process.

339. Five Ways to Be a Really Good Friend

"To have a friend, be a friend"—there's obvious truth to this saying. But how can you be a *really* good friend? Here are some ideas that will help you go the extra mile in your friendships.

1. Show encouragement at events in which your friend is involved, such as art shows, concerts, and fundraisers.

2. Pay attention to your friend's likes and interests, and remember them when considering gifts or other kind gestures. If your friend likes a specific type of food, for example, make it or order it for a special treat.

3. Be helpful in good times and in bad. Offer to watch your friend's pet when he goes on vacation. Loan a friend a dress for her big night out. Drive your friend to the mechanic when her car dies. Pick up your friend's homework assignment when he's sick.

4. Listen. When your friend talks with you, show him or her that you care by listening attentively.

5. Keep confidences. Don't divulge secrets or share information that has been given to you in confidence.

340. Interpreting Body Language— Theirs and Yours

Humans are expressive even when we're not trying to be. This is because we use body language—physical gestures, facial expressions, and postures—that sends messages without words. Being aware of body language and what it says helps to promote understanding and avoid miscommunication. Here are some typical expressions and what experts say they mean.

Eye contact. Experts say that making eye contact 50 to 60 percent of the time is normal for Americans. More than this might indicate to the other person that you're intense or romantically interested;

less might indicate that you're untrustworthy.

Folded arms. Folded arms are traditionally seen as a sign of defensiveness. A person who has his or her arms crossed over the chest is saying, "I'm not interested," or, "Keep your distance."

Hand gestures. Hands in the pockets often signal submission or withdrawal. However, they may be saying, "I'm interested in what you have to say." Liars are known to keep their hands in their pockets for fear that their hands will give their lies away.

What Body Language Do You Speak?

It's dangerous to think that everyone's body language is the same. For example, body language primers say that arms folded across the chest mean the person is closed to new experiences. Perhaps this is true. Or perhaps the person is cold. Or has a stomachache. Be wary of making assumptions.

Hair. Most body language experts state that preening or touching one's hair is a sign of romantic interest—or at least a desire for the other person to like him or her.

341. Five Ways to Jump-start Your Creativity

Looking for inspiration that will help get those creative juices flowing? See if any of the following turn on the tap.

1. Revisit passages of a book that you love, look at artwork by an artist whom you admire, or give your favorite album another listen. Pondering other creative works can help you to get "in the zone."

2. Browse creativity-sparking Web sites. For interior design ideas, try ApartmentTherapy.com; for photography, try Flickr.com; for a quick education about a random topic, try Wikipedia.org and click on "Random Article."

3. Visit your local library and check out books on a subject about which you know nothing; then do a project that utilizes the information you found. For example, you could research pin-

hole cameras and then make your own, or read up on French cooking and then attempt a homemade crepe.

4. Get together with a friend for a creative "playdate," such as a collaborative art project, an impromptu jam session, or a crafting workshop.

342. Breaking Through Mental Blocks

We all get stuck from time to time, but it's doubly frustrating when there is no real good reason for your difficulties. Here are some strategies that productivity experts use when they're paralyzed by mental blocks.

> ### Face the Fear
> Many mental blocks are the results of fear of failure—but if you don't try, you'll never succeed. Failure is a natural part of everyone's personal evolution; acknowledge that, and your block may just dissolve.

Change the scenery. Humans are creatures of habit, and so we tend to associate certain places with certain feelings, rituals, or ways of thinking. If you find yourself unable to focus, try taking your work elsewhere. Sometimes, a new environment is all it takes to get a fresh start.

Do something. Anything. A blank sheet of paper, an empty canvas, or a blinking cursor can be daunting. Just put down whatever comes to mind for a few minutes. Having something to work with is better than having nothing at all.

Change your attitude. Sometimes, a little positive thinking is all that it takes to remove a mental block. If you tell yourself, "I can't," then you won't. All projects and tasks seem a little easier if you believe you can do them.

343. Trust Your Intuition

Sometimes, you need to dispense with rational thought and simply trust your intuition. That little voice inside your head and that feeling in your gut aren't silly, and they're not to be ignored. In fact, according to experts who have studied human behavior, your emotions can lead you to the right decisions when your brain cannot. Gut instinct, it turns out, is informed by a combination of our life experiences and our practical knowledge, while the rational mind pulls from a smaller data set. Overthinking—continuing to weigh the pros and cons of a decision—can overwhelm your rational mind. Following your intuition can lead to smarter decisions, more meaningful relationships, and more effective solutions. So the next time you have to decide which restaurant to go to or whether the person on the other side of the street is dangerous, consult your gut—it is unlikely to lead you astray.

344. Roommate Etiquette

You can minimize conflict and maximize harmony with a roommate by practicing proper etiquette. This doesn't mean that you should act in an unnecessarily formal way or tiptoe around each other; it just means showing simple courtesy—treating your roommate the way you want to be treated. Establish policies about borrowing each other's possessions. Is it allowed? How much of an item can you use? If you finish the last of a food item or household product, be sure to replace it. Decide which chores need to be taken care of and discuss how you will divide the responsibilities; then make sure that you follow through and complete your assigned tasks. Talk about noise levels and sleeping patterns, and be mindful of each other's schedules. Remember that living with a roommate involves compromise and keeping lines of communication open. It's often the little things that end up causing conflict, so speak openly, clearly, and often to make sure that you're on the same page.

345. Seven Ways to Be a Bad Roommate

Keep your home harmonious by avoiding these classic roommate blunders.

1. **Forgetting to pay the bills.** Roommate relationships can get pretty chilly if the heat is shut off because you didn't send the check.

2. **Using your roommate's toiletries.** Using a roommate's bath sponge, toothpaste, and/or razor is rude and unsanitary.

3. **Eating your roommate's food.** If you drink your roommate's milk, don't add water to the carton to replace the level; replace the milk.

4. **Playing music loudly at inappropriate times.** Use headphones so your roommate can enjoy the apartment in peace and quiet.

5. **Letting your significant other move in without asking permission.** Some roommates won't mind if your boyfriend or girlfriend is hanging around all the time. You should find out if yours is one of them before your love life sours your apartment life.

6. **Leaving your personal belongings strewn about.** Having a messy bedroom is one thing, but leaving your clothes, dishes, papers, etc., all over the house is quite another.

7. **Leaving dirty pots on the stove.** Wash everything you use when you're finished using it.

> ### Talk It Out
> The best way to be a good roommate is to communicate. You can have monthly "state of the union" talks or simply check in on a daily basis. Simple and direct communication is always best.

346. How to Choose a Roommate

It may seem counterintuitive, but great friends often aren't the best roommates. The qualities that make you enjoy hanging out with your friend are not necessarily those with which you will be happy living. The most important quality in a roommate is lifestyle compatibility. Are you a neat freak? Look for a fellow order-craver. Do you like to stay up all night? Look for another night owl—or at least someone who won't be disturbed by your late hours and who won't disturb you at the crack of dawn. Think about the home environment that you want to create, and then look for a roommate who wants a similar one. When considering and interviewing prospective roommates, make sure you are open about your preferences and policies (talk about noise, houseguests, pets, chores, and food sharing, for

example), and make sure that you have similar expectations for your relationship. The more up-front you are and the more you find out from the candidate, the better the match will be. In addition to lifestyles, be sure to discuss finances; the last thing you need is a deadbeat roommate.

347. How to Read a Supermarket Supplement

You can save lots of money by using the supermarket sale supplement to help create your menu. But don't blindly buy items just because they're on sale—or appear to be on sale. Use these tips to use the advertisement to your advantage.

Check your list. It can be cost-effective to buy sale items that aren't on your list—particularly nonperishables that you will eventually use, such as paper towels. In general, however, don't buy a product simply because it's on sale. Think about it: If those cookies weren't on sale, would you really want to buy them?

Take Advantage

If you have freezer space, consider loading up on vegetables and meats when they go on sale. Many of these items last for months when frozen, and they taste almost as good after they're frozen as they would if you were to eat them fresh.

Compare brand-name and generic items. Store flyers are often littered with sales on brand-name products. But these are not necessarily cheaper than store-brand or generic items. Compare prices and sizes before making a choice.

Make sure that it's on sale. Some sneaky supermarkets will advertise nonsale items in the sale flyer, often adjacent to items that are being offered at deep discounts. Check the item's price to determine if you will be saving any money before putting it in your cart.

348. Why You Should Make a Grocery List

Making a grocery list will save you both time and money. You'll avoid wandering the store's aisles aimlessly trying to remember what you need, and you'll be more likely to resist unnecessary—and usually more expensive—items that tempt you while you shop. List-making will become a habit if you keep a pad of paper in a kitchen drawer or on the refrigerator. Write down items when you think of them. If you plan to make a dish from a recipe, write down the ingredients you'll need. Even better, plan a menu for the week, jot down all ingredients you'll need to purchase, then get everything during one shopping trip. If you shop at the same grocery store most of the time, make your list according to the store's layout to save even more time.

Repeat Business

If you buy the same items every week, make a list of them and keep it handy. Each time you go to the store, you can simply check off the ones that you need to purchase.

349. Cheap Healthy Foods

Ask any college student about cheap eats and "ramen" will likely be the immediate reply. But a person can't live on ramen alone! There are lots of other cheap eats that are just as tasty—and better for you.

Beans. Among the cheapest and best sources of protein available, beans can help to stretch your food budget. Mix black beans with rice for an inexpensive, easy, and nutritious meal.

Bananas. Loaded with nutrients, bananas are cheap and available year-round. Eat them plain, or slice them into cereal or yogurt. They're also tasty when placed on top of an open-face peanut butter sandwich.

Eggs. Unless you have a serious cholesterol problem, eggs can be a cheap, nutritious, and versatile part of your diet. They are loaded with protein, have brain-boosting nutrients, and are easy to whip up whenever you need a snack.

Sweet potatoes. Sweet potatoes aren't just for Thanksgiving. Whether baked or microwaved, they are filling and loaded with important nutrients.

350. Five Quick, Nutritious Lunches

Take charge of your health and your wallet with these quick, nutritious alternatives to the fast-food lunch.

Hummus dip with fresh-cut vegetables. Buy ready-made hummus and vegetables that you like. Clean and cut the veggies. This lunch is easy to tote to school or work.

Wraps. Put some black beans, fresh tomatoes, and salsa inside a tortilla for a lunch that's fresh and filling. Try wrapping other foods you like. Peanut butter and bananas or turkey and lettuce with mustard are other quick wrap options.

Yogurt with toppings. Fruit, crushed granola bars, raisins, and trail mix make tasty toppings for yogurt.

Baked potatoes. Baked potatoes are packed with nutrition. Top them with cheese, vegetables, refried beans, or salsa—or anything else your taste buds desire.

Whole-grain muffins. Slice them and add low-fat cream cheese, slices of boiled egg, a couple of pieces of lunch meat, or dried fruit.

351. How to Make a Good First Impression

Making good first impressions will take you far in life, and doing so doesn't require special skills. Whether you're in a social or a professional situation, the most important thing to do is show genuine interest in the people you are meeting. Look them in the eye, offer a firm handshake, and actively listen to what they have to say. Smile warmly. Speak clearly and confidently, but don't dominate the conversation. Dress appropriately for the situation or occasion, and pay attention to your posture—people who stand up straight and tall appear confident and attractive to others.

352. How to Be a Great Conversationalist

To become a great conversationalist, you have to learn to be a great listener. This may sound like a contradiction, but it's not. No one wants to talk with someone who does all the talking—or who talks only about him- or herself. If you listen intently, people will want to talk with you. Give verbal and physical cues that convey that you are paying rapt attention. While you're listening, think of questions to ask that show you're interested or move the conversation forward. If someone says something that triggers a comment or story of your own, then share it—just make sure that the other people don't feel "steamrolled" (that is, interrupted or talked over). Try to avoid adding a competitive edge to the conversation—saying something like, "That's nothing! You'll never believe what happened to *me*!" is a conversation killer. Try to remember previous conversations or details about people so you can follow up with them the next time you speak. Show sensitivity and look for verbal and nonverbal cues to guide your interaction.

353. Four Easy Ways to Find People Who Share Your Interests

Sometimes it seems that despite the fact that there are billions of people in the world, it's impossible to find one who shares your interests. Don't despair—with these tips, you're bound to find someone who shares even the most obscure passion.

1. **Check out the library.** Your local public library can provide you with information about community organizations, and it offers workshops and seminars on everything from knitting to financial planning.

2. **Frequent the places that interest you.** If you love collecting coins, hang out at the coin shop; if you're passionate about exercise, head to the gym.

3. **Go to a conference or workshop.** Just about every hobby, interest, or ideology has its own association or organization, and these groups often have conferences or workshops. Subscribe to e-mail newsletters to keep tabs on upcoming events.

4. **Join an online group.** Web sites like Meetup.com will help you find like-minded people in your area—and you can virtually hang with people from all over the world via the Web.

> ### Look Outside the Box
> When trying to find places frequented by people with similar interests or views, don't just look in the most obvious places. Yoga enthusiasts might be at a vegetarian restaurant, for example, and book lovers might be in a coffee shop on a Friday night.

354. Social Skills for Shy People

If you're shy, you're probably a great listener—which is a very important social skill. So your problem isn't getting to know other people—it's allowing them to know you. If you find yourself nodding silently through too many conversations, try this: Every time you ask a question, add a little bit of information about yourself. Making friends is easier when conversation is a two-way street. If you feel that you don't have anything to talk about, participate in activities that involve team effort—volunteer with an organization that has a mission in which you believe or with a community project. You'll have to interact with others in order to get things accomplished, and you'll have something in common to talk with these people about. Push yourself out of your comfort zone a little at a time. Don't just paint scenery at the community theater—audition for a small speaking role. Once you've learned to use a carpenter's level, teach someone else the skill. Get the idea? Taking risks is, well— *risky*, but it's also worth the effort.

355. How to Deal with Loneliness

When you're lonely, you feel empty and disconnected from other people and the world at large. You may be surrounded by many people—roommates, classmates, teachers, coworkers, family, friends, and acquaintances—but you don't feel emotionally connected to anyone. It can be tempting to wallow in your isolation, but loneliness breeds more loneliness and can lead to depression. The best thing to do when you recognize that you're feeling lonely is switch up your routine—get out and become more active. Go on an adventure. Do something that involves creative expression. Think about people who you'd like to get to know better and get in touch with them. Reach out to family or friends who you think might be supportive—or simply fun to be around. It's important to recognize that the loneliness will pass. Everyone—even the most social of butterflies, even a person who you think "has it all together"—experiences loneliness. It's part of being human.

356. How to Develop Basic Leadership Skills

Even if you don't consider yourself to be a natural leader, you can hone your skills by following these guidelines.

1. Have a plan and goals, and make your expectations clear to the people with whom you are collaborating. Assign roles and tasks so everyone is invested and feels valued.

2. If someone offers a great suggestion or does something well, give positive feedback.

3. If someone does something that you don't like, tactfully suggest an alternative way to handle the situation.

4. Communicate clearly—not just in person, but also via e-mail—and listen actively.

5. Be open to feedback.

357. How to Travel with a Friend

Traveling with a friend can be an amazing experience; it can also be extremely trying. Avoid frustration and preserve your friendship by following these suggestions.

1. Be choosy about your travel partners. Just because you get along with someone does not mean that he or she will make a good travel buddy. Make sure that your companion is adaptable, upbeat, and a great problem-solver.

2. Decide how you will divide expenses ahead of time. Determine how you will you split the costs of meals, accommodations, tours, and taxi rides. Be mindful of how much money each of you has to spend.

3. Plan a rough itinerary to ensure that you both get to do what you want to do.

4. Talk about issues and problems immediately; don't let anything fester. If you don't get everything resolved right away, the conflict will likely reemerge later.

5. Make sure that you both take cameras. This will ensure that you will have a lot of photographic documentation of your vacation, not to mention some awesome shared memories.

358. How to Use a Taxi

Taxis are convenient—albeit expensive—ways to get around. They are especially helpful late at night, when public transportation is absent, or when you aren't able to drive your own car. Here's a guide to basic taxi procedures.

Finding a taxi. You can call taxi companies and ask them to pick you up, but if you're in a city, it is often far easier to hail a passing taxi by waving to it.

> ### Taxi Safety Tips
> + Only use licensed taxis. In most states, taxis are required to display their licenses prominently.
> + Always enter and exit a taxi curbside. Opening a door into traffic is dangerous.

Getting to your destination. As soon as you enter a cab, let the driver know where you are going. Most taxi drivers know major tourist attractions and restaurants, but giving an address or intersection is always a good idea.

During the ride. Pay attention to the route. Most taxi drivers are honest, but unscrupulous ones will take "the long way" in order to increase the fare. You have the right to choose the route to your destination, so don't be shy about giving directions.

Paying. The driver will calculate the fare at the end of the ride. While some taxi companies have credit card machines in their cars, many do not, so it's always a good idea to have cash on hand. In the United States, tipping is appropriate; most experts say that a 15 percent gratuity is acceptable, with a little extra thrown in if the driver helps you with your bags.

359. How to Use Phone Cards

Prepaid phone cards are incredibly handy, especially if you need to make international calls or use a pay phone, or if you are traveling overseas. They are also excellent for emergencies.

Phone cards are widely available from telecommunication companies, major retailers, and even convenience stores. Rates vary depending on the card you choose, which is why it's important to know what types of calls you're going to be making before you purchase one. Phone cards are very easy to use—just dial the toll-free number on the back and, when prompted, enter the PIN number provided. You will then be given instructions for making the call. The issuing company keeps track of the minutes you use and lets you know when they are running out.

> ### Cell Phone Warning
>
> If you're using a cell phone with a phone card, make sure that you *manually* dial the number you're calling when prompted. If you choose the number from your phone book, you'll disconnect from the phone card and call directly from your cell phone provider, which may lead to an unpleasant phone bill.

A few tips to keep in mind:

✦ Many phone cards charge a connection fee—which can vary from just a few minutes to many—just for making a call.

✦ Some phone cards have expiration dates, after which they become useless. If you plan to carry a phone card for emergencies, try to find one that doesn't have an expiration date.

360. How to Make a Collect Call

Calling cards and cell phones have made the collect call nearly obsolete. But if you lose your cell phone and get lost or stranded, a collect call can save the day. To make a collect call, dial zero, followed by the area code and number of the person who you are trying to reach; listen for and comply with the recorded instructions that follow. Or you can simply dial zero and request that the operator place your call for you. When the recipient answers, he or she will be asked to accept the charges. But beware: Collect calls can have hefty fees—sometimes as much as $15 a minute.

361. What to Keep in Mind During a Road Trip

There's no better way to explore America than by driving the nation's highways and byways. Here are a few things to keep in mind before taking off on your next road trip.

Rest stops. Always use well-lit, busy rest stops and travel plazas. Many state turnpikes have official travel plazas, which are often safe choices. Avoid unused, secluded rest stops.

Lift the Lids

If you get drowsy and can't find a place to stop, try singing along to the radio, opening the window, and/ or drinking a cold beverage. If you can't make it as far as you thought, so be it—your road trip will end much more quickly if you get in an accident.

Hitchhikers. This is simple: Don't pick up hitchhikers.

Gas. Don't assume that there will be another gas station a few miles down the road. Keep an eye on the fuel gauge and don't let it get too low. Rural areas usually offer cheaper gas than urban areas, which means that it's smart to gas up before passing through a city.

Contacts. Make sure that you leave your itinerary and contact info with at least one other person.

Maps. GPS units break, smart phone batteries die, and cell phones lose reception, but a good map is fairly reliable.

Emergency kit. Pack blankets, extra food and water, a first-aid kit, and a flashlight in case your car breaks down.

362. How to Use a Road Map

Thanks to the popularity of GPS technology, many people don't keep a road atlas in the car, much less know how to use one. Technology is great, but it can also fail—so map-reading skills can certainly come in handy.

Find your destination. Road maps have an alphabetical "place index" at the bottom of each map, while a road atlas has one at the back of the book. Find your destination in the index and locate it on the map using the coordinates provided.

Trace the route. Figure out which roads lead to your destination. Larger roads are represented by thicker or differently colored lines—check the key or legend to identify which symbols are being used. In general, highways and interstates allow for faster traffic than narrower routes.

Newer is Better

Always use a new map or road atlas. Highways are constantly under construction, new roads are always being built, and exits sometimes disappear completely. If you're not sure how old your map is, get a new one.

Find the distance. Calculate the distance to your destination. Some maps list mileage on the routes themselves, while others have a "mileage scale" in one of the map corners.

Track your progress. Follow your route as you go. By identifying the towns and landmarks on the map as you pass them, you'll know that you're still on the right track.

363. Understanding Interstate Signs

Unless you're stuck in traffic, you'll have only a couple of seconds to read a highway sign. You'll be able to decipher them at glance—and avoid getting lost—if you know what the numbers and symbols mean.

Interstates. These highways are marked with blue shields that are topped with red crowns and feature white letters. Odd-numbered routes—such as I-95—are north–south routes; the numbering of these roads begins in the west (I-5 is in California, while I-95 runs along the east coast from Miami to Canada). Even numbers indicate east–west routes (I-80 runs from San Francisco to Teaneck, New Jersey); the numbering of these roads begins in the south.

Auxiliary interstates (loop roads or alternate routes). Highways that bypass interstates have three digits—a single digit added to the front of the two-digit number of the associated interstate. For example, auxiliary interstate 285 is associated with I-85 and is a loop route around Atlanta. Signs for auxiliary routes are the same shape and colors as interstate signs.

U.S. highways. These roads are marked with black signs with white shields and black two-digit numbers. The numbering system of U.S. highways is completely different from that of the interstate system. Odd-numbered routes generally run north and south, and the lowest numbers begin in the east. Even-numbered routes run east and west, with the lowest numbers beginning in the north. Three-digit black-and-white highway signs signify spurs of two-digit highways or alternate routes.

364. What to Do in a Snowstorm

You may have fond memories of childhood snowstorms, but resist the temptation to head out into one—they're dangerous. Here's what to do the next time you encounter a blizzard.

- Stay indoors. You don't know how long you'll be trapped inside, so be cautious about food and fuel usage.

- If you're outside during a snowstorm, find shelter immediately. If you can't find haven indoors, look for a wind-protected spot so you can stay as dry and warm as possible. Beware of snowdrifts; they can be deeper than you expect. It's incredibly easy to get lost during a whiteout, so don't try hiking anywhere.

- Don't drive during a snowstorm unless you have no other choice. If you must drive, do so only during the day, staying on major highways. If it's impossible to see, pull to the side of the road. Use your cell phone to call a friend or relative so someone will know where you are. Run the engine for about ten minutes out of every hour to generate warmth while conserving fuel, and be sure not to run down the car's battery.

> **Breathe Easy**
>
> If you're trapped in a car during a blizzard, get out every once in a while to clear snow from the exhaust pipe. Running the engine with a blocked exhaust can cause carbon monoxide poisoning.

365. How to Avoid Frostbite

You don't have to be a mountain climber to experience frostbite. When the temperature dips below 20 degrees Fahrenheit and the wind is blowing, it only takes a few minutes for exposed skin to succumb to the chill—and it only takes seconds when the thermometer dips significantly lower.

Frostbite affects the extremities, the ears, and the nose first and foremost. This is because the body protects its core temperature by routing blood away from the extremities and to the heart, lungs, and other organs.

Signs of frostbite include numb skin that is white, red, or purple. The affected area may get hard and blisters may appear.

It's easier to avoid frostbite than to treat it. Here's how.

- Wear mittens over a pair of gloves or two pairs of gloves, and two or three pairs of socks.

- ✦ Wear a hat that covers your ears and a ski mask when facing a wicked windchill. Cover your nose and mouth with a scarf if you don't have a mask.

- ✦ Wear long underwear. Look for fibers—such as silk or synthetics—that wick moisture away from the skin.

- ✦ Wear a water-resistant outer layer.

If you're suffering from frostbite, get to a warm place as soon as possible. Don't stop moving. Tuck your hands under your armpits to keep them warm. Call 911, explain your situation and follow the instructions that you receive. Once indoors, remove wet garments and wrap yourself in dry blankets. Gently bathe frostbitten areas in warm water. Seek medical attention as soon as you can.

366. How to Avoid Getting Struck by Lightning

A thunderstorm is beautiful, but it can also be dangerous. In fact, in the United States, more people are killed each year by lightning than by tornadoes, floods, or hurricanes.

If you're caught outdoors during a lightning storm, seek shelter immediately. Avoid trees, picnic shelters, or open metal structures (like lean-tos or sheds). Metal attracts and conducts electricity, so stay away from metal objects such as fences or machinery. Above all, avoid water. If you can't find shelter, get into the lightning safety crouch—keep your feet close together, and crouch as deeply as you can without putting your knees or hands on the ground.

It's safer to be indoors, but you should still be vigilant. Avoid using electronic equipment or landline telephones, as lightning can strike telephone and electrical poles, sending shocks into the equip-ment. Turn off running water (this means no showers) and stay away from windows and external doors.

> **It's Not Nerves**
>
> If your skin starts tingling and your hair begins to stand on end during a thunderstorm, it could mean that a lightning strike is imminent. Assume the lightning safety crouch immediately.

367. How to Control Your Online Presence

Job recruiters, acquaintances, potential clients, and even prospective dates will type your name into a search engine to try to find out more about you. Follow these steps to make sure that the information about you on the Web is accurate and positive.

Search your name. Put quotation marks around your name when you type it into a search engine. You'll get hits that range from social network profiles to newspaper reports to political contributions.

Clean up your profile. Google is the most-used search engine, so it's the best place to begin. Remove old self-generated content from your search profile by visiting Google's "Remove Your Own Content" page. Remove personal information by using the "Webpage Removal Request Tool." To remove information that's controlled by another Web site, contact its webmaster by clicking on the "webmaster" link, which is usually located at the bottom of the Web site's homepage.

Monitor social networks. You can use professional networks to tout your expertise and social networks to keep in touch with friends and family. Just be sure to delete any controversial or negative information (or, better yet, don't post it in the first place).

Register on professional Web sites. You don't have to post information, but it's worth the trouble of signing up to keep someone else from getting the name first.

Report all malicious activity. If someone is cyber-bullying you by posting inaccurate or malicious information, contact local law enforcement.

368. How to Check a Web Site's Credibility

The Internet is an excellent place to obtain information, but it's important to consult trustworthy Web sites. The Internet is a public domain, so anyone—from eminent scholars to your kid brother—can post information or create a Web site. Here's how to determine if a particular site is a reputable source of information.

1. Look for the author's name and background (which are often listed in the "bio" link). Check his or her title, position, and organizational affiliation. Reliable Web sites will always include information about the site and the people who post on it. (You can also find this information by following the "About" link on the home page.)

2. Look for a date. If the information is old, look for a more recently updated source.

3. Assess the quality of the information. Does it seem fair, credible, clear, and accurate? Inconsistency in tone, spelling errors, and clear bias are signs that you should seek your information elsewhere. Web sites that include source documentation and contact information (in case you need to follow up with the author) are more likely to be reputable.

4. Community-generated sites—such as Wikipedia—are wonderful, but they're not always accurate. It's best not to use them as your sole source, but if you do, be careful. Check out the footnotes that Wikipedia provides for substantiation.

369. How to Use Craigslist Safely

Between apartment listings, job listings, and items for sale, you could conceivably set up an entire life without leaving Craigslist. Use the site safely by taking a few precautions.

Meet in person. When buying and selling items, always deal with the other party in person. Scammers have concocted dozens of ways to commit fraud through e-mail and snail mail, so never send money through the mail or online, and be especially suspicious of any request involving "escrow" or deals in which the other party pledges to send you any kind of check.

Bring a friend. Don't go to a stranger's house alone—bring a friend or relative. Likewise, if you're selling something from your house, make sure that other people are present when a buyer comes by. It's even better to suggest a public meeting place.

Get the job description. Craigslist is one of the most popular job boards on the Web, but not every job that's posted is legitimate—or safe. If a job posting seems vague or sketchy to you, contact the poster for more information before sending your résumé or other personal information.

370. How to Efficiently Search the Web

Search engines help you locate content on the World Wide Web; without them, you'd be lost in a sea of unsorted information. Yet there are ways to search for online content even more quickly and efficiently. Try these tips to help improve your next Internet search.

✦ Use quotations around the phrase you want to look up to get results for only those exact words used in that sequence.

✦ Conversely, if you want to filter a word from a search, put a hyphen before it (e.g., if you search "skiing-downhill," you will be directed to sites with the word "skiing" but not the word "downhill").

✦ For definitions of a word, type in "define:" followed by the word (e.g., "define:optimization").

✦ For current weather conditions, type in "weather:" followed by a zip code (e.g., "weather:60602").

✦ If you're using Google, look in the upper left corner for links to "Images," "Videos," "Books," "Maps," "News," and more. Use these for a more detailed search within these specific categories. Use the "Advanced Search" link next to the search box to really home in on a piece of information.

371. How—and Why—to Back Up Your Data

Most of us store huge parts of our lives—including music, photos, bank statements, personal correspondence, and schoolwork—on our computers. And that puts us at the mercy of tiny electronic chips and some hardware. Pretty scary, isn't it? That's why it's a good idea to have a backup of all your data, just in case.

You can use either an on-site or an off-site back-up method. When you back up on site, you put a copy of your data on a separate device, such as a DVD, CD-R, USB flash drive, or external hard drive. There are pros and cons to each of these types of media—DVDs and CD-Rs are cheap, but they hold less data than hard drives; flash drives are convenient because they are portable; and external hard drives are handy because they can back up all your data. Having a local backup is great, but if disaster—like a flood or fire—strikes, both copies of your data will be lost forever. That's why having an off-site backup is also a good idea. There are dozens of companies that provide unlimited off-site backup, often for a low cost. To back up with these companies, you'll need to download a small program that communicates with the company's storage servers. Your information will be stored, encrypted, and password-protected, so if you ever have a disaster at home or the office, it won't be lost forever.

372. How to Choose an E-mail Password

You can reduce the odds of having your e-mail account hacked by choosing a strong password—one that is easy to remember, uses both numbers and letters, combines upper- and lowercase letters, includes special characters, and doesn't feature any words that appear in a dictionary.

Avoid using passwords that include names, birthdates, and Social Security numbers—these are the first things that a hacker will try.

An easy way to develop a password is to start with a favorite quote, such as, "To be or not to be, that is the question." Take the first letter of each word (in this case, you'll get "Tbontbtitq"). To make it even stronger, consider mixing up the case: TBOntbtITQ, for example. Then throw in a couple of weird characters for added security, and you've got yourself a strong password: TBO&ntbt%ITQ. (Of course, we don't recommend using this particular example.)

Even though you have a good password, don't use it with every one of your online accounts. If hackers get access to it, they'll have access to all your Web-based information.

Once you've got a great password, you need to protect it. Never give out your passwords, no matter how convincing the request.

373. How to Secure Your Wireless Network

If you have an unsecured wireless network, *anybody* can get onto it. This means that not-so-nice people can use your wireless network for malicious activity—including conducting illegal business that will be traced to you—or even directly attack your computer. You can stay safe by securing your network. The manual that came with your router will give instructions on how to complete these steps.

Public Insecurity

Free Wi-Fi "hotspots," such as those available at public libraries and bookstores, often lack any kind of security—and you share the network with dozens or even hundreds of other people. Don't engage in sensitive online activities—such as banking and credit card transactions—from them.

✦ **Make your wireless network invisible.** Disabling the broadcasting of your network's name—known as its SSID—makes your network harder to detect.

✦ **Change your network name and password.** Most routers come with a default name and password—settings that are well-known to hackers. Change these as soon as you can, making sure to choose a long, difficult-to-guess password.

✦ **Encrypt your network.** The two most common forms of wireless network encryption are WEP and WPA. Most newer computers and routers support WPA, which is considered to be a more secure method of encryption.

374. How to Stay Safe When Shopping Online

If you need to find a bargain, shopping online is often your best bet. You need to be careful when handing out your financial information, however. Here are some pointers that will help you stay safe.

Go with the big names. In terms of security, bigger—as in big online retailers, such as Amazon—is better.

If it seems too good to be true, it probably is. Do you really think that this retailer you've never heard of can offer a new MacBook for $50? Unlikely.

Use a credit card. Federal laws protect you from paying for fraudulent credit card charges; this safety net is not available to all debit cards. If you send money through the post or with a wire service, forget about it.

Keep a receipt. Save confirmation e-mails and receipts—they'll provide substantiation if you have a problem getting what you pay for.

Use a secure connection. Always look for "https:" at the start of a checkout URL, and make sure that the online store uses encryption for its transactions.

> ### Shop at Home
> Never use a public computer—such as those you'll find at the library—to conduct financial transactions. Public computers may be infested with spyware and are easily rigged by hackers to log personal information.

375. How to Be Smart About Online Relationships

These days, it's common to have online relationships with people you barely know—or don't know at all—in real life. This means that you should be conscientious about how and with whom you're interacting online.

Real people. Your interactions may be virtual, but the relationships you build are real. Treat those with whom you interact online as you would in person. Behind that avatar or picture or chat room message is a real human being, with *real* feelings.

Safety. The anonymity of the Web means that anybody can be anybody, no matter how they present themselves to you. Don't give out too much personal information—and never send anybody money.

Turn off the computer. Online relationships can hurt off-line relationships if you start sacrificing time with friends and family for "virtual" friends.

376. How to Recycle

Recycling reduces waste, saves energy, helps the economy, decreases pollution—and more. Here's how you can help the environment.

What to recycle. Paper (almost all types except waxed or sticky—stickers and address labels cannot be recycled), cardboard, cereal boxes, aluminum or steel cans, glass bottles and jars (although some types of colored glass can't be recycled), detergent containers, and all other plastics labeled "1" and "2." (Some recycling centers take other numbers, too; check with your local center.)

How to recycle. Rinse out food residue; recyclables should be dry and clean. To save room in your recycling bin, crush milk cartons and aluminum cans and crumple paper. Find out if your city requires you to presort or if you can put everything in the same bin. If your area lacks a curbside pickup service, you may have to transport your stash to a recycling center; visit the Web site Earth911.com to find the facility nearest you.

377. Garbage Disposal Basics

A garbage disposal helps to keep your kitchen smelling fresh by quickly getting rid of old, smelly foods—just grind them up and flush them down the drain. Here are some tips that will help you make sure that your garbage disposal stays friendly. Always use cold water, and make sure that the water is running *before* you turn on the disposal. Pack the disposal loosely—otherwise, it could jam. Allow the disposal to grind and empty before you turn the motor off.

> **Deodorize the Drain**
> Even if you completely flush your disposal after each use, it's bound to get a little, shall we say, *aromatic* after a while. Keep your disposal smelling fresh by using it to grind a few lemon peels every week or two.

The disposal is designed to deal with soft food and liquid waste, but it can't handle everything. Plumbers recommend against introducing fibrous foods, eggshells, pasta (which swells and can cause clogs), or large bones into the disposal. Don't pour grease, oil, or fat into a disposal—it will harden and clog the pipes. And don't ever put your fingers into it—the blades are sharp enough to cut them even if the unit isn't on, and disposals can activate accidentally. If the disposal breaks or gets clogged, turn it off immediately.

378. What Not to Throw in the Trash

It can be incredibly satisfying to rid your house of garbage and items that you no longer use—but not everything should be tossed into the trash.

- **Recyclables.** Check with your municipality's recycling program to find out what it accepts. If it doesn't take computers and electronic equipment, find one that does nearby. Just be sure to wipe out your hard drive before you recycle it.

> **Don't Flush!**
>
> Don't throw expired or unwanted prescription drugs down the toilet— they can contaminate waterways.

- **Legible sensitive paperwork.** Bank statements, credit card bills, and paycheck stubs are all attractive to identity thieves. Shred any documents that contain sensitive personal information before disposing of them.

- **Batteries.** Batteries contain acids and chemicals that are environmental hazards. Check with local authorities to learn how to dispose of hazardous waste.

- **Prescription drugs.** The best way to dispose of medication is to bring it to a local facility, such as a village hall or police station. If you must throw drugs into the trash, remove identifying information from the label and try to put the bottle inside something opaque or undesirable to make it unrecognizable or unattractive to scavengers.

379. When Not to Use the U.S. Postal Service

There are lots of delivery services—including UPS, FedEx, and DHL—but are they really better than the U.S. Postal Service? The post office is probably adequate for most mail, but sometimes you might consider an alternative service.

Same-day service. If you need a package to arrive on the day that you send it, you'll be out of luck at the post office. Other services offer this option, but it will cost you.

Next-day service. The USPS offers overnight service, but it doesn't guarantee delivery at a particular time. Other carriers offer options for morning delivery or delivery by a certain time in the afternoon, usually for a higher rate.

Cost. In most cases, the USPS is cheaper than its competitors, especially if you take advantage of its special "flat-rate" priority and express packages. However, its rate might be higher, so it's worth checking online shipping calculators to figure out the best service for your needs.

Pickup/Tracking options.

The USPS does offer free package pickup through your mail carrier, but other delivery services offer more flexibility and have more advanced online tracking features.

> ### Self-service
> If you buy a cheap, small postal scale, you can weigh and stamp your packages without having to go to the post office. You can print shipping labels and postage at USPS.gov.

380. How to Pack a Box for Mailing

Whether you're shipping stuff home from college or sending Christmas gifts, packing items securely will help to ensure their safety en route. Here are three steps that will help you become a packing guru.

1. Use a sturdy box. If you're shipping with the USPS's Priority Mail service, you can get boxes for free from the post office (or order them online).

2. Put a layer of packing material on the bottom of the box—bubble wrap, Styrofoam peanuts, or even old newspaper will work. Then place the object you're shipping in the box; if it's fragile, you can put it in a smaller box or encase it in bubble wrap. Fill the rest of the box with more packing material.

3. Seal the box with packing tape, which is available from any office supply store or shipping office. (Be sure to reinforce the sides and bottom flaps of the box with tape as well.) When you're finished, shake the box gently to make sure that the object isn't flying around.

381. How to Stop Junk Mail and Solicitation Calls

If the majority of your mail is junk and most of your phone calls are solicitations, it's easy to become disenchanted with those forms of communication. But you can put a halt to third-class mail (a.k.a. bulk advertisements) and telemarketing. Whenever you write your address on a form, charitable donation, or newspaper subscription, add this line: "Please do not sell my name or address." Say this same sentence to telemarketers when they call. A little sleuthing will help you discover who is selling your contact information. Use a different middle initial when filling out a form and then watch to see if that initial shows up on any junk mail; if it does, contact the group that is selling your name and insist that they stop. To halt unwanted mail, fill out the Direct Marketing Association's "Opt Out" form, which stops 75 percent of the DMA's mailings to you for five years; to stop calls, tell telemarketers to permanently remove you from their lists or register your number at DoNotCall.gov, the National Do Not Call Registry.

382. How to Stop Your Mail

If you are leaving town for an extended period of time—for vacation or a school trip—you'll need to decide what to do about your mail. The best option is to have a friend or family member pick it up for you, on a daily basis if possible. This way, your mail doesn't pile up, and it's not immediately obvious to neighbors or strangers that you are out of town (overloaded mailboxes have the potential to attract burglars and vandals). You can also request that the post office hold your mail; go to your local branch and fill out the appropriate form. (You can also make this request online at holdmail.usps.com.)

383. How to Fold Clothes to Avoid Wrinkles

Folding clothes neatly helps to keep your wardrobe wrinkle-free. For best results, fold your clothes when you take them out of the dryer; don't heap them in a pile in the laundry basket. Quickly hang items that you won't fold—such as skirts, dresses, dress pants, and dress shirts—then separate your foldable items into groups: pants, T-shirts, socks, underwear, pajamas, etc. Fold pants in half lengthwise, taking care to line up the outer and inner seams; smooth them out, fold the bottom of the pants to the

Speed-folding

Learn how to fold a T-shirt in two seconds by watching an online video that demonstrates the "Japanese" shirt-folding method, which involves a short series of fluid motions. It's amazingly efficient!

top of the back pocket, and then fold the top of the pants over the folded legs. To fold a T-shirt, lay it face down and smooth out any wrinkles. Fold one sleeve lengthwise to the midpoint of the back; do the same with the other sleeve. Fold back the sleeve, flat against the shoulder. Fold the bottom third of the shirt up. Fold the top of the shirt over onto the folded third and smooth it out. Stack your neatly folded clothes in drawers or baskets.

384. Ironing Basics

Potato chips can be crinkled; your dress shirt should not be! Here are ironing tips that will help you smooth out your wardrobe.

1. Check your clothing tags for ironing instructions.

2. Using steam can help to remove wrinkles. Fill the iron's reservoir with water (distilled water works best). Misting some water or using spray starch can help to release stubborn wrinkles if you don't have a steam iron. Don't use steam with nylon or polyester fabrics or if the garment's tag says, "dry iron only."

3. Use a heat-resistant cover on the ironing board or surface.

4. If you're ironing multiple items, begin with those that require the coolest temperatures. Use low temperatures for delicate fabrics like satin and silk and higher temps for cotton (shirts, linens, jeans, etc.).

5. Iron the inside of the garment first, and always iron away from your body. Keep the iron moving to avoid scorching the

clothes. If you must stop for a moment, stand the iron up and place it away from the fabric.

6. To finish, iron the outside of the garment. Immediately hang it up or fold it to prevent wrinkling.

385. How to Tie a Tie

Every guy should know how to tie a tie—and it's a helpful skill for women to have too. Here's a step-by-step guide to tying the most basic of all knots—the "four-in-hand."

1. Drape the tie around your neck. The wide end should hang on the right side, about twelve inches longer than the skinny end.

2. Cross the wide end over the skinny end.

3. Loop the wide end underneath the skinny end, back to the right side, then loop it right back in front of the skinny end, back to the left side. This is the start of your knot.

4. Bring the wide end through the loop around your neck, up toward the ceiling.

5. Slide the tip of the wide end through the loop-knot you created earlier, and carefully pull it through, keeping your hand on the knot to maintain its shape.

6. Tighten and adjust the knot.

386. How to Remove a Stain

Taking prompt action is critical when attempting to remove a stain. In general, you should wipe or blot away as much of the staining agent as possible before treating it with a stain-removal product or laundry detergent. Here are additional directions that will help you remove some common stains.

Line-dry

When laundering stained items, skip the dryer and opt for air-drying on a rack or clothesline. The heat of a dryer can set the stain, which can make it hard to remove.

Ink. Apply water to the stain and blot the ink up with a clean towel. Then apply liquid laundry detergent and let it sit for a few minutes. Wash in warm water and let the item air-dry.

Candle wax. If the wax hasn't hardened, freeze the item and then scrape off the wax. Place a paper towel over the stain and press it with an iron (don't use water) to transfer the wax to the paper towel. Repeat this process until the towel has absorbed all the wax.

Blood. Soak the stain in cold water before laundering the item.

387. How to Build a Smart Wardrobe on a Budget

You can assemble a great, versatile wardrobe without spending a fortune. Low-cost apparel can be found at thrift stores, outlet malls, and department store sales. Choose basic, mixable pieces—a smart wardrobe includes a jacket, a skirt or dress pants, a top for any occasion, a great-fitting pair of jeans, and a sweater or cardigan that goes with everything—to get the most from your purchases. Here are some tips that will help you shop on the cheap.

✦ Have a clothing swap with friends. You can get rid of items that you no longer wear or don't fit and perhaps get something useful in return. Take any unswapped duds to a store that buys and sells used garments; it will give you store credit in exchange for your clothes.

✦ Frequent thrift stores that sell high-quality clothing that's been discarded by wealthy donors.

✦ Shop at outlet malls, where manufacturers sell directly to the public. You can score great deals on out-of-season items.

✦ Visit department stores during storewide sales. Clip coupons and browse the clearance racks carefully.

388. What to Expect During Your Annual Physical

One of the primary purposes of a physical is to discuss health maintenance and prevention strategies, including diet and exercise.

A typical physical begins with a conversation between you and the doctor about how you've been feeling and if you've experienced any health problems or unusual symptoms. The nurse will check your vital signs (your pulse, blood pressure, and temperature) and measure your height and weight before the exam begins. The doctor will then examine your eyes, ears, mouth, abdomen, and lymph nodes and listen to your heart and lungs; he or she may also check your reflexes. The doctor will likely order a blood test to get a more complete picture of your current health. If you're a guy, the doctor will perform a testicular exam or another inspection of the genitals; you'll also be asked to turn your head and cough so the doctor can check for hernias. If you're a woman, the doctor may examine your breasts to check for unusual lumps or masses; if you don't have a separate gynecologist, the physical may also include a pelvic exam and a pap smear.

389. The Importance of Good Posture

"Stand up straight!" Maybe you've shrugged off this admonition before, but good posture will instantly make you look more attractive and self-assured—and it's important for your health too. Standing up straight strengthens your spine and helps to protect your back's natural curves, while poor posture overexerts your muscles and ligaments, which can cause back pain and fatigue. Good posture doesn't just make us look confident, though—it inspires us to feel confident too. Here's how to be a fine, upstanding citizen: Keeping your feet parallel, hold your chest high and your shoulders back in a relaxed position (slouching your shoulders forward shortens the muscles in your chest); pull in your abs and rear end; and balance your weight on both feet and relax your knees. With practice, you will naturally default to good posture

Sit Up Straight!

Good posture is equally as important when you're seated (if not more so). Slouching over a keyboard and slumping in your chair can cause severe strain of your vertebrae. Press the small of your back against your chair and relax your shoulders.

rather than a slouchy stance, and then you'll really stand out from the crowd!

390. Floss Your Teeth

Using mouthwash and sprays to mask bad breath is like using perfume to cover body odor: You'll smell better if you wash—whether it's your underarms or your mouth. The key to avoiding bad breath is to get rid of odor-causing bacteria. Bacteria hides between the teeth, growing on trapped, rotting food particles; flossing at least once a day will get rid of these particles.

> **Brush Your Tongue!**
>
> Bacteria also collect on your tongue, so brush it every time you brush your teeth to remove bacteria and freshen your breath.

Flossing is also important for your health. It helps to prevent tooth decay and gum disease, and it keeps bacteria from traveling into your bloodstream, where they inflame and thicken arteries, setting the stage for heart disease.

Floss right after brushing your teeth but before rinsing with mouthwash. Wrap a long piece of floss around each pointer finger and hold the ends securely with your hands; leave two exposed inches pulled taut. Using your thumbs, gently guide the floss between teeth in a sawing or rubbing motion, moving it up to the gum line and then curving it around each side of the tooth, into the space between the tooth and the gum. Floss between every tooth and at the outside of the very back tooth on each side, upper and lower. You can ask your dental hygienist to show you how, or you can watch a video explanation on the American Dental Association's Web site.

391. How to Choose Effective Birth Control

Knowledge is power when it comes to birth control, so be sure to rely on facts instead of hearsay when choosing how to protect yourself during sexual activity. The following is a quick guide; visit

PlannedParenthood.org or talk to your doctor for more comprehensive information.

Contraceptives. The pill, contraceptive injections, the patch, the diaphragm, male condoms, and the contraceptive vaginal ring are 97 percent effective in preventing pregnancy. Your doctor or a health clinic can help you decide which method is best for you, based on your sexual activity, health, menstrual regularity, and existing medical conditions.

Spermicides. Spermicides kill sperm, but they are much less effective than other contraceptives.

Withdrawal method. This method requires the male partner to withdraw before ejaculation. It can be about 96 percent effective if the man is experienced and has considerable self-control.

Emergency contraception. This is a backup method of birth control that you can use if you have had unprotected intercourse or if your birth-control method failed. You can take these pills up to five days after you have unprotected intercourse; they contain the same hormones as birth control pills.

> ### Beware Antibiotics
> Antibiotics can interfere with the effectiveness of birth control. Use a backup method if you are sexually active while taking antibiotics.

Emergency contraception (also called "the morning-after pill") does not cause an abortion.

392. Where and Why to Get a Flu Shot

You can protect yourself from the miseries—and potential dangers—of the flu by getting vaccinated every fall. The flu vaccine introduces a dead flu virus into your body (despite rumors to the contrary, a dead virus can't make you sick), and your immune system responds by creating antibodies to protect against the virus. Taking this vaccine can reduce your odds of getting the flu by up to 90 percent.

Flu vaccines are widely available. If you're a student, try your school's health center. If you're not a student, the easiest place to get one is probably your local pharmacy; many of the large pharmacy chains—such as CVS and Walgreens—offer low-cost flu vaccines every fall and winter. You can also get a shot at a doctor's office. Some employers even sponsor flu vaccination clinics.

Talk to your doctor before getting a flu shot. Some people, such as those with chronic illnesses or certain allergies, shouldn't be vaccinated.

393. How to Prevent Hearing Loss

Excessive noise is the leading cause of hearing loss among teens and young adults, so if you regularly pump up the volume on your personal music player, you're at considerable risk. These devices can expose you to 105 decibels—significantly more than the 85 decibels (the volume of heavy traffic) that can lead to gradual hearing loss. Regular exposure to noise levels of 110 decibels (the volume level of a rock concert) or above for more than one minute at a time may cause permanent hearing loss.

Listening to music is great, but hearing loss is forever. What can you do about all those decibels? First, keep your MP3 player at a moderate volume. If you work with or around heavy machinery, wear protective ear gear—you can buy it at hardware and sporting-goods stores. If you attend rock concerts, use earplugs—they're available at pharmacies, and some concert venues even sell them. Don't sit right next to the speakers, and if you notice ringing or buzzing in your ears, take a break.

FAST FACT

Dolphins have some of the best ears in the animal world—they can hear 14 times better than humans. Now if we could only figure out what their squeaky voices are saying . . .

394. High-Fructose Corn Syrup

When you're reading food labels at the grocery store, you may notice a recurring ingredient: high-fructose corn syrup (HFCS). It's a popular sweetener and preservative that shows up in everything from sodas and granola bars to packaged bread and processed meats, as well as many varieties of ketchup, cereal, salad dressing, and sports drinks. HFCS is made by changing one sugar molecule in cornstarch (glucose) to another (fructose). Food manufacturers use it because it's cheap, versatile, and extends shelf life.

You almost certainly consume lots of foods with HFCS, so it's worthwhile to learn some of its potential health risks. Foods and beverages that contain HFCS often have a lot of calories but little nutritional value. Frequently consuming the sweetener may increase your appetite, which is why some researchers have linked the widespread use of HFCS to the rise in obesity, which can lead to a variety of other health concerns (e.g., high blood pressure, type 2 diabetes, and coronary artery disease). Scientists are still studying the ways our bodies react to sugar, but a good rule of thumb is to practice moderation when eating or drinking any kind of sweetener. Give it a try: The process of cutting out processed foods—and opting instead to consume healthier stuff, including fresh fruits and veggies—can be very sweet indeed.

395. How to Just Say "No"

Why do we say "yes" when we really mean "no"? We often disregard our true feelings because we're trying to please others or we want to improve their opinions of us. So we agree to do things that we can't do (they're not within our skill sets or we're too busy to tackle them) and things that we don't want to do (they don't interest us or they compromise our goals or values). If "no" sticks in your throat but you want to be able to release it, try some of these strategies.

✦ Acknowledge that you're not a bad person for saying "no." In fact, saying "no" might help you to be an even *better* person by freeing you up to do the things you really need to do.

✦ Say "no" politely but firmly. Don't be wishy-washy or you'll be tempted—or others might try to convince you—to change your answer to "yes."

✦ Offer an alternative—but only if necessary and if you really mean it. For example, say, "I can't edit your résumé tonight because I have a term paper due, but I can help you tomorrow." The other person might be willing to negotiate.

✦ Leave the door open. If you say "yes," you're committed; saying "no"—or "no" with a qualifier—gives you the ability to change your mind and say "yes" later on.

396. How to Set Boundaries

Learning how to set emotional and physical boundaries in all the areas of your life helps you to establish your identity, as well as to gain respect from others.

At home. It's extremely important to set and maintain clear boundaries when you're living with someone else in a confined space. Carefully consider how you feel about sharing your things with your roommate, for example, and how much time you want to spend with him or her. Establishing boundaries through tactful, clear communication early on will help prevent misunderstandings and make life easier in general.

At work. When you're starting a new job, it's natural—even smart— to go above and beyond the call of duty to impress your boss and coworkers. While that might be okay in the short term, eventually people will take advantage of you if you don't ever say "no."

With family. *You* know that you've moved out on your own, but it might take your parents longer to recognize that you aren't under their thumbs anymore. While it's important to maintain close relationships with your parents, it's okay to gently remind them that you're an adult now and you need to make your own decisions and mistakes.

Stand Firm

Boundaries need to be enforced—otherwise, they're worthless. If you allow others to trample on your boundaries, the ones that you set in the future won't be respected—by others, or by you.

---

397. The Art of Making a Deal

Here's the deal: You can learn to negotiate—it just requires patience and practice. Here are some tips that will help you get a good deal.

Be prepared. Think about the points that you want to bring up ahead of time. If you're negotiating a price, decide the price that you will offer or accept; if you're negotiating a salary, know your bottom line. Be prepared to compromise—a negotiation usually requires meeting somewhere in the middle.

State your points clearly, then stop talking and listen. It's easy to ramble on passionately, but there is power in silence.

Follow your instincts. If the other party is acting like a bully or using bribes, trust your gut and do not give in. On the other hand, if you feel that the other party has come up with a reasonable offer, be willing to accept it. You may not win, but at least you will negotiate successfully.

398. Understanding Fallacies

A fallacy is an error in reasoning—and many people use them consciously and unconsciously during an argument. Fallacies are different from factual errors, which have nothing to do with the logic behind an argument. By watching out for common fallacies, you'll be better equipped to refute an argument calmly and logically. Here are some of the most common fallacies.

Ad hominem. When someone makes a personal attack that has nothing to do with the claim being disputed, it's called an *ad hominem*—"against man"—argument.

Appeal to authority. When a person claims to be an authority on the subject that is up for debate—but is decidedly not.

> ## Hone Your Skills
> Watch a political talk show and see if you can identify different types of fallacies that are employed by the host and guests. Recognizing these will develop your arguing expertise.

Red herring. This kind of fallacy occurs when someone introduces a subject that has no relevance to the original topic, which is abandoned.

Slippery slope. In this fallacy, someone claims that one event must necessarily follow from another without providing proof of the event's inevitability.

Bandwagon. This fallacy is employed by appealing to the popularity of an idea regardless of its merits.

399. How to Admit That You Are Wrong

Everyone gets things wrong sometimes—lots of times!—but very few people will admit it. Some will hold on to their convictions, even in the face of overwhelming evidence against them. But admitting error is a sign of maturity, and it goes a long way toward defusing conflict and strengthening relationships. Here are some tips that will help you out the next time you're wrong about something (and you will be).

✦ Not admitting a wrong will not make that wrong right. In fact, it compounds the problem.

✦ Admit to yourself that you're wrong. You can't admit to others that you are wrong if you don't believe it yourself.

> ### Shades of Gray
> Remember that there isn't always a right and a wrong; things aren't only black and white. Life is lived mostly in the gray.

✦ Recognize that being wrong does not cast aspersions on your character. Most of the time, it just means that you took a risk.

✦ You won't save face by refusing to admit that you're wrong; in fact, you'll actually make yourself look worse. Most people respect somebody who can admit being wrong much more than somebody who can't.

Then again, we could be wrong about that. Of course, we'd admit it if we were.

400. How to Speak Your Mind

The freedom of speech is a fundamental right in the United States. Unfortunately, many people are afraid to exercise it, whether because of a fear of rejection, a fear of confrontation, or a fear of being wrong. Learning how to speak your mind is a key to developing your personality. Here's how to do it.

Recognize that your opinion is valid. It's difficult to speak your mind unless you believe that what you have to say is important. You are a thinking, feeling human being, and your thoughts and opinions matter.

Don't be afraid to make a mistake. Worrying about blundering or making a verbal faux pas can be a self-fulfilling prophecy. Remember, *everybody* makes mistakes.

Speak confidently. You know that your opinion counts, but nobody else will care unless you present it clearly and confidently. Project your voice, enunciate, and make eye contact with your conversational partners.

Practice in a safe environment. Ask a trusted friend or family member to help you practice speaking your mind. A little experience with people who won't dismiss your opinions will help you express yourself with others.

Stand Up

Maggie Kuhn, one of the great social activists in American history, gave this advice about speaking up: "Stand before the people you fear and speak your mind—even if your voice shakes."

401. How to Repair a Bicycle-Tire Puncture

Whether you ride a bicycle for pleasure or for transportation, a flat can be troublesome—not to mention costly, if you have to take your bike to a repair shop to get it fixed. Save money by learning how to repair a punctured bike tire yourself. You'll need a replacement inner tube, a tire pump, tire irons (tools that are designed to pry the edge of a tire away from the wheel), and a tire patch kit (which should contain sandpaper, rubber patches, and glue). Here's a step-by-step guide that will help you fix your tire.

1. Remove the wheel from the bike, and then remove the tire and inner tube from the wheel.

2. Inspect the tire inside and out for gashes or objects that may have caused the puncture.

3. Inspect the inner tube, then inflate it and listen for a hissing sound, which will indicate that air is escaping.

4. Locate the hole and lightly rub the area with sandpaper.

5. Apply glue to both the tube and a rubber patch, then apply the patch to the tube and let it dry for a few minutes.

6. Inflate the tube and check the patch—as well as the tube—for additional leaks, then deflate the tube and put it back in the tire. Put the tire onto the wheel. Inflate and enjoy the ride!

402. How to Stay Safe on the Trail

Hiking in a state park is a great way to enjoy the natural beauty of the United States. Here's how to stay safe on the trail so you can fully enjoy your outdoor adventures.

A safe hike begins with appropriate dress. Proper footwear—such as hiking boots or sturdy walking shoes—will help to prevent twisted ankles on rough paths. Wear thick socks, long pants, and long sleeves to protect against twigs, thorns, ticks, rocks, and poisonous plants (such as poison ivy and poison sumac).

The human body can last for weeks without food but only three days without water, so it's critical to bring plenty of potable water on your hikes. Never drink from streams, ponds, or lakes, even if they seem clear and clean; microorganisms that live in these bodies of water can make you very ill. If you're going for a long backcountry expedition, consider taking a water-filtration system; you can buy one at an outdoor recreation store.

It might be tempting to hike off into unmarked territory, but it's never a good idea to leave the trail. If you lose your way in a large park or forest, you could be lost for days. Always bring a compass with you, just in case.

403. How to Remove a Tick

Ticks are sneaky, bloodsucking parasites that spread disease from one host to another. They range in size from tiny pinpoints to bulging grapes. It's not ticks' bites that are dangerous, though—it's the bacteria that they inject when they bite. There are several tick-borne diseases that are serious—even deadly.

Check your body for ticks after walking in the woods, sitting in a grassy meadow, or playing with your pets. They prefer warm, moist areas such as groins, underarms, and scalps. Here's what to do if you find a tick attached to your body.

1. Grab the tick with tweezers placed as close to your skin as possible and hold it gently so you don't tear off its head or mouthparts. Pull up with a steady, even pressure so your skin is also pulled up a bit.

2. Keep up the pressure for three minutes or so; this is usually enough time for the tick to release and back out.

3. Don't kill the tick by squeezing or crushing it—its body fluids may contain bacteria. Once removed, flush it down the toilet or put it in a plastic bag and freeze it. If you get sick, you can take the dead tick with you to the doctor's office for examination.

4. Clean the area around the bite with soap and water to disinfect.

404. How to Open a Stubborn Jar Lid

You're in the middle of making a peanut-butter-and-jelly sandwich, but the lid of the jelly jar won't budge. Here's a surefire way to get it open before you starve.

1. Place the top of a spoon underneath the lid so the bowl of the spoon is facing out.

> ### Warm It Up
> If the jar has previously been used, food may be stuck around the rim. Run hot water over the top of the jar to soften the food and then try opening it again.

2. Working around the lid and using the jar as leverage, rock the top of the spoon back and forth underneath the lid. You will know that the seal is broken if you hear a slow release of air or a sudden pop.

If the spoon trick doesn't work, try whacking the rim of the lid with the handle of a knife. This may well release the vacuum seal, which will allow you to open the lid.

405. How to Open a Bottle of Wine

Are you scared of "screwing up" when you open a bottle of wine? Never fear: Opening a bottle of wine is as easy as 1–2–3.

1. Standard corkscrews come with a small, serrated knife that's designed to help you remove the foil. Pull out this knife and cut around the top of the bottle, just under the lip. Discard the foil.

2. Click the knife back into place and position the corkscrew in the center of the cork. Twist it in, turning clockwise a few times until you're able to place its first bottle rest onto the lip of the bottle. Lifting the handle, pull the cork only halfway out.

3. Place the second bottle rest onto the lip and pull the cork all the way out. *Voilà!* Your bottle is open.

406. How to Sharpen a Knife

You will work quickly, easily, and safely if you use a sharp kitchen knife for food preparation. A sharp knife cuts cleanly without sawing or tearing, and it requires less pressure so it's less likely to slip off food (and onto your finger).

There are three different tools from which to choose for routine knife sharpening—a commercial knife sharpener (manual or electric), a sharpening steel, and a sharpening stone. Using a steel or stone requires practice—it's helpful to watch online videos that demonstrate the techniques. Each method will take about six to ten strokes per side.

✦ **Commercial sharpener.** Insert the knife into the slot and pull slowly through, toward your body, working from the bottom of the knife to the tip.

- **Stone.** Place the stone on a cutting board, coarse side up. Holding the stone securely, pull the knife blade against the coarse surface toward your body. Work slowly and apply moderate pressure, holding the knife at an angle to create a beveled edge. Turn the stone over to use the fine-grit side to polish the blade. Some experts recommend that you wet the stone with water or oil to refine sharpening.
- **Steel.** Rest the steel's tip securely against the cutting board, then pull the knife blade across the shaft, toward your body, while simultaneously gliding it down the steel.

407. Food Safety Tips

There are more than 250 types of food-borne illness, according to the Centers for Disease Control and Prevention; you can avoid many of them by handling and storing food properly. Here are some tips that will help you keep food—and your intestinal tract—bacteria-free.

- Always check sell-by and expiration dates on perishable foods before buying them. Look for products that have dates that are as far from the current date as possible. When buying meat and poultry, check the "packed-on" date, and try to buy those that were most recently packed.
- Wash your hands after handling raw meat, fish, and poultry.
- Clean knives and cutting boards after each use. Use separate cutting boards for meat products and vegetables to avoid cross-contamination.
- Make sure that food packaging is airtight. Food will perish much faster if the container is left open—even a tiny bit.
- Check the seals on bottles for punctures or signs that they have been opened. (You should always hear a "pop" when you break the suction on a lid.) Check cans of food for dents or other damage.
- Refrigerate perishables immediately after you get home from the grocery store.
- Don't leave leftovers or cooked perishable foods out for more than two hours.
- Wash your fruits and vegetables under cold running water.

408. How to Store Leftovers

If you don't finish your food at a restaurant or if you make extra servings of a delicious meal, you will have leftovers to enjoy. Here's how to store them—and prevent food-borne illness in the process.

1. Package leftovers in secure airtight containers. If a restaurant puts them in a flimsy bag or piece of foil, transfer the food to a plastic or glass container with a lid after you return home; this will keep the food from spoiling right away. If you prepare a large dish at home, divide the leftovers into several clean storage containers.

2. Eat leftover restaurant food within a day or two. Eat prepared food that contains meat within three days and meatless prepared food within five or six days. Examine the food—smell it and look for changes in color or texture that could signal spoilage—to make sure it is still safe to consume.

3. Store bread, soup, vegetables, and sauces in freezer-safe containers in the freezer.

4. Separate refrigerated containers by at least two inches so air can circulate between them.

5. If you put milk or cream into a pitcher to serve at the table, don't pour it back into the original container if it isn't finished; just put a piece of plastic wrap or aluminum foil over the pitcher and store it in the refrigerator.

6. If you don't use all of a canned product (such as tomato sauce), transfer what's left to a plastic or glass container before you refrigerate it; do not leave it in the can.

409. Cooking Equipment That Every Kitchen Needs

Having the right cooking equipment is just as important as having the right ingredients. If you'd like to do more than prepare ramen noodles in your kitchen, you'll find these pieces of cooking equipment essential.

1. Large frying or sauté pan with lid (to sauté vegetables and scramble eggs).

2. Two-quart (or larger) saucepan with lid (to make or heat up soups and sauces, and to cook rice and vegetables).

3. 13×9-inch pan (for lasagna, cakes, brownies, and more).

4. Mixing bowl—choose glass, heavy plastic, or stainless steel.

5. A set of measuring cups and spoons, including a separate measuring cup that has ounces marked on one side.

6. Chef's knife with 8-inch blade.

7. Paring knife with 4-inch blade.

8. Cutting board—choose wood or lightweight plastic.

9. Wooden spoon.

10. Vegetable peeler.

11. Colander (for straining pasta, among other things).

12. Nonstick baking sheet (to roast vegetables, toast nuts, and bake cookies).

410. A Guide to the Refrigerator

Refrigerators are designed so that each shelf and drawer is an ideal storage spot for a different type of food. Getting to know your fridge will help you store food properly.

Meat drawer. As you might expect, meat goes in the meat drawer. It's colder in there.

Butter compartment. Butter can certainly go here, but experts actually suggest that you use this compartment—which is often found on the top shelf of the door—to store herbs. You can store butter (covered in a butter dish) at the front of the top shelf.

Crisper. It's called a "crisper" because it's designed to keep vegetables, well, *crisp.* The slits on the front of the drawer help to control the amount of humidity in the crisper. Vegetables need moisture to stay crisp (which is why the produce department mists their vegetables), and humidity helps to provide that. Fruits require less humidity than vegetables, so store them in a separate drawer and adjust its openings to create a less humid environment.

Door. Shelves on the door are the warmest parts of the refrigerator, since they are exposed to room temperatures every time you open the door. Use them to store items that won't go bad if they're exposed to warmer temperatures, such as salad dressings and mustards.

411. What Not to Put in the Microwave

If you're not intimately familiar with a microwave yet, you will be soon. You can't put just anything in the microwave, however. Here are a few things that you should never nuke.

Metal/tin foil. Metal doesn't absorb microwaves—it reflects them, potentially creating sparks, electrical arcs, and fire.

Styrofoam. Putting most Styrofoam—especially the kind used in restaurant takeout containers—into the microwave is a no-no. Styrofoam tends to melt (or, occasionally, catch fire) in the microwave, which will ruin last night's leftovers and create a stink.

Some kinds of plastics. In general, plastics have lower melting points than liquids, which means that they may melt in the microwave. Avoid putting water bottles and the plastic tubs that are used for yogurt into the microwave. Tupperware, on the other hand, is designed for microwave use. When in doubt, look for the microwave-safe label.

Nothing. Never run a microwave with nothing inside of it. The radio waves will bounce off the internal walls, potentially damaging the microwave, if there isn't anything to absorb them.

412. Tools for the Person Who Isn't Handy

If you're a renter, odds are that you won't need to make too many major repairs by yourself. But having a few tools around can be handy. Here are some must-haves.

1. **Hammer.** Choose a lightweight claw hammer for maximum versatility.

2. **Tape measure.** Make sure that you choose a tape measure with a decent length—about 20 feet—and a thumb lock.

3. **Screwdrivers.** A basic Phillips-head, which has a cross-shape tip, and a flathead screwdriver should be sufficient, but if you want to splurge, you can get a screwdriver with a replaceable tip.

4. **Utility knife.** X-Acto knives or box cutters are incredibly handy; just be sure that you get the retractable kind or use a safety cap so you don't accidentally cut yourself.

5. **Pliers.** You'll be surprised by how often you need these.

6. **Adjustable wrench.** This is another tool that you'll need surprisingly often—even if you're not planning to do any serious plumbing work. Lots of household objects use nuts, and you'll need a wrench to remove them.

413. How to Clean a Stainless-Steel Sink

Stainless-steel appliances are sleek and modern-looking—but just because they're called "stainless" doesn't mean that they don't get dirty. Stainless-steel sinks take the most abuse, but fortunately they're a snap to keep clean. Here's how.

✦ Use a soft cloth that's been dipped in warm water and a little mild detergent. Wipe the sink gently with this solution and then use a clean cloth to dry it and prevent streaks. Basic window cleaner works well on fingerprints and common food stains, but undiluted white vinegar is a less expensive and equally effective cleaner; just spray it into the sink and wipe it down with a soft cloth.

✦ For tougher jobs, such as old grease or paint stains, invest in a special stainless-steel cleaner. Whatever you do, though, do not use steel wool or abrasive cleaners, as they will permanently scratch surfaces. Also, avoid chemical cleaners that contain chlorine, which will damage and corrode the sink.

FAST FACT

Though stainless steel is pretty durable, it can develop rust spots, so try not to leave wet sponges or cloths on it for extended periods of time. If you do get rust, use a paste of cream of tartar mixed with lemon juice to remove it.

414. How to Clean a Toilet

Moving into your own place has many upsides—and some downsides. One of the downsides is cleaning the toilet. Harness your best "mind over matter" approach to this household chore and your porcelain throne will be sparkling in no time.

First, assemble your supplies. You'll need a toilet bowl brush, a cloth or rag, an all-purpose disinfectant, and toilet bowl cleaner in a spray or squeeze bottle. (If your toilet is really gross, wear rubber gloves.) Lift the lids and then spray the inside of the toilet with the cleaner. Aim it under the rim and along the sides—don't just spray it in the toilet water; in fact, you don't really need to spray it in the water at all. Let the cleaner sit for a few minutes. Use the toilet bowl brush to scrub under the rim, along the water line (where you may have a ring of dirt), and into the trap (the hole where the water goes). Flush the toilet, and as it refills, assess the bowl's cleanliness; if you're not satisfied, repeat the process. Next, spray disinfectant under and on top of all the seat surfaces. Spray the porcelain on the back of the toilet, as well as the sides. Using your cloth or paper towels, wipe down the lid surfaces and the entire outside of the toilet, then wipe around the inside top rim of the toilet bowl. Put away your supplies, hang the cloth to dry before placing it in the laundry, wash your hands, and admire your handiwork.

415. How to Remove Lint from the Dryer

If drying your clothes costs a lot more in quarters and/or time than you think it should, the problem could be the dryer's lint screen. Lint buildup inhibits air circulation, which causes the dryer to work inefficiently. But lint costs more than wasted time and money: Every year, tens of thousands of fires are caused by lint that builds up around the heating elements in dryers. Be sure that you know how to prevent this hazard.

If you do your laundry at a commercial facility or in your apartment building, empty the lint trap before you load your clothes. (The location of the trap should be identified on the machine—if it isn't, ask a custodian or attendant.) If the dryer is in your home, empty the trap often, and be sure to vacuum behind and underneath the dryer every couple of months. If you notice a lot of buildup (particularly if you use fabric-softener sheets), wash and thoroughly dry the lint trap by hand.

416. How to Open a Utility Account

Once upon a time, opening a utility (electric, gas, phone, etc.) account meant you had to stand in line, fill out paperwork, and then schedule installation. Well, guess what? Times haven't changed all that much. Some companies allow you to do everything online, but most still require you to do it the old-fashioned way—you will have to show up in person to complete the forms and pay a deposit. Here's what you'll need to do to get started.

✦ If you're under 21 years old, some companies will require that a parent or guarantor open or cosign your account (so in case you "forget" to pay your bills, they'll have someone to go after). Check the company's policy in advance.

✦ Make sure that you take the required identification— usually a driver's license and Social Security card—as well as cash or a check for your connection fee. A deposit may also be required, so make sure that you have enough money to cover it. (You'll get the deposit back if your account is in good standing when you move or cancel your service.)

> ### Don't Pay Late
>
> It's not enough to just pay your bill—you have to pay it on time. Many utility companies charge a fee if you pay late, and if you are more than 30 days past due, they may disconnect your service and then require you to pay a reconnection fee on top of what you already owe.

✦ Be prepared to block out at least half a day for installation. Most companies schedule two- to four-hour windows of time for hook-ups; if the technicians are running late, you may end up waiting all day.

417. How to Dust

Household dust may seem harmless, but you'll never look at it the same way after you find out what's in it. Dust is actually nasty stuff that's composed of dirt particles, pet dander, human skin cells, insect parts, and dust-mite excrement. Surface dust makes a room appear dirty (because dust *is* dirty!), and it can damage wood furniture. More importantly, it can trigger allergic reactions that cause hives and/or breathing difficulties. Here's how to dust your living space safely and effectively.

✦ Sweep linoleum and hardwood floors every day, making sure to get into corners and under furniture. Once a week, damp mop using a vinegar and water solution.

- Use a soft cloth or feather duster to clean desks, tables, shelves, electronics, etc. Don't forget to dust doorframes, ceiling fans, and baseboards.
- Books and magazines collect lots of dust, so occasionally wipe them all over with a slightly damp cloth.
- Try to wash your bedding once a week (wash mattress covers at a laundry facility that has large-capacity machines). Dry-clean large curtains and comforters (if so advised by the manufacturer).

418. Terms of Address and How to Use Them

"Excuse me, miss." "Can I help you, sir?"

If you sometimes struggle with terms of address when greeting someone, making an introduction, starting a letter, or calling someone on the phone, you're not alone—this can be a challenging area of etiquette. Here are some pointers for situations that you may encounter.

Academics. Dean: Dean Smith; President: President Smith; Professor: Professor Smith.

Elected officials. U.S. President: Mr./Madam President; Vice-President: Mr./Madam Vice-President; State or U.S. Representative: Representative Smith; State or U.S. Senator: Senator Smith; Governor: Governor Smith. When addressing envelopes, use "The Honorable" plus the person's full name, followed by his or her position: The Honorable John Smith, Governor of Utah.

Attorneys. Mr./Mrs./Miss Smith.

Physicians. Doctor Smith.

419. How to Make an Introduction

After you move away from home, you'll meet lots of new people—and introduce them to lots of other people. Old friends will meet new friends, new friends will meet siblings, significant others will meet parents, etc. Knowing how to properly introduce them to each other will make everybody more comfortable.

When introducing others:

✦ Introduce the younger person to the older person first. This is an old-fashioned rule of etiquette, but it is still considered the polite way to go about it.

✦ Be sure to say each person's full name during an introduction. A bad introduction: "Hey Mom, this is Jessica." A good introduction: "Mom, I'd like to introduce you to my friend Jessica Johnson. Jessica, this is my mom, Mary Smith."

✦ Use titles when appropriate. If somebody is a doctor, introduce him or her as "Dr. [last name]. If you are introducing someone who holds a position of authority—such as a professor—use "Professor" or "Mr." with the last name; don't include his or her first name. For example, "Professor Johnson, this is my roommate, John Williams."

When introducing yourself or being introduced:

✦ Say your full name. Never use "Mr." or "Ms."
✦ If you're sitting down, stand up.
✦ Smile and make eye contact with the other person.
✦ Offer a handshake. The handshake should be firm and not overly long.
✦ Express your pleasure at meeting the other person.

> ### Old Formalities
>
> In the old days, formal introductions always took the form of "presenting" someone—as in, "Mrs. Smith, may I present Mr. Jones?" Men were always "presented" to women. This is no longer common, but you can still introduce people in this way if you'd like. After all, being old-fashioned is better than being rude.

420. How to Shake Hands

A handshake can make a powerful first impression—good or bad. A limp handshake after finishing a job interview? Bad. A firm but quick handshake when meeting your girlfriend's parents? Good. Even better than a firm traditional handshake is the "double handshake," which experts have deemed the most effective grip for making positive first impressions. Here's how to do it.

1. When shaking hands, cup your left hand (this is standard practice, regardless of whether you are right- or left-handed) under the clasped hands. This "double handshake" method shows enthusiasm and conveys friendship.

2. Don't shake. A handshake is really a hand*grip*, with two or three very small shakes. Shaking a person's entire arm is annoying.

3. Use a firm grip, but don't squeeze. If you clutch too tightly, you come off as aggressive. Conversely, if your grasp is too loose, you will seem wimpy.

4. Make eye contact and smile. Looking away signifies guilt or dishonesty.

5. Say the person's name and introduce yourself. Conversing is an essential part of an introduction.

6. Take your time. Hold the handshake for a couple of seconds. Letting go too soon will make you seem anxious or hurried.

421. How to Negotiate a Good Price

Just because you see a price on items such as clothes, cars, and electronics—or even rates for hotel rooms—doesn't mean you have to pay that amount. In many cases (and within reason), you can negotiate a better price. Here are some tips that will help you get a good deal.

✦ Ask, but don't assume. If you know that something will go on sale soon or you think that you should get a discount because of a small flaw in the item, don't be afraid to ask. On the other hand, don't assume that you are guaranteed a discount. Be polite, and know when to back down.

✦ Sometimes, big chain stores can't be flexible with prices the way that mom-and-pop stores can. At a larger chain store, let a manager know—in person—that you saw the item priced lower at a competing store and ask if he or she will match that price.

✦ If you are a loyal customer at a smaller store, its employees will know you, and that should work in your favor. Make larger stores aware that you shop there frequently, and be sure to mention that you refer others to the store or business.

422. How to Get Free Auto Diagnostic Help

If that dreaded "Check Engine" light—which signals a potential problem with the engine or emissions system—comes on in your car, don't panic, and don't head straight to the dealership; sometimes, dealers will charge a fee just to diagnose the problem and turn off the light. The first thing you should do is check the dashboard for any other lights or abnormal gauge readings that might signal a serious problem, such as low oil pressure. If you have a problem that requires immediate action (which may be indicated by a flashing—rather than steady—warning light), pull over to the side of the road as soon as it is safe and turn off the engine. If you don't have an emergency, take your car to an auto parts store as soon as it's convenient. The car's computer will have stored a code in its memory that indicates the source of the problem that caused it to turn on the warning light. The code can be read with an electronic scan tool or diagnostic computer, and auto parts stores will often provide this service for free. The store will give you the code, tell you what it means, and let you know if there's an easy fix that it can do for you. If there isn't, it will refer you to a mechanic, or you can choose to take your car to the dealership for repair. There are also many Web sites and message boards—many of them specific to vehicle makes and models—that can assist you in troubleshooting your car's problems.

423. How to Research a Used Car

Buying a used car is a practical way to become a vehicle owner if you've got limited funds. Used cars are significantly cheaper than new cars initially, they cost less to insure, and they have a slower rate of depreciation. Make sure that a used vehicle isn't a lemon by knowing what to research before plunking down your cash.

1. **Vehicle history.** Every car has a unique number that's known as its "vehicle identification number" (VIN). Several reputable companies offer comprehensive reports for every VIN, with

information about accidents, odometer readings, and more. There's a fee to view these reports, but it's a small price to pay to avoid dropping a lot more on a clunker.

2. **Reviews of the model's year.** Just because some car brands have solid reputations doesn't mean that every model year is of uniform quality. Find reviews of the specific year of the model that you're considering from reputable sources such as *Consumer Reports*.

3. **Cost.** A car's cost isn't limited to its sticker price or Blue Book value. Several car-oriented Web sites offer "total cost" calculators that factor gas mileage, insurance, and average repair costs into the equation.

4. **Test drive.** Take the car for a spin before buying it. If your car IQ isn't very high, bring along somebody who knows how to evaluate the ride and performance. Ask to have the car inspected by an independent mechanic whom you choose.

424. How to Decide Whether to Buy an Extended Warranty

Replacement Cost

Be sure to compare the cost of an extended warranty to the cost of a replacement. It makes little sense to spend $40 on a three-year extended warranty for a $200 tech product that will be obsolete in three months.

If you buy a high-price item—a car, an appliance, or a computer, for example—you're probably going to be offered an extended warranty for it. These warranties extend the original manufacturers' warranties (which often cover repairs and replacements for a year or less) for another two or three years—and sometimes even longer. They can be costly, though, so are they necessary?

According to a *Consumer Reports* study published in 2008, extended warranties almost never pay for themselves. This is because the kind of catastrophic failure that would be covered by an extended warranty simply doesn't happen very often with the vast majority of products.

This doesn't mean that you should flat-out reject all extended-warranty offers. Just remember that what these companies are selling with their extended warranties is peace of mind.

425. How to Buy Tires

Many people don't give their tires a second thought. They should, though, because tires affect safety, gas mileage, and comfort.

Check the wear. The easiest way to check tires for wear is to look at the tread—if it's worn away, it's time for new tires. (Use the penny test: Insert a penny into the tire's groove, with Lincoln's head upside down and facing you. If you can see all of Lincoln's head, it's time to replace the tires.) Bulging, lopsided, or misshapen tires also need to be replaced.

Read the owner's manual. Your car's owner's manual will specify exactly what type of tires you need.

Learn the code. If you're feeling really bold, learn how to read those serial numbers that are printed on the side of every tire—the ones that say something like "P215/65R 15 95H M+S"—by spending some time on the Web site of the National Highway Traffic Safety Administration (nhtsa.dot.gov).

Compare brands. Once you've familiarized yourself with the kind of tire you need, check out consumer reviews from reputable sources such as *Consumer Reports*.

Buy a full set. Tires can be expensive, and it may be tempting to only replace the ones that look *really* bad. However, experts agree that cars run best when tires are replaced as a set.

426. The Real Cost of Driving

If you own a car, you probably don't consider taking public transportation very often. After all, driving is free—isn't it? Well, no. Actually, driving—even a quick trip to the grocery store—has many associated costs besides gasoline. Understanding how to calculate the real cost of driving can help you decide when public transportation is a wise fiscal choice.

The most obvious driving expense is gasoline, but there are other costs, too. Consider the wear-and-tear on your vehicle: Every mile that you drive moves you one mile closer to a tune-up, an oil change, new tires, and new shocks. Other expenses include auto insurance, parking fees, and tolls. To illustrate this point, the IRS has assigned a cost of driving in its deduction guidelines—in 2009 it was 55 cents per mile.

The true cost of driving varies from driver to driver, however. Internet sites, such as AAA.com, have interactive driving-cost calculators that can help you to determine the actual cost of driving your vehicle. You might find that it's cheaper to pay for the subway after all.

427. How to Prevent a Car Break-in

Car break-ins are common in the United States, and they can happen anywhere—from the big city to rural hamlets. Here are a few simple measures that you can take to prevent a break-in.

1. **Lock the doors.** This seems obvious, but almost 25 percent of car burglaries occur in unlocked vehicles.

2. **Leave nothing out.** Hide electronics such as GPS units, high-end audio equipment, and iPods, as well as their telltale accoutrements (such as adapters and charging units). Even smaller items—such as sunglasses and loose change—could lure those who are looking for something to steal.

3. **Engage the car alarm.** The ineffectiveness of car alarms is a cliché that's mentioned in many stand-up routines. Still, anything that draws attention to your vehicle might deter thieves.

4. **Park smart.** It might be tempting to park your sweet ride far away from other vehicles in order to avoid dings from inattentive drivers and passengers. However, thieves are far less likely to break into cars that are parked in well-lit, high-traffic areas.

428. How to Calm Your Nerves

When it comes to dealing with any situation that life throws your way, the Boy Scouts have it exactly right: Be prepared! Preparation is especially critical when it comes to dealing with nerve-racking events, such as a tests, job interviews, speeches, and performances. If you have prepared adequately (i.e., studied or rehearsed), it's less likely that you will succumb to pre-event jitters. If you've done all that you can to prepare but still feel anxious and abuzz with adrenaline, try some of these coping techniques

✦ Make sure that you're not holding your breath, then focus on your breathing, gently inhaling and exhaling.

✦ Close your eyes and visualize a peaceful place.

✦ Stretch or do some basic yoga poses.

✦ Tense and then relax different muscle groups, starting with your toes and feet and working your way up through the rest of your body. This will help to relieve tension.

✦ Avoid sugary foods and caffeinated beverages, as they can increase agitation and put you on edge.

✦ Take a break—turn off your computer, close your textbook, and step out for a brief walk or sit with your eyes closed for a few minutes.

429. How to Stay Cool Under Pressure

Everybody—including movie stars, politicians, athletes, and CEOs—gets nervous sometimes. But what separates the truly successful people in any field from the rest is their ability to stay cool under pressure. Here are a few tips that will help you maintain your composure when the going gets tough.

1. **Breathe.** Simply taking a few deep breaths can help you stay calm in high-pressure situations.

2. **Get perspective.** Sure, writing a five-page English paper might seem stressful, but consider how many people never have an opportunity to go to college. Sometimes recognizing that others have much more difficult situations than yours can help you keep yours manageable.

3. **Exercise regularly.** Studies have shown that engaging in regular exercise helps people to maintain focus and composure in strenuous situations.

4. **Identify your stressors.** Making a list of what makes you nervous in pressure-packed situations can help you recognize and deal with stressors when they come up in real life.

430. Asking for Help

Being independent is great, but we all need a little help sometimes. Asking for it, though, can be tough. There are many reasons why people don't ask for help. Some feel that it's a sign of weakness or incompetence; others are afraid that people will feel put upon by the request. (Oddly enough, people who don't ask for help are often the ones who are quickest to help others.) However, being able to ask for help is a sign of maturity.

When to ask. Obviously, you should first try to solve the problem on your own. Once it's clear that you won't be able to accomplish the task yourself, however, go ahead and ask for help.

How to ask. Be direct—clearly express your problem and how the other person can help you. Acknowledge that your request may be an inconvenience. And if you need lots of help—say, on moving day—solicit enough people so you don't have to rely on one person for everything.

FAST FACT

We underestimate the helpfulness of others by as much as 50 percent, according to recent research. So go ahead and ask for help—chances are, you'll get it.

431. Which Receipts to Keep and Why

Whether you're picking up groceries, buying a latte, or purchasing new clothes, you will be offered a receipt after you've paid. Don't leave your receipts on counters or crumple them in your pocket; these are valuable tools that will help you keep track of purchases and manage your finances, as well as provide documentation for your tax filings. Tracking expenses via receipts is also a good way to stay on solid financial footing.

It's possible that you don't need to hold onto *every* receipt (depending on how you handle your transactions), but here are a few that are worth keeping.

Restaurant receipts. If you use a credit card to pay for a meal, hold onto the receipt for a month to make sure that the tip is entered properly. If the meal is a business expense, attach the receipt to your expense report or hold onto it until tax time.

Medical expenses. Keep receipts for visits to your doctor and for medication. You'll need these when filing insurance claims.

Large purchases. Receipts for expensive purchases or items that are under warranty—such as bicycles, computers, and televisions—are critical if you need to make a return or if the product fails during the warranty period.

Job-search receipts. If you spend money hunting for a job—on travel, for example—you may be able to deduct some of these expenses. Job-related moving expenses may also be deductible.

432. How to Pay Off Debt

Perhaps you had an unexpected vehicle expense or uninsured medical bills—or you made excessive purchases with a credit card. Whatever the reason, if you find yourself in debt at some point, keep in mind that you're hardly the first— many others have emerged unscathed. Debt can be scary, but it will be less so with these techniques, which will help you tackle it.

1. **Snowball.** If you have multiple debts, some personal finance experts recommend that you "snowball" your payments. This technique involves paying as much as you can each month

> **Settle Yourself**
>
> Personal finance experts urge consumers to beware of "debt settlement" services that promise to erase debt for a fee. The vast majority of these services are merely moneymaking operations that do nothing more to erase your debt than you could do on your own for free.

toward the debt with the highest interest rate while paying the minimum required on the other debts. After the first high-interest debt is completely paid off, take the amount that you were paying per month on that first debt and roll it into your existing payment toward the debt with the next highest rate, and so on until all your debts are paid off.

2. **Stop accruing debt.** You can't do much about the debt that you've already accrued, but you can avoid accruing more. Create a budget, spend less, and start paying attention to where your money goes. Above all, stop using your credit cards.

3. **Consider credit counseling.** Credit counselors can help you negotiate lower payments to creditors and plan for a more responsible financial future. However, it is critical that you choose a reputable counselor; one can be found through the National Foundation for Credit Counseling (NFCC.org).

433. How to Avoid Bankruptcy

Young people aren't immune to bankruptcy; in fact, 19 percent of those who file for bankruptcy in the United States are college students. Bankruptcy is a legal protection that is offered to people who owe more than they can pay—the debts are forgiven, and the debtor is given a clean slate. If you're drowning in debt, bankruptcy may seem like an easy solution, but you will have to deal with its consequences far into your future. A bankruptcy filing will stay on your credit report for up to ten years, and you will have to reveal a bankruptcy on most credit and loan applications. This will make it much more difficult to buy a car or house—and it may even affect your ability to lease an apartment or get a job.

Clearly, it's a good idea to avoid bankruptcy if at all possible. If you're drowning in debt, start by cutting everything extraneous out of your life—pare down to the bare necessities (food, shelter, basic clothing, and transportation). Learn how to budget, making sure that you're realistic about how much you are earning each month. Consult a credit counselor, who will help you evaluate your alternatives and assist you in making a budget.

434. What to Do When You Can't Pay Your Bills

It happens to the best of us. Even if we're working and careful with our spending, it's sometimes tough to pay the bills, especially if unexpected medical or vehicle expenses pop up. Regardless of the reason why you're short on cash, there are steps that you can—and should—take to limit the damage.

1. **Prioritize.** If you can't pay all your bills, figure out which ones need to be paid first. If you have credit cards, for example, it's important to pay their minimums to avoid fees and rate hikes.

> ### A Raw Deal
> While it may be tempting to take out a payday loan if you're short on cash at the end of the month, resist the urge. These companies charge exorbitant fees and interest rates that will only drive you further into debt.

2. **Communicate.** Most companies are fairly flexible when it comes to paying bills. They may offer you a payment plan that will break your bill into smaller monthly payments, or they may offer hardship waivers. If you're a good tenant, your landlord may be willing to let you pay late once or twice. Whatever you do, don't simply ignore bills; they won't go away.

3. **Seek help.** Many states have assistance programs that can help you pay for utilities, and most hospitals have uncompensated-care programs for those who can't afford medical bills. Never assume that you're out of luck.

4. **Plan.** Falling behind on bills can happen, but don't make a habit of it. Figure out what went wrong and plan ahead so it doesn't happen again. It may be that you need to work more hours, and perhaps you should eliminate your extravagant cable package or daily coffee purchase. Whatever sacrifice you have to make, it will be a small price to pay for financial security.

435. How to Apply for a Loan

Cars, education, dental expenses—the important things in life are expensive, and there may be times when you need to take out a loan to help pay for them. Here's how to get the financial boost that you may need.

Auto loan. If you absolutely must have a car but don't have the cash to pay for it, you may decide to apply for an auto loan. These are available through banks, though if you buy a new car or a certified pre-owned vehicle, you might be able to qualify for financing through the dealer.

Student loan. The best place to find a student loan is through your school or through Sallie Mae, the student financial-aid arm of the government. Many banks and private firms offer student loans, too. You'll need to fill out a Free Application for Federal Student Aid (FAFSA) form, providing your income (and if you're a dependent, your parents' income). There are many federal student loan programs that are good choices because they usually have very low interest rates.

Personal loan. Personal finance experts urge most people to stay away from personal loans. If you must obtain a personal loan, apply for one at a credit union or bank rather than from an online loan company. And no matter what, stay away from loan-sharking payday loan companies, which gouge borrowers with enormous fees and interest rates.

436. Why You Should Contribute to an IRA

At your age, retirement is probably the furthest thing from your mind. But planning for your golden years now is the best way to enjoy a comfortable and financially secure retirement. Young people have a huge advantage over their older counterparts due to the magic of compound interest (interest that's paid on interest). This accumulates over the years, so investing early can reap big rewards down the line.

Individual retirement accounts (IRAs) are the primary investment vehicles for retirement. IRAs have many benefits, the greatest being that they provide tax-free earnings. There are several different kinds of IRAs, and each has its advantages. The most important thing to understand is that contributing to *some* kind of IRA is a key to a comfortable retirement.

Employee Retirement Plans

If your company offers a 401K retirement plan, consider enrolling in it. These are excellent investment tools because they offer tax benefits—and many employers will match a percentage of your contribution to the plan.

Because IRAs have so many tax benefits, the government limits the amount of money you can put into these accounts per year. However, the IRS also gives you a tax credit for deductions that you make during the year, which is an added incentive to get started with an IRA sooner rather than later. Check with your bank for more information about how to open an IRA.

437. How to Make a Million Bucks Without Trying

Who wants to be a millionaire? The better question is: Who *doesn't?* What if we were to tell you that you could become a millionaire without really doing much of anything at all? You'd probably think that an e-mail from your spam folder accidentally got into this book.

Of course, you have to do *something*. You have to work to earn money. And you have to invest your money. But if you invest your money—not even a lot of money—wisely, you can save a million dollars or more without doing much of anything else. This is all possible because of the magic of compound interest—interest that accrues on top of interest.

Here's what we mean. Suppose you put $100 into an account that earns 10 percent interest, which compounds annually. After the first year, that $100 would be worth $110 (10 percent of $100 = $10, which is added to the original balance). The next year, the money earns 10 percent interest again—but this time, it's paid on the new $110 balance. (10 percent of $110 = $11). Your original $100 has become $121 in two years, without you doing a thing.

It's even better if you keep adding money to the account. In fact, an 18-year old who adds $100 a month to an account that earns 10 percent compound interest will have more than one million dollars in that account by the age of 65. So what are you waiting for? Get down to the bank!

438. Understanding Social Security Benefits

It may come as a surprise to you, but Social Security isn't just for old people. In fact, the money that's taken out of your paycheck for Social Security helps Americans of all ages.

- ✦ **Senior citizens.** When most people think of Social Security, they think of retirement. A large percentage of Social Security benefits are distributed to those who are age 62 and older.
- ✦ **Disabled individuals.** If you're unable to work because of a disability, you may be able to receive Social Security benefits, regardless of your age.
- ✦ **Survivors of deceased workers.** If someone who is receiving Social Security benefits passes away, his or her survivors might still receive benefits, depending on the individual situation.
- ✦ **Dependents.** If your parents receive Social Security benefits and you're under the age of 18, your family might be entitled to additional benefits.

For more information about Social Security, check out the Social Security Administration's Web site at SSA.gov.

439. What to Consider Before Enlisting

The ads make the military seem glamorous: They promise that you'll travel the world, serve your country with honor, help the downtrodden, learn new skills, and experience a unique brand of camaraderie. But while the military may be a good option for some, it's important to make the decision to enlist with your eyes wide open. Here are some things that you should consider.

A recruiter is a salesperson. Just as a car salesman will gloss over a vehicle's low gas mileage or poor safety record, military recruiters aren't going to tell you about the harsher aspects of military life.

Which skills you'd like to acquire. One of the advantages of military service is the on-the-job training that you receive. Identify your interests and then talk to a recruiter about which branch of the service would best suit your goals.

Your views on war and killing. Ultimately, it's important to remember that a military's purpose is to fight wars, not to train people for civilian jobs. Would you be able to kill another human being under any circumstances? If the answer is no, the military is not for you.

What veterans have to say. Seek out the opinions of multiple service members before making the decision to enlist. For every veteran who speaks highly of military experience, there is probably one who will have the opposite view.

FAST FACT

While the military was once considered to be an excellent place to train for jobs in the real world, this may no longer be the case. According to a recent survey, 60 percent of employers say that the military does not adequately prepare servicemen and -women for the workforce, while more than 80 percent of veterans feel unprepared for job hunting.

440. How to File for Conscientious Objector Status

Federal law requires men to register with the Selective Service System (SSS)—the organization responsible for organizing military drafts in the United States—within 30 days of their 18th birthdays (or within 30 days of becoming a U.S. resident for those between the ages of 18 and 26). Although there hasn't been a draft in the United States for several decades, men are still required to register in order to qualify for federal student loans and other benefits. If you're morally or religiously opposed to war, you must still register, but you can file for conscientious objector (CO) status if a draft is instituted. If you intend to file as a CO, it's best to state your views on the SSS registration form; just write, "I'm opposed to participation in war in any form because of my ethical, moral, or religious beliefs." You can't do this online; you'll have to fill out a form by hand and send it in the mail. To be granted CO status, you will need to prove that you're deeply opposed to war of all kinds (not just a current war, if there is one) by filing a CO status claim with your area's SSS Local Board, then appearing in person for an interview. The process is somewhat tedious, but it's a small price to pay to stand up for your beliefs. By filing as a CO, you will become exempt from placement in combat situations, but CO status won't necessarily get you off the hook from all military duty.

441. Pros and Cons of the National Guard

If you're interested in joining the military but aren't prepared to enlist in one of the primary branches, you might want to consider the Army or Air Force National Guard. The National Guard's primary duty is to protect domestic targets, so it is under state—rather than federal—jurisdiction. For example, if there is a domestic disturbance in Illinois, the Illinois governor will call out the Illinois National Guard, not federal military units. However, if the federal government decides that the regular Army or Air Force needs to be bolstered, it can call up Guardsmen from any state to supplement those forces.

National Guardsmen are often called "weekend warriors" because they are required to train one weekend a month (in addition to a two-week stint once per year). For this reason, the Guard appeals to men and women who are interested in obtaining military benefits—such as tuition assistance, skills training, and cash bonuses—without making full-time service commitments. National Guard benefits vary by state and individual, though, so be sure to check which apply to you—and get them in writing—before signing up.

FAST FACT

For many years, joining the National Guard was considered to be a way to enjoy military benefits without the risk of combat. Not anymore. In the past decade, tens of thousands of National Guardsmen from every state have been mobilized to fight in Iraq and Afghanistan.

442. How to Get Free Legal Help

Every year thousands of lawyers in the United States provide free legal help to those who can't afford to hire attorneys. If you ever need to consult a lawyer but don't have the money to hire one, here are some options.

Legal hotlines. These are staffed by lawyers who answer basic legal questions. The American Bar Association maintains a directory of free legal hotlines on its Web site.

Pro bono programs. *Pro bono* is a Latin term that means "done without compensation for the public good." In plain English: It's free. Pro bono legal programs exist in every state, and the Legal Services Corporation (a government-run organization that offers free legal aid to low-income individuals; check out its Web site at LSC.gov) oversees many of them. Also check with state, city, and local governments and agencies.

443. Copyright Protection for Creative Types

Copyright protection prevents your original creative work from being copied by others. It's offered by the government to ensure that creators get the credit—financially and professionally—for original works of art.

How to get it. By simply being produced, your work is automatically copyrighted. However, if you ever have to prove that you are the original creator of a work, a copyright from the U.S. Copyright Office can be good evidence. The easiest way to register a copyright is online, through the U.S. Copyright Office's Web site (Copyright.gov). Although there are Web sites and companies that offer "help" in registering copyrights, they often charge exorbitant fees for a simple task.

Poor Man's Copyright

Sending a copy of your work to yourself—so it is dated with a postmark—is not a substitute for registering with the U.S. Copyright Office. This "poor man's copyright" is not recognized, nor does it provide protection.

What can't be copyrighted. Some things cannot be copyrighted. Ideas, concepts, domain names, slogans, titles, and band names cannot be copyrighted, nor can original works of art that are not created or owned by you.

Do you need to copyright? Whether you need to register a copyright for your work depends on the situation. If you're self-publishing a novel, obtaining a copyright is probably a good idea. A class paper? Not so much. The main reason to register is so you can bring legal action for copyright infringement (someone claiming your work as his or her own).

444. A Guide to Permissions for Creative Works

So you've finished your class essay or your latest blog post, but you'd like to add an epigraph of some sort—perhaps a poem by your favorite writer. Can you just use somebody else's material without asking?

Before you can use another person's work, you must determine if you need to seek permission to do so. The best way to do this is to find out if the work is copyrighted. Most contemporary creative works in the United States are copyrighted, and you will probably need to request permission to use them. If a work is very old, the copyright may have expired.

To get permission, contact the copyright holder or the publisher of the creative work you want to use. Most companies and artists charge a fee for the use of their copyrighted material, so be prepared to put out some cash.

There are circumstances in which you don't need permission to use copyrighted material, however. If you're only using a small excerpt—a quote from a scholar for a class paper, for example—you don't need permission. This is known as "fair use," and it is a complicated and nuanced aspect of copyright and permissions law. (You do need to acknowledge the source of the work, but this is not considered to be a substitute for obtaining permission.)

445. The Importance of Reading the Fine Print

Sale! Zero-percent financing! Free! No money down! Save! You've probably come across all of these phrases recently. But there's always more to the story than what's conveyed in these enticing come-ons, so take some time to investigate before you sign on the dotted line, send in that credit application, or pull out your debit card. Unfortunately, the rest of the story is often buried at the bottom of the page in minuscule type that you need a microscope to read.

It may seem like a pain, but it's essential to read the fine print of each contractual agreement, whether it's for a purchase, a credit card, or a gym membership. The fine print is where you'll find the details—especially the details that the institution offering the deal would rather you didn't notice. Think the "no money down" deal sounds pretty good for a new flat-screen? You may change your mind when you discover that you're being charged 23 percent interest on your payments. (You'll uncover this in the fine print.) Cell phone contracts, cable and Internet introductory deals, trial offers, leases, etc.—by law, all of these are required to include complete information about terms and rates. It's up to you to find the information and read it—no matter how small the type is.

446. Creative Ways to Wrap Gifts

Wrapping a gift in an interesting or beautiful way is like icing on a cake—it adds pleasure to the experience. There are all kinds of ways to wrap a present; you don't have to take the traditional paper-and-bow approach. Instead, try some of these more imaginative ideas.

✦ Use nontraditional wrapping materials, such as maps, newspaper (the Sunday comics section makes for a colorful wrapping), pages of old children's books or cookbooks or *National Geographic*, vintage postcards (cut and stuck to another piece of paper), wallpaper, or fabric.

✦ Match the wrapping to the gift. If you're giving kitchen items, pack them in a reusable canvas shopping bag. If you bought toys, books, or clothes for a baby, wrap them in a baby blanket and tie it with a soft ribbon. Wrap beach-theme gifts in a towel and music-theme gifts in sheet music.

✦ Tie packages with interesting items, such as twine, yarn, old ties, or measuring tape.

✦ Add touches of the natural world by topping gifts with decorative acorns, pinecones, and sprigs of evergreen or dried flowers.

447. How to Give a Thoughtful Gift

Forget the gift cards—here's how to choose something that's *really* meaningful.

✦ **Encouraging gifts.** If the prospective recipient has expressed an interest in a new skill or hobby, buy a gift that will support it. An aspiring musician might love a music lesson, for example, while someone who wants to get in shape could use a pass to a gym.

✦ **Do things together.** For many people—especially family members or significant others—the best gifts are those that bring you together. Dance lessons, dinner out, or theater tickets for the two of you are great ways to do something fun and spend time together. Just make sure that you choose something the other person wants to do too.

✦ **Make something.** Anybody can go buy something—this is why a handmade, creative gift can be extra-special. If you scrapbook, make a book about your friendship; if you're a musician, write and record some songs that are inspired by your relationship.

448. How to Give a Compliment

Everybody loves to get compliments—they make people feel good, increase the positive energy in the room, and help break down social barriers. Yet for many, giving compliments is more difficult than solving a calculus problem. Here are some tips that will help you give meaningful and appropriate compliments.

Be specific. Saying things like, "You're great," is nice and all, but a compliment works best when it is specific. Saying, "I really admire the way you give your undivided attention when you're speaking with someone," for example, is much more specific and will be better appreciated.

Be appropriate. Telling your girlfriend that she looks sexy in her new dress? Good idea. Telling your friend's wife the same thing? Not so much.

Be timely. Knowing when to give certain kinds of compliments is another skill that takes time to learn. Telling your boss you love his new haircut just after he conducted a meeting is less appropriate than telling him how much you enjoyed the meeting itself.

If you're not used to giving compliments, it might feel awkward at first. Don't worry—with practice, it will get easier.

449. How to Accept a Compliment

Being able to receive a compliment graciously is just as important as being able to give a compliment. When someone compliments you—on doing a great job on a school presentation, say—do not look away or at the ground, and don't shrug or say "That's not true!" or "I already know that!" It doesn't matter whether you agree or disagree; what matters is that someone cared enough to compliment you. Acknowledging the compliment with a smile and a simple, warm, "Thank you," will validate the other person's observation and maintain the positive energy that was created by the compliment. You don't need to elaborate, though saying, "That means a lot," is a lovely way to express your gratitude. Accepting compliments can take a little practice—many of us are not comfortable being in the spotlight—but in time, you will learn to handle them with grace and dignity.

450. A Guide to Diplomas

You can't underestimate the value of having a diploma. The more advanced your education, the higher your income is likely to be and the easier it will be to get a job. But there are many different kinds of diplomas. Here are a few of them, along with a quick explanation of what it takes to earn each.

GED. Even if you didn't finish high school, you can still earn the equiva-

> ## Certificate Programs
>
> Many schools offer certificate programs, which are similar to, but different from, degree programs. Certificate programs are often focused on building "real-world" experience.

lent of a high-school diploma by passing the General Educational Development (GED) test.

Associate's degree. If you successfully complete the academic requirements of a junior college, you'll receive an associate's degree. Some four-year institutions also award associate's degrees for completion of their programs' first two years.

Bachelor's degree. A bachelor's degree is conferred upon graduation from a four-year college or university.

Master's degree. A master's degree is the next rung in the academic ladder. Each discipline and school has different requirements, but in general, a master's degree requires one to two years of coursework beyond a bachelor's degree, plus the successful completion of a thesis (a really, really long paper).

JD. The "JD" stands for *juris doctore*, and it is the diploma earned upon finishing law school.

Ph.D. The Ph.D. is the crowning achievement of an academic career—it requires at least four years of coursework beyond a bachelor's degree, plus a dissertation that requires research and can end up being hundreds of pages long. Ph.D.s often take more than four years to complete.

MD. Chances are, your doctor has the letters "MD" after his or her name. That "MD" (it stands for *medicinae doctor*) is hard-earned—it recognizes the successful completion of medical school, a process that can take the better part of a decade.

451. How to Apply for Financial Aid

If you want to receive financial aid for school (and who doesn't?), you'll need to fill out a Free Application for Federal Student Aid (FAFSA). First, gather all the necessary documents, including your driver's license, Social Security number, current bank statements, and your current federal income tax return. Assess your dependency status (do this at FAFSA.ed.gov). Check the application dates to make sure that you meet the deadlines. Fill out the FAFSA, which asks questions about you, your plans for school, and your financial status. Follow up online to view the results of your application. If you do not qualify for federal aid, you can pursue other financial assistance opportunities, including scholarships, student loans, and military aid. Visit the Web site FinAid (FinAid.org) for help.

452. How to Prevent and Treat a Hangover

Consuming too much alcohol—or combining the wrong kinds of alcoholic drinks—can result in a hangover, an unpleasant condition that causes pounding headaches, nausea, and sometimes vomiting. This is because alcohol consumption dehydrates your body, inhibits the liver's ability to produce glucose (the sugar that fuels your cells), inflames your blood vessels, and disturbs your sleeping patterns.

How to prevent a hangover. Eat a meal (or at least a snack) before you drink. Try to stick to clear beverages. Dark-colored beverages, such as whiskey and red wine, contain a chemical that can intensify hangover headaches. Stick to one kind of alcoholic beverage. Drink plenty of water between alcoholic drinks and before going to bed. Sip slowly.

How to treat a hangover. Drink water or fruit juice. Have a snack to settle your stomach. Try something bland, such as crackers or toast. Take a pain reliever, but avoid aspirin, which can cause stomach irritation, and acetaminophen (i.e., Tylenol), which can severely damage your liver.

453. What to Do if Someone Has an Epileptic Seizure

Epilepsy is a surprisingly common disease—it affects almost three million Americans. Since so many people live with the condition, you may be present when someone has a seizure. By following a few guidelines, you can help without hurting.

Remain calm. In some cases, people who suffer seizures are aware of their surroundings. If you freak out, you will add to their trauma.

Don't move the person. Moving a seizing person can lead to injury. The only reason to move someone who is having a seizure is if he or she is in immediate danger.

Remove dangerous objects from the immediate area. Protect the seizing person from sharp and hard objects lying nearby.

Don't put anything into the person's mouth. Keep your fingers— as well as all other objects—out of the person's mouth.

Place a cushion beneath the person's head. This will protect the individual from further injury—just make sure to be gentle when placing the pillow.

Turn the person on his or her side after the seizure has ended. This is known as the "recovery position."

Stay with the person until he or she is recovered. Don't offer any food or drink until the person is completely recovered.

If a seizure lasts longer than a minute or two, or it's the person's first seizure, call an ambulance as soon as possible.

454. Common Poisons and What to Do About Them

Poisonous substances aren't always marked to warn you that danger lurks inside. Among the most common household poisons are cleansers, drain cleaners, antifreeze, turpentine, varnish, and pesticides.

If you're with someone who has swallowed poison or overdosed on medication, call 911 or poison control (800–222–1222). If you have a container of the substance ingested, read the label to the operator. *Do not* make the victim vomit unless instructed to do so by the operator. If the

Carbon Monoxide Danger

Carbon monoxide is a colorless, odorless, tasteless gas. Inhaling it can be lethal. Symptoms of carbon monoxide poisoning include drowsiness, headaches, dizziness, vomiting, and seizures. If you experience two or more of these symptoms, get outside into the fresh air immediately and find medical care as soon as possible.

substance swallowed is not medication, it may be all right to give the victim a small amount of water or milk, but do not force liquids unless told to do so.

Toxic substances can be inhaled or absorbed through the eyes or skin. For inhaled poisons, open windows and doors and get the victim outside into the fresh air immediately. Rinse poison out of the eyes with cold running water—a shower is helpful for this—for 15 to 20 minutes. If poison is spilled on clothing or skin, remove any clothes that may have absorbed the poison and rinse the skin with cold water for 15 to 20 minutes. In all cases, call emergency services.

455. How to Become an Organ Donor

Every day, an average of 18 people die while waiting for transplants. Nobody likes to think about the worst-case scenario, but consider that death can also be about life. If you want to be an organ donor, all you need to do is register with your state's donor registry—you can find it online at OrganDonor.gov or by calling your state's department of health. (If you own an iPhone, there's even an app that will guide you through the process.) Be sure to sign any cards and forms that you receive in the mail, and carry your donor card in your wallet. In most states, you can also indicate your intention to be an organ donor on your driver's license. Make sure that you talk to family members about your desire to be a donor; they are the ones who will have to carry out your wishes.

456. How to Perform the Heimlich Maneuver

You can save a choking person's life if you know how to perform the Heimlich maneuver. The technique has two steps.

The Hold. Wrap your arms around the victim's waist. Make a fist and place the thumb side of your fist against the person's upper abdomen, just below the rib cage and above the navel.

The Thrust. Grab the back of your fist with your other hand and press it into the victim's upper abdomen with a quick upward thrust. The thrust should be forceful but direct; you don't want to squeeze the victim's ribs while thrusting. Repeat these thrusts until the object is dislodged and out of the victim's mouth. (This technique can also be used to save drowning victims—it forces water out of their lungs, which jump-starts breathing.)

457. How to Give a Great Speech

Delivering a great speech is all about preparation; rarely does a great speech come from off-the-cuff remarks. You need to plan exactly what you're going to say in advance. Great speeches focus on a theme that is expressed in clear, concise language and is enhanced by plenty of examples, anecdotes, and/or statistics. Don't use clichés or excessive jargon. Once you've developed your script, practice, practice, practice! If you practice out loud, you'll find spots where the language trips you up, and you'll find a rhythm that suits your delivery. The more you practice, the more confident you will be and the less likely you will be to fall back on verbal fillers like "um" and "uh." Being comfortable with the material will free you to make eye contact with the audience and use gestures for emphasis. A great speech is only great if it can be understood, so speak slowly and enunciate.

458. How to Make a Toast

It's quite an honor to be asked to make a toast. Are you ready? Mind these tips and you will be.

✦ Be brief. A good toast is only about two or three minutes long.

✦ Name those whom you are toasting and the occasion. For example, say, "To my dad, on his 50th birthday."

✦ Say something special about the person or persons who you are toasting. Use an anecdote to illustrate your point.

✦ Be a little funny if you want; just remember—a toast is not a stand-up routine.

✦ Add a short quote or favorite poem if you like.

✦ Close with good wishes for the future.

At most events, toasts are given after dinner but before dessert. (Follow the host or coordinator's instructions.) When the moment comes, here's what to do:

✦ Take a sip of water to clear your throat.

✦ Stand up. Don't clink your spoon against your glass at formal events. Wait until everyone's quiet and all the glasses have been filled.

✦ Raise your glass to the guests of honor.

✦ Speak at a natural pace. Don't rush.

✦ At the conclusion of the toast, tap your glass against that of someone next to you and take a drink.

✦ Sit down and let the toasting continue!

459. Responding to Invitations

In the good old days, invited guests would respond to invitations with hand-written cards or notes. Nowadays, more and more event invitations are being issued via Facebook and Web-based invitation services, which make the whole idea of RSVP cards seem quaint. Generally speaking, your RSVP should reflect the invitation—or conform to a specific request from the host. If you receive an e-mail invitation, for example, it's okay to respond via e-mail. Sometimes the host may request that guests respond by phone or by postal mail regardless of the format of the invitation.

> **It's French**
>
> The acronym *RSVP* stands for *répondez s'il vous plaît*, a French phrase that means "please respond."

No matter what the format, the important thing is that you *do respond*. The host needs to know how many people are coming so he or she can plan accordingly.

460. How to Show Respect

Everyone likes to be respected—it makes us feel valued and considered. There are plenty of ways to show respect to the important people in your life. Here are some ideas.

- ✦ Give others your full attention when they are speaking to you. Respect what they have to say, even if you disagree.
- ✦ Admit when you are wrong and learn from your mistakes.
- ✦ Take care of things you borrow and return them quickly.
- ✦ Say "please" and "thank you," "excuse me," and "you're welcome." These simple phrases go so far!

461. How to Know if an E-mail Chain Letter Is a Hoax

A trusted friend who never passes along hoax messages has sent you an e-mail chain letter that promises a free dinner at Applebee's. E-mail chain letters that promise all kinds of free stuff are abundant and enticing, especially if you get one from someone you trust. But corporations don't often give out freebees. And if they do, they surely don't spread the word with long, poorly written chain letters.

Here's a quick and easy way to determine if a message is a fake: If it claims that the company is "tracking" the e-mail, it's a hoax. There are no tracking systems that can tell who passed on a chain letter and who didn't. Likewise, messages that promise substantial cash rewards or other gifts for doing nothing other than passing along a note are suspect. When in doubt, check one of the Web sites that reveal Internet hoaxes, such as Snopes.com.

462. How to Block a Person from Calling You

If you've got a landline, blocking a number is easy. Many companies allow you to block a limited amount of numbers for free by dialing *60. Other companies offer call-blocking services for a fee.

Blocking a number from calling your cell phone is a different story. Most cell-phone providers don't offer incoming-number-blocking features. First, check with the manufacturer of your phone; the phone itself might have a call-blocking feature. If you've got a smart phone, there are likely a variety of applications you can download to block unwanted calls.

Finally, you might want to look into alternative voice-mail providers, such as YouMail and Google Voice. These services route your phone number through their voice-mail servers, and they offer a host of options, including the ability to designate numbers as spam or block callers. Some of these services even offer the option to play a "This number is no longer in service" message to make bothersome callers think that your number has been changed.

463. How to Forward E-mail Jokes

You might love receiving jokes in your inbox, but that's not the case for everyone else. Here are a few things to keep in mind before you hit that "send" button.

Consider the sensitivities of your e-mail contacts. Jokes about religion and politics should only be shared with those who agree with your views.

Never send forwarded jokes to certain people. This group might include your boss, professors, and colleagues with whom you don't have a personal relationship.

Fwd: Fwd: Re: HA!

Change the subject line of the e-mail you're forwarding to reflect its contents. Writing "Forwarded joke" in the subject line is a courteous way to alert recipients that the e-mail isn't urgent.

Use the BCC field. Always protect your contacts' privacy by using the blind carbon copy (BCC) field, which hides their e-mail addresses. To use this feature, you'll need to put one address in the "To" field; that address should be your own.

When in doubt, don't forward a joke at all. Save it for the next party, so you can tell it in person.

464. How to Organize Your Personal Files

Your important personal papers will get lost in no time if you don't have a system for storing them. Your files should include completed applications for school and work; your birth certificate, Social

Security card, and marriage license (if you are married); school transcripts, diplomas, and certificates; insurance documents; health records; warranties; bills; and income tax forms. A little up-front maintenance will help to control paper pileups.

Put all your important papers—anything at all that you want to save—in one place. Decide where and how to store your papers. An accordion file, file cabinet drawer, or even a bin that slides underneath your bed will work. Divide your papers into categories and create a label for each category; place each category into a separate folder. File your documents. Stay on top of future paperwork by filing items as soon as you receive them.

465. How to Make a Useful List

Creating a list does more than help you get organized—it can motivate you too. If you're feeling overwhelmed by your mental to-do list, here are some tips that will help you make lists effectively.

> ### List-making Templates
> Web-based programs, such as those at TadaList.com and PrintableChecklist.org, make list-making easy. Also, many mobile phones come equipped with list-making functions or applications.

Make it detailed. The more you get down on paper, the more you'll free up your mind.

Prioritize. List the most important things first to make sure that they get done.

Categorize. Put like activities together. If you have three errands to run, you will accomplish more in less time if you group them together.

Break it down. A big task, like planning a birthday party, can't be done all at once. Write down the steps—making a guest list, sending invitations, etc.—so you can get it done little by little.

Make a list of daily tasks. This is a handy way to remember the things you keep forgetting to do, such as taking out the garbage or paying the bills. Try posting the list in a prominent spot.

Make a project list. If you write projects down, you're more likely to start chipping away at them.

466. How to Control Your Emotions

Even the most unflappable among us have emotional tipping points. For some, it can be a bit of criticism; for others, it might be a fight with a significant other or an unreasonable parental rule. With practice, however, you can control these flare-ups. Here's how.

✦ Take a deep breath and pretend that you are looking at the situation from a stranger's perspective. How would a neutral party react?

✦ Take a five-minute time-out before you say or do anything. This will give you a chance to calm down, reassess, and gather your thoughts. Your emotions may subside in the interim.

✦ Try to identify the emotional trigger. Remember, controlling your emotions means facing them head-on and learning why you feel the way you do.

467. How to Accept Criticism

The ability to maturely and gracefully accept criticism can take a lifetime to master. It's not easy to listen to critical comments, but with the right mind-set, it can actually be a constructive experience. Here are some techniques to use.

✦ **Acknowledge that you make mistakes.** No matter how confident you are in your abilities, you *will* err. Why else would pencils come equipped with erasers?

✦ **Listen carefully.** If you tune out anything and everything that's hard to hear, you'll never improve or grow.

✦ **Try your best not to take it personally.** It's easy to be defensive or overly sensitive when someone criticizes you; instead, try putting the criticism in context. Don't immediately assume that the person's chief goal is to hurt you or bring you down.

✦ **Let the critic know that you agree with some parts of his or her critique.** This shows a great deal of maturity.

468. How to Shake Off a Bad Mood

If you weren't in a bad mood every once in a while, your good moods wouldn't seem so good, would they? But nobody likes being around a grouch. Here are a few tips that will help you shake off your grumpiness.

Exercise. Study after study has shown that exercise pumps up the body's endorphins (the chemical agents that are responsible for producing good moods). Hop on the treadmill, take a bike ride, hit the courts, or just go for a walk.

Get it out of your system. Don't brood silently. Instead, let it out—moan, whine, complain, etc.—even if it's to a mirror.

Change your surroundings. Sometimes this is all you need. Take a stroll through your neighborhood, visit a friend, or browse the bookstore.

Get creative. Play some music. Draw a picture. Write a poem. Giving your creative muscles a workout will increase your body's endorphin output, which in turn will elevate your mood.

469. How to Get in Touch with Your Feelings

Sometimes we dismiss feelings as silly or invalid, and sometimes they scare us, so we sublimate them, keeping busy to avoid dealing with them. But no matter how we bury our emotions, they are bound to resurface. If you have trouble getting in touch with your feelings, here are some suggestions.

1. **Keep a journal.** You may not even realize what you're feeling until you write it down.

2. **Talk to a friend or trusted adult.** Similarly, you may not realize what you're feeling until you verbalize it. What's more, another person can help you zero in on your true feelings by asking questions.

3. **Contemplate your situation.** Allow yourself to feel different shades of emotion and to imagine different outcomes.

4. **Practice positive self-talk.** Encourage—rather than disparage—yourself.

470. How to Get a Prescription Filled in an Emergency

Losing your medication while you're away from home is a drag, but it doesn't have to affect your plans. Here's how to get your meds so you can resume your activities.

If you normally fill your prescription at a chain store and there's one in the area, you're in luck. Many chains share the same patient database, so your prescription will probably be on file. If you don't use a chain, head for the nearest open pharmacy. To get an emergency refill, you'll need to give the pharmacist your physician's contact information—including an emergency number—and present a valid ID. If the pharmacist can't reach your doctor, he or she may still be able to give you a single dose or a limited supply to get you by until you can get a complete refill. State laws regarding this practice vary, however, so be sure to ask.

If you can't locate an open pharmacy, call a nearby hospital or the local police department. If you think your medication may have been stolen, be sure to report your suspicion to the police.

When you travel, always carry a copy of your prescription, or at least a card listing the name of the medication, the dose, and the date of your last refill. This can help to speed things along.

If you have insurance, bring your insurance card. If the pharmacy is outside of your insurer's network, you will have to file a claim in order to be reimbursed, so be sure to keep your receipt.

When Disaster Strikes

If you are forced to leave your home without your medication because of a natural disaster, federal law permits a pharmacist to issue an emergency refill, even if your medical records have been lost or destroyed. Contact a hospital or talk to a relief worker for details.

471. Handy Things to Keep in Your Medicine Cabinet

Here are some helpful items that you won't find in a first-aid kit.

1. **Petroleum jelly.** Softens calluses and helps heal cracked skin.

2. **Baby oil.** Soothes razor burn and dry skin.

3. **Cornstarch-based powder.** Absorbs moisture and can pinch-hit as a deodorant.

4. **Witch-hazel.** A mild antiseptic that reduces inflammation of minor cuts, acne, and hemorrhoids, and can be used as a rinse for oily hair.

5. **Epsom salts.** Relieves bruises, swelling, and sprains—add a cupful to the bath and soak.

6. **Antifungal cream or ointment.** Use on athlete's foot and jock itch.

7. **Baking soda.** Add a cupful to your bath and soak to relieve sore muscles and mild rashes. Can also be used as toothpaste in an emergency.

8. **Styptic pencils.** Stops bleeding from minor shaving cuts.

472. How to Water Houseplants

Plants need water to survive, but do you know how much water your plants need? Overwatering can be just as deadly to a plant as underwatering. Here's a quick guide to watering your plants.

When to water. The best time of day to water houseplants is in the morning. How often you need to water depends on the type of plant, the type of pot and soil, and the room conditions (such as the amount of light and the humidity level). Stick your finger about one inch into the soil. If it is dry, hard, or crumbly, it's time to water; if it's damp or spongy, wait a couple of days. You can also use moisture strips or gauges (which are available in the lawn and garden aisle of the hardware store) to obtain more accurate readings.

How to water. Use room-temperature water—cold water can shock the roots and leaves, damaging the plant. Pour slowly and gently into the pot, making sure to saturate the entire area. It is okay—even good—if some water leaks from the pot's drainage holes to the tray underneath, but don't let the plant sit in it for very long; check after an hour and pour off any remaining water.

473. Practical Uses for Superglue

If you're stuck on duct tape because of its versatility, your loyalties may change after you find out what superglue can do. Check out some of the things it can fix.

FAST FACT

In 2008, British doctors used superglue to seal leaking arteries in a newborn's brain, saving his life.

✦ **Shoes.** If your soles are falling off your shoes but you don't have the money to replace them, try a little superglue.

✦ **Broken ceramic.** Superglue works well on broken dishes and other ceramic objects. Just be careful—not all superglues are heat-resistant, and almost all are toxic.

✦ **Fingernails.** That's right—superglue is great for sealing cracked nails; it can also prevent them from splitting more.

✦ **Skin.** Liquid bandages made with superglue—such as Band-Aid Liquid Bandages—seal minor cuts, keeping dirt out while letting moisture in. Unlike regular adhesive bandages, a superglue bandage won't fall off.

474. What to Consider Before Getting a Pet

A pet can be your most loyal friend and a companion, but it is also a long-term commitment. If you're contemplating pet ownership, consider the following before taking the plunge.

Time. A dog has to be walked daily; a cat's litter box has to be cleaned daily and overhauled weekly. Plan to spend at least 30 minutes to an hour per day caring for and socializing with your pet.

Money. Even if you get your pet from an animal shelter, you'll have to spend money on vaccinations, vet visits, food, toys, medicine, carpet cleaning, training, pet-sitting, and boarding.

Patience. Puppies chew, cats claw, and older pets develop set routines. You will need lots of patience to see your pet through its life stages. Read a breed-specific book so you know what to expect.

Space. You'll need room for a litter box and litter supplies, pet food, and a place for the pet to sleep. You'll also need a place to stash a crate, a dining area for food and water, and an exercise area.

Responsibility. Pets require daily contact and care—think hard about your lifestyle and whether you have the time and discipline to care for a pet day in and day out.

475. How to Write a Personal Essay

Does the idea of putting yourself out there in a personal essay give you cold feet? Here's a little advice that will make it easier.

1. **Think of it as a story, not an essay.** You're telling a story about yourself. Compelling stories revolve around change, so focus on something that changed your ideas or attitude.

2. **Start small.** Choose one episode from your life. A good writer works like a filmmaker—setting up the scene, zooming in for a close-up, and then pulling back to reveal the big picture.

3. **Use details.** Describe sound, smell, and feel. The details make your writing come alive.

4. **Don't explain too much.** Resist this urge. Rely on your images to convey your ideas. Writers call this "showing not telling."

5. **Make your ending memorable.** Close your essay with a "snapshot"—a single, vivid scene from your story that your reader will remember.

476. How to Write a Sympathy Note

The times when you don't know what to say are often times when you need to say something the most. When a friend or relative experiences a traumatic event—such as the death of a loved one, a miscarriage, the loss of a job, or a divorce—your sympathetic words can help him or her cope. Here's how to say the right things.

Acknowledge the loss. Address the issue and say how sorry you are for what happened. "I am so sorry to hear about your mother's death. My heart aches for you and your family." If you have trouble finding the right words, use a quote or poem that expresses your feelings.

Keep it brief and personal. You don't have to say a lot in your note. However, it's lovely to share an anecdote that recalls happier times or a special memory if you can.

Offer to help. Mention that you'll call about bringing over a meal or that you would be happy to meet for coffee and talk.

End on an encouraging note. Here's one example: "Don't take the layoff personally; your infectious enthusiasm and go-get-'em attitude will help you land another job in no time."

477. How to Become an Expert

Turn on any talk show or news program and you'll find an expert being interviewed about the subject du jour. If you aspire to having such expertise, here's how to get it. Who knows—you may just end up on *The Daily Show*.

> ### Practice Makes... Expertise
>
> So how long does it take to become an expert on something? According to writer Malcolm Gladwell, it takes about 10,000 hours. That's about five years of full-time, 40-hours-a-week practice.

✦ **Choose a narrow topic.** It's much harder to become an expert on "marketing" or "the Internet" than it is to become an expert on "Internet marketing."

✦ **Find other people who are experts.** Learn from other experts. Seek out Web forums, conferences, and talks by authors to meet others who are interested in the same topic.

✦ **Learn the jargon.** Every field, from Web development to literary theory, has its own lingo.

- ✦ **Read one book on the topic per month.** Ask other experts to recommend the best books to read.
- ✦ **Devote time each day.** You can't become an expert on a subject without spending time learning about it. Start by devoting one hour per day to reading or research.
- ✦ **Subscribe to publications about the field.** This is how to keep up with the latest news and ideas.

478. How to Network

Networking is the process of cultivating professional relationships and building a strong group of contacts—which is critical to advancement in any field. Here are some networking tips.

1. When you meet people who are already working in your desired field, ask questions, express interest in their work, and exchange contact information if possible. Ask if you can contact them in the future, and if so, ask if they prefer that you get in touch via e-mail or telephone. Then be sure to follow up.

2. Set up an informational interview. E-mail your dream employers or people whose work you admire to see if they'd be willing to answer a few questions about how they got their professional starts and the qualities and kinds of experience they look for in an employee. If they agree to meet with you, be sure to ask thoughtful questions and follow up within 24 hours with a thank-you note.

3. Find public events—workshops, conventions, seminars—in your field of interest and attend them.

4. Seek out an internship, apprenticeship, or mentorship—even an unpaid one. This is a great way to get your foot in the door.

479. How to Communicate with Older Adults

Interacting with older adults is a rewarding experience. Their insights and perspectives will enrich you, and your time and attention will help them feel respected and valued. Aging is often accompanied by health issues, so be sensitive to infirmities such as hearing loss, poor eyesight, and impaired speech (this may be due to a stroke). Be patient, and speak slowly and clearly. Some senior adults may be easily confused, so use hand gestures and facial expressions as nonverbal cues. Make eye contact and smile. If you feel comfortable with the person, communicate through touch—put your hand reassuringly on an arm or pat the back. Sometimes, however, physical contact is unwelcome; if this is the case, avoid it. Listen carefully and ask questions, which will let seniors know that you are paying attention.

480. How to Hold a Baby

Holding a newborn for the first time can be scary—they're tiny and delicate, and their necks are like rubber. In fact, their necks can't support the weight of their own heads until they are about four months of age, so the cardinal rule of baby-holding is to always support the head and spine. If you worry about dropping or injuring the baby, you're not alone—everyone worries about that. With a little practice, however, you will become a confident baby-holder. Here are the two most basic baby holds.

1. Cradle the baby's head in the crook of your arm with the spine lying along your forearm and the bottom secured in the palm of your hand. You can place your other arm underneath for additional security. This is the classic position for feeding and rocking.

2. Hold the baby upright facing behind you, and place its head over your shoulder. Put the palm of your hand behind the baby's head and your forearm along the spine. Use your other hand to hold the baby's bottom. This is a good burping position.

481. How to Stay Up-to-Date on the News

When you're busy at school and at work, you may lose track of what's going on in the world outside your bubble. But keeping abreast of current events is part of being a thoughtful, active citizen. The more sources you use and the more conversations you have, the better your judgments will be. Here are some tips that will help you stay up-to-date.

✦ Read the daily newspaper.

✦ Read newsmagazines (*Time, Newsweek*, etc.) that provide opinion columns and go in-depth on the issues.

✦ Watch the news on TV or listen to public radio.

✦ Visit online news sites, such as CNN.com, BBC News Online, Google News, Reuters, etc.

✦ Try to get your news from a variety of sources that offers a range of perspectives.

✦ Engage others (coworkers, friends, etc.) in discussions about current events.

482. How to Find Out if a Charity Is Legit

If footage of natural disasters and photos of starving children tug at your heartstrings, they may also open your wallet. That's a human impulse—and you should give as generously as you can to worthy causes. But be careful to whom you direct your dollars. Some charities are simply scams, while others are legitimate but don't use your hard-earned money wisely. Here are some tips to help you make sure that those in need get the most bang for your donated buck.

1. **Use the IRS.** The Internal Revenue Service's Web site (IRS.gov) maintains a list of charitable organizations that are eligible to receive tax-deductible contributions.

2. **Visit the American Institute of Philanthropy's Web site (charitywatch.org).** This charity watchdog group provides a wealth of information about charities and grades them on performance to help you refine your donation decisions.

3. **Check with the National Association of State Charity Officials (NASCO).** Each state has its own requirements and procedures for forming charitable organizations, as well as for soliciting charitable contributions. You can find the charity officer for your state on NASCO's Web site (NASCOnet.org).

4. **Consult the Better Business Bureau.** It has a helpful Wise Giving Alliance list that you can access at bbb.org/us/charity.

483. Wet Cleaning vs. Dry Cleaning

Back in the old days, cleaners washed all garments with water and detergent. This was a time-consuming and laborious process, so the industry developed chemical solvents to clean garments without water. This is called "dry cleaning." Unfortunately, these chemical solvents include perchloroethylene, or "perc," which has been shown to produce serious negative environmental effects.

As a result, many cleaners have adopted a "wet cleaning" system, which uses water-based technology to clean garments. Wet cleaning does just as thorough a job as dry cleaning, but without the harmful environmental effects. It is more costly, however. While wet cleaning technology can clean almost all types of fabric, there are a few items—such as antique satin garments—that need to be cleaned using the old dry-cleaning technology. When in doubt, ask your local cleaner.

484. Laundromat Etiquette

When you're doing laundry in your parents' house, you don't have to worry much about etiquette. But when you do your laundry at a Laundromat, you'll need to follow these rules.

Don't touch other people's clothes. It can be annoying to wait for a stopped dryer full of other people's clothes, but it's never okay to remove them. Talk to an attendant, if there is one on duty. Otherwise, wait it out for as long as you can.

Remove your clothes from machines promptly. Machines are in high demand at many Laundromats.

Use the proper amount of detergent. Too much detergent can cause a washing machine to overflow, creating a huge mess.

Don't be a dryer hog. There's no need to separate a single washer load into six dryers—clothes actually dry best when part of a full load. And don't stand at the dryer folding one piece of clothing at a time while others wait to use the machine.

485. How to Get a Cheap Haircut That Doesn't Look Cheap

Your hair is getting unruly, but you don't want to spend big money for a haircut. You can get a free or low-cost haircut at a high-end salon by booking an appointment with a salon apprentice—a stylist-in-training who needs practical experience before getting his or her own chair. Apprentices often advertise on special Web sites, in local newspapers, and on Craigslist. You can also call a salon and ask for an appointment with an apprentice. The apprentice will be supervised by a master stylist, which means that the haircut will take a while longer—probably at least an hour—because the master stylist will interrupt frequently to explain techniques or make suggestions.

Gratuity Not Included

Just because the haircut is free or cheap doesn't mean that you shouldn't tip the apprentice. Even after your tip, your haircut will still have been far cheaper than it would be if you'd gone to the local discount chain, and it will probably look better, too.

486. How to Deal with Gossip

Gossip is toxic. It can impair our interactions and poison relationships. It makes its subject feel frustrated, humiliated, and helpless.

Even though we know gossip is destructive, most of us have listened to and even spread some. So how do you deal with catty talk and how do you break the cycle? If the gossip is about you, confront the gossiper and explain how hurtful it is. If it's about someone else, tell the gossiper that it's not right to spread harmful information—whether or not it's true—and refuse to listen or pass the gossip along. You can also make a point to change the subject. Confide only in your closest, most trusted friends. Finally, if someone insists on gossiping about you or around you, move on and let it go. The person who is spreading the gossip will notice that you've lost interest and will tire of spreading rumors.

487. Getting Help from a U.S. Consulate While Abroad

If anything goes awry while you're abroad, you can get help from a U.S. embassy or consulate. Embassies are outposts of the U.S. government; they provide diplomatic services such as reissuing passports for U.S. citizens and negotiating with local governments on behalf of Americans living or traveling abroad. Consulates are junior embassies; they provide an American presence in foreign countries but only perform minor diplomatic tasks.

Before traveling overseas, you can register your travel plans with the U.S. State Department. This allows the embassy or consulate to contact you in an emergency, such as a natural disaster, political unrest, or terrorist activity. Registration is free and confidential via the State Department's Web site: travelregistration.state.gov. You never know when you might encounter a problem, so carry the address and phone number of the consulate in the area to which you are traveling. A consulate can provide emergency assistance to Americans who encounter legal, financial, and health issues; suffer lost and stolen passports; and become victims of crime. The consular office also provides nonemergency assistance with absentee voting, transferring Social Security and other U.S. government benefits for payment abroad, completing tax forms, notarizing documents, registering American children who are born out of the country, and Selective Service registration.

488. How to Safely Stay at a Hotel or Motel

Safely staying at a hotel or motel requires common sense and some extra caution.

1. Make sure the hotel/motel is located in a safe, low-crime area, and that it is clean with well-lit hallways.

2. Park your vehicle as close to the lobby door or your room as possible, especially if you are arriving late at night. Don't keep valuables in your car—or at least make sure they're out of sight.

3. Make a reservation so you don't get stranded on the road due to a lack of vacancies.

4. As soon as you enter your room, check the locks to make sure that they work properly. Rooms with electronic locks are safest, as the lock combination is changed for every guest. Familiarize yourself with the locations of the emergency exits.

5. When you go out, leave a light on in your room and hang the "Do Not Disturb" sign on the doorknob.

6. Store valuables in a hotel safe rather than in your car or room.

> ### Inside Is Best
>
> Try not to stay at hotels or motels that have doors and windows that open to the outside instead of to an interior hallway; they're not as safe. If you must stay in one of these inns, ask for a room on the second floor. The worst place you can stay is in a ground-floor room that opens to a parking lot.

489. How to Be Helpful

Being helpful is about the little things as much as the big ones. It's about paying attention to other people, anticipating what they might need or want, and then providing it. Here are some easy ways in which you can lend a hand.

- Volunteer to help a friend who is moving.
- When you're invited to someone's house for dinner, ask if you can bring something and help with the after-meal cleanup.
- When using public transportation, give your seat to someone who is older, pregnant, infirm, or struggling.
- Offer to pick up mail for a friend who is going out of town.
- Notice when a friend or family member is overbooked and volunteer to take something, such as running an errand, off his or her hands.
- Provide a night of free babysitting to parents who can't afford a babysitter.
- Make hot soup or tea for a roommate who is sick.
- Troubleshoot a computer problem.

490. The Importance of Saying "Please" and "Thank You"

You probably learned to say "please" and "thank you" as a toddler—but do you remember to use those words frequently now that you're a young adult? They aren't called "magic words" for nothing—they can engender cooperation, relieve tension, and alter perspectives. Saying "please" when you want something and "thank you" when you're grateful for something is a sign of respect and civility. If you use good manners, other people will see you in a positive light and you'll feel good about yourself. The words may be small, but their dividends are huge.

491. How to Refuse a Second Date

Dull first dates can be awkward—but not nearly as awkward as that moment when the other person says how much he or she would love to get together with you again. What do you do? Here are a few tips that will help you make sure you don't send the wrong message.

Be honest . . . but not too honest. It's sufficient to say that you don't think you're compatible.

Close the door completely. Don't lead the other person on by hinting at a possible future date. Avoid making an excuse like, "I'm really busy right now," or, "If this were another time in my life, it might work out," if it's not the truth. All this will do is make your date think that he or she can try again in a few months.

> ### Don't Hide
> Refusing a second date by ignoring phone calls and e-mails is the height of bad form; the same goes for refusing or breaking dates via text messages. Mature adults communicate with thoughts that are longer than 160 characters.

The "compliment sandwich." Letting someone down gently is tough to do, but it is easier if you couch the bad news with some positive comments.

492. How to Look Great in Photos

Taking photographs has never been easier—there are point-and-shoot cameras for every budget, and most cell phones now come with cameras. It's one thing to be the photographer and quite another to be the subject, however. Here's how to look your best when the lens is pointed in your direction.

1. **Don't pose.** The stiffer you are, the worse you will look.
2. **Turn your head slightly.** Photos taken from a bit of an angle rather than straight-on are more flattering.
3. **Talk.** You'll appear animated and more natural.
4. **Smile spontaneously.** If you prepare your smile in advance, it will look forced and fake.
5. **Stand or sit up straight**. And keep your shoulders down. Good posture makes you look thinner, confident, and attractive.

493. How to Avoid Losing Yourself When You Fall in Love

How do you keep your feet on the ground when you fall in love and your head is in the clouds? Try some of these tips.

- **Take things slowly.** Don't start making wedding plans when you're just getting to know each other. Enjoy the moment.
- **Spend some time apart.** Stay in touch with your friends and family, and take some time for yourself. It will only strengthen your romantic relationship.
- **Write about your feelings in a journal.** This can help keep you grounded and put things in perspective.
- **Get to know each other's friends.** Don't make a habit of isolating yourselves. Go out with friends and get to know each other's backgrounds.

494. What Your Elected Officials Can Do for You

Local, county, state, and federal elected officials represent you. But do you have any idea how they can be helpful to you? Here's a basic guide to the people who are elected to serve you.

Local municipality, township, and county officials are concerned with street maintenance, zoning, taxes (including those on sales and property), education and school funding, local economic development, parks and recreation, housing, crime, fire, and recycling and garbage removal. Contact them through your local city hall or attend a city council meeting.

Your state congressperson can handle many of the same concerns, but on the state level. The best place to start is with the congressperson from your district, but you can also reach out to other state congresspeople, particularly when you wish to discuss certain issues. Visit your state's Web site to find contact information for any state representative or senator.

On the federal level, there's an enormous range of things that congresspeople can do for you—including providing Washington, D.C., tourist information; copies of bills, laws, hearings, and other government publications; and tickets for White House tours and passes to the House and Senate galleries. Congresspeople can intervene if you have a request from the Library of Congress, need a passport expedited, have adoption or immigration issues, or need help negotiating or communicating with a federal agency. You can find a wealth of information on the Web site Congress.org.

495. How to Give Blood

Every three seconds, someone in the United States needs a blood transfusion, yet only five percent of the population donates blood. You can help save a life by donating your blood—it's easy and relatively painless. Here's what you need to know.

Eligibility. In general, you must be at least 16 years of age, weigh a minimum of 110 pounds, and be in good health. You cannot donate if you have had hepatitis or HIV or are pregnant—or if you are ill, are on an antibiotic, or just had a vaccination.

Where to go. The American Red Cross and your local hospital can help you find a blood donation center. The AABB Web site (AABB.org) has a blood bank locator; just type in your zip code, and it will give you the locations of nearby accredited blood banks.

The donation process. You will need to present identification and fill out a medical history form. A staff member will talk to you privately about your history and ask some questions. He or she will check your blood pressure, take your pulse and temperature, and prick your finger for a blood sample to check your iron level. If you're healthy, you will go to the donor room, where a needle will be inserted into a vein to collect a pint of blood. The whole procedure, from sign-in to recovery, takes only about an hour.

> **FAST FACT**
>
> The O negative blood type is considered to be the universal donor. Most people can accept this blood type, no matter what their own blood type is.

496. The Danger of Drinking Too Much Water

We've become hyperconscious about hydration, and carrying around a water bottle is *de rigueur*. But the drink that we consider healthy and benign can be lethal if consumed in excess. If you drink too much water too quickly, you can develop a condition called water intoxication, in which the body's nutrients, particularly sodium, become so diluted that they cannot perform their essential functions. The symptoms of water intoxication—or hyponatremia— are similar to those of alcohol intoxication and include nausea and vomiting, confusion, headache, and muscle weakness. Severe water intoxication causes brain swelling and death. Athletes and marathon runners are particularly susceptible because they drink lots of extra water to compensate for fluid loss from sweating. If you plan to exercise intensely for more than an hour, choose a sports drink that contains sodium to maintain the appropriate concentration of salt in your blood.

497. How to Fail Gracefully

Failure, the cliché goes, is not an option. It's an old saying—and it's also untrue. *Everybody* fails once in a while. What separates successful people from others, though, is *how* they fail. Here are three tips for making sure that the next time you fail—and you *will* fail—you do it gracefully.

1. **Don't point fingers.** Even if you think somebody else is partially to blame for your failure, resist the urge to scapegoat. Admit your failure and move on.

2. **Get perspective.** A failure isn't truly a setback unless you learn nothing from it. Figure out what went wrong and fix it. If you can't fix it, find another way to your goal.

3. **Give 100 percent to the very end.** It's tempting to give up when you have an inkling that a project is not going to work out. But if you don't give it your all, you won't be left just with failure—you'll also be left with regret.

498. The Importance of Being Positive

Do you consider a partially filled glass of milk on the counter half-empty or half-full? If you said, "Half-full," you may be better off than those who say, "Half-empty." Scientists have linked positive thinking to a host of health benefits, including longer life spans, better physical health, lower rates of depression, and a greater ability to handle stress.

But being positive (or negative, unfortunately) doesn't just affect you—it actually spreads to other people via a phenomenon called "emotional contagion." This means that when you're happy, everybody around you tends to be happy. Behavior experts suggest that you surround yourself with positive people and learn to identify and eliminate negative forces in your life. Turning negative thoughts into positive ones—finding "the silver lining" in any situation—takes practice. But by becoming a positive person, you might find that the glass isn't just half-full—the milk also tastes better.

> ### It's Sickening
>
> Negativity might not just breed negativity—it might also breed the flu. According to a 2003 study conducted at the University of Wisconsin, negative emotions weaken the body's immune response to the flu virus.

499. How to Find Your Passion

At this point in your life, you're probably hearing a lot about what you *should* be doing. Try to drown out the chatter and focus on what you *want* to be doing.

What is your passion? It's easy to figure out what you *don't* want to do. What work responsibilities do you avoid like the plague? What classes do you dread attending? Do you hate being cooped up inside behind a desk? The answers to questions like these will help you narrow your choices to those that best suit you. On the flip side, what comes easy to you? What activities are so captivating that time flies by when you are engaged in them? What makes you smile? If money weren't an issue, what would you do?

What's holding you back? Failure stinks, but trying—and sometimes failing—is the only way you'll know if you are on the right path. To reach your goal, you're eventually going to have to do something uncomfortable and terrifying, whether it's moving to a new city to study in a particular program or quitting your stable job to give your start-up business your full attention.

What are your goals? Focus, keep your eyes on the prize, and clear your calendar so nothing stands between you and your goals. Break your goals down into manageable, achievable steps.

500. The Benefits of Volunteering

After you move away from home, you will establish new communities and forge new friendships. In the process, you will learn about yourself, your priorities, and what kind of adult you want to become. One of the most rewarding ways to do this is through volunteering. Consider which causes, organizations, and/or interests are important to you. Do you enjoy caring for animals? Working outdoors? Interacting with senior citizens or individuals with special needs? Are there specific ways in which you'd like to effect change in your community? Do you have a special skill that you'd like to teach others? Look for volunteer opportunities posted on community bulletin boards at coffee shops, libraries, stores, schools, and religious centers. Consider becoming an after-school tutor or a regular visitor to a nursing home or animal shelter. Help

> **Make It Happen**
>
> Having trouble finding just the right volunteering opportunity? Consider starting your own service project. Get the word out by soliciting a sponsor or teaming up with a partner organization. For help with recruiting volunteers, visit Serve.gov and click on "Register Your Project."

at a soup kitchen or food pantry. Browse the opportunities posted on VolunteerMatch.org, Serve.gov, and Idealist.org. Programs such as AmeriCorps and the Peace Corps provide long-term volunteering placement, both domestically and abroad. No matter where you volunteer, you will meet new people, get a better sense of the things that really matter to you, learn new skills, and experience the particular joy of making a difference in the lives of others.